Is Japan really remilitarising?

Is Japan really remilitarising?
The politics of norm formation and change

by Yasuo Takao

Monash University Press
Clayton

Monash University Press
Building 11
Monash University
Victoria 3800, Australia
www.monash.edu.au/mai

All Monash University Press publications are subject to double blind peer review.

© Yasuo Takao 2008

National Library of Australia Cataloguing-in-Publication entry:

Takao, Yasuo.
Is Japan remilitarising? : the politics of norm formation
and change / Yasuo Takao.
Clayton, Vic. : Monash Asia Institute, 2008.
ISBN: 9781876924607 (pbk.)

Series: Japanese Studies Centre monographs
Notes: Bibliography.
Subjects: Remilitarization--Japan.
           Japan--Armed Forces.
           Japan--Military policy.

Other Authors/Contributors:
           Monash University. Monash Asia Institute.
           Japanese Studies Centre (Melbourne, Vic.)
Dewey Number: 355.033552

Cover photograph and design by Jenny Hall.
Printed by BPA Print Group, Melbourne, Australia - www.bpabooks.com

contents

	List of tables and figures	vii
	A note on convention	viii
	Preface	ix
Introduction	New developments	1
Chapter one	Existing explanations of Japanese security	17
Chapter two	Norm formation	53
Chapter three	Norm compliance	65
Chapter four	External structures	87
Chapter five	Norm changes	99
	Conclusion	133
Appendix 1	Chronology	145
Appendix 2	Article 9 of the constitution of Japan and related documents	149
	Glossary	159
	Notes	163
	Bibliography	175
	Index	197

About the Author

Yasuo Takao is Senior Lecturer in Political Science at Curtin University of Technology, Western Australia. His current research interests include society-initiated transnationalism at the grassroots level in Japan. His recent publications include *National integration and local power in Japan*, *Reinventing Japan: from merchant nation to civic nation*, and numerous articles on local governance and transnationalism in international academic journals.

List of tables and figures

TABLE 1.1	Average Defence Burden as Percentage of GDP/GNP, 1969–2003	33
TABLE 1.2	Japan's Defence Budget, FY1969–FY2006	36
TABLE 5.1	Voting behaviour in single-member districts under the new electoral system	124

FIGURE 2.1	Japanese perception of armed conflict involvement, 1969–2003	60
FIGURE 2.2	Japanese perception of national security, 1969–2003	61
FIGURE 2.3	Japanese perception of defence spending levels, 1969–2003	62
FIGURE 5.1	Japanese Support for the US Attack on Iraq, August 2002–March 2003 (%)	112
FIGURE 5.2	Japanese Public Support for Dispatching the SDF, June 2003–April 2004 (%)	113
FIGURE 5.3	Japanese Public Support for Continuing SDF Deployment, January 2004–November 2005 (%)	117
FIGURE 5.4	Trends in Midterm Defence Program Estimates	130

A note on convention

Japanese personal names throughout the text are presented in Japanese form, that is, with the surname followed by the given name, in reversal of standard Western practice. Newspaper citations refer to morning editions, or else are specifically cited.

preface

This book is about the politics of state compliance with national security norms. It emphasises the important role played by domestic norms in Japan's post-Second World War military security policy. It examines how the Japanese government's decision-making has been embedded within a series of norm compliance mechanisms. These mechanisms sustain national security measures in order to be broadly acceptable to the general public within the context of military dependence on the United States.

I was born in Japan after the end of the Second World War, but I feel as if I were still dragging it along with me. My father, Haruo, was born in the Taisho era and grew up with a military government. My grandparents farewelled him on his journey to Manchuria as an engineer soldier. My grandmother once told me,

> We went to the local station to say goodbye to Haruo. He was looking out of the window [on a train bound for Japan's gateway port to Northeast Asia, Shimonoseki] and your grandpa and I were shouting out at the tops of our voices—'Don't get ill!' When the steam whistle blew, I just ran along and chased after the train as far as I could.

My grandfather said to her, 'Haruo will come home!' My mother, Misao, who met my father after the war, was teaching at a high school located next to a munitions storage site in Kyoto. She recalled,

> Your father and I were the lucky ones and survived well. Before the war ended, he was repatriated alive from Harbin [Manchuria]. Unlike other major cities, Kyoto was never targeted for air bombing. All of my students were alive though suffering from starvation.

The end of the war brought feelings of release but my mother was ashamed to face her children again. She suffered a crises of personal guilt for not having the courage during the war to tell her students her true opinion—not about honourable death, but that all the solders should come home. None of my father's close friends returned alive from the South Pacific. He later learned that many had died in a ditch by their own hand, or of starvation and malaria, not 'glorious' deaths in real combat. My father never showed emotion in front of me, but he had been scarred by the war and lost confidence. He never asked me to sing the national anthem, respect the flag or think of Japan as a beautiful nation. I am still dragging my parents' war memories along with me. I wonder if my generation is coping with their parents' horrific experience.

By the spring of 1945, neither the Japanese military nor the Allied forces differentiated civilians from combatants any longer. In the early summer of 1945, the bloodiest battle, the Battle of Okinawa, resulted in the deaths of as many as 150,000 Okinawan civilians. On the single night of 9 March 1945, B-29 bombers killed 100,000 Tokyoites. These bombers reduced most of the major Japanese cities to ashes. By the end of 1945, another 140,000 individuals had died from the atomic bomb dropped on Hiroshima, and a further 70,000 deaths from the atomic blast in Nagasaki.

In the Philippines, 480,000 Japanese servicemen had died in the war. In New Guinea, 16,000 Japanese soldiers died and the surviving Japanese POWs did not even have the strength to dig graves for the bodies of their comrades. About 40,000 Japanese defenders died in the battle of Saipan; thousands of Japanese women, children, and elderly were driven to the cliffs of the island and committed mass suicide. In spring 1945, over 200 student nurses and 18 teachers of elite girls' high schools in Okinawa were forced to serve as a nursing unit which became known as the 'Lily Corps'. Most of the girls were killed by the random firing of US soldiers' and others threw themselves from the southern cliff of Okinawa. In a similar way, about 2,000 middle and high school students were mobilised and more than half of them died in the course of the battle.

In June 2007, the Japanese government gave a directive to Japanese school textbook publishers to delete references to the Japanese Imperial Army ordering Okinawans to commit group suicide (*shudan jiketsu*) instead of surrendering to US forces. Okinawans reacted furiously to this decision and called on the government to retract its instruction. In this event, I believe that each Okinawan found himself or herself with a personal obligation to remember the dead, to sustain the memories of the Battle of Okinawa, but I am interested in the collective understanding of their *shudan jiketsu* memories or the norm that exists because Okinawans collectively believe it exists and act accordingly. In general terms, I seek to examine when and why such collective understanding or expectation influences the domestic structures, such as electoral systems, of political opportunities in a government's policy-making. Public opinion surveys conducted by the Prime Minister's Office reveal that, in the event of a foreign invasion of Japan, one-third of respondents from 1978 to 2006 consistently favoured unarmed resistance or no resistance at all and slightly over 5% during the same period said that they would join the SDF and fight. This trend has remained intact amid the direct military threat posed by North Korea against Japan. I hypothesised that social norms would greatly matter in Japan's military security policy-making.

Nonetheless, the unsolved problem is that in the war's aftermath many individual Japanese felt that the responsibility of war and aggression had already been settled, and that they had been victims of Japan's militarism. Although harboring resentment, distrust and ill-feeling against a military that had mobilised the nation into an aggressive war, the Japanese people neither held themselves accountable for the war, nor took action to indict and punish those deemed responsible. In December 1937, the Japanese military carried out a horrific rampage, executing some 300,000 civilians (the Chinese official estimate) in the city of Nanjing. The Japanese soldiers raped and killed thousands of Filipina women and girls in the course of the war. These historical events had been ignored or omitted from Japanese textbooks. By the early 1990s, these history textbooks at last became more accountable for sufferings of non-Japanese victims of war and described Japan's wartime atrocities in much greater detail. In the 1990s, it was argued that Japan should not confine itself to 'inward-looking pacifism' but open up in order to be accepted and understood by the rest of the world. As social norms evolved, Japan's military security policy may have changed. I seek out views of how norms changed and affected the nature and direction of Japan's military security policy.

In any democratic nation, we expect that the weight of popular pressure, to some extent, influences the process of decision-making in government policy areas including military security policy. In fact, the formation of foreign policy seems to be increasingly influenced by popular opinion in the midst of ICT-based application. But realists argue otherwise, that military security policy is largely made in isolation from domestic politics. In their view, too much fragmentation in policy confuses allies and encourages enemies. It is true that critical security decisions have often been made in the absence of public consensus. It is the nature of military security policy that a greater degree of secrecy and discretion is required to deal with the sensitivities of other nations and military intelligence. The conventional wisdom in the literature suggests that military security policy views are elite rather than mass opinions. This understanding corresponds to the notion of elitism or state-centric realist assumptions. It is assumed that national consensus is a function of the elite consensus: public ideology is manipulated and shaped by political leaders as security issues are less significant and seemingly too remote from the public. However, this elite-led approach needs to reconcile with counterevidence: the public are increasingly informed and less subject to manipulation and national leaders thus take the power of masses more seriously than ever before. Likewise, the mass-led approach requires an explanation of how the weight of popular pressure might influence military security policy decisions, which must be made decisively to respond to the problems the world outside is constantly throwing up.

In post-Second World War Japan, there have been contending elite opinions over Japan's military security, that is, about how to protect the nation. These opinions have continually been skewed to changes in the external strategic environment in their application, but they have been consistent in essence. Two groups share the view that Japan should keep the United States at a greater distance and seek autonomous defense. But they take diametrically different approaches to the proposed way of protecting the nation. The anti-militarists on the old left seek security through 'unarmed neutrality.' In the post-Cold War environment, the idea of neutrality is marginalised because of the collapse of the Soviet Union. In 1994, even socialist Prime Minister Murayama Tomiichi recognised the constitutionality of Japan's Self-Defense Force (SDF) and the continuation of the US–Japan Security Treaty. The nationalists on the right also criticise Japan for subordinating itself to the United States yet see its independent military strength as the way to autonomy. After the Cold War, we saw a resurgence of nationalists (or 'neo-nationalists'), such as Ishihara Shintaro and Nakanishi Terumasa, who are troubled by US unilateralism and propose Japan's strong identity and self-reliance. Nonetheless, few mainstream politicians take such a nationalist stance seriously, particularly at the expense of electoral fortune.

Two other groups have dominated elite discourse over the past decade. These groups believe that Japan cannot stand on its own feet and must seek security through alliance with the United States. A new group in this pro-US mainstream, which has emerged in the past decade, are the revisionists, such as Ozawa Ichiro, Koizumi Jun'ichiro and Ishiba Shigeru. They share the view that Japan as a 'normal nation' should seek security through its military contribution at a level commensurate with the nation's economic strength and build a more equal partnership with the United States. Perhaps the most dominant group in the elite discourse are the pragmatic conservatives, the conventional practitioners of the Yoshida Doctrine, who continue to oppose the use of force and see economic prosperity as a better way for Japan to make an international contribution while relying on US security guarantee.

Security specialists have examined how Japan's elite security discourse is actually transformed into policy-making. One of the most influential accounts for Japanese security is the realists' interpretation that argues Japan has pursued an active, rational strategy consistent with defensive and offensive realism. In their view, Japan has actively chosen the strategy of 'back-passer', first relying on the protector, the United States, to restore the balance-of-power by transferring the cost of this shift to the United States, and second to increasing Japanese military contributions if the United States is unable or neglects to do this. This realists' account appears to support the observation that Japan is now in the midst of a transition from pragmatic conservatism to revisionism. My close research tells otherwise; that domestic norms largely inhibit Japan's strategic security decision-making. In other words, Japan's military security policy is inconsistent with defensive and offensive realism. I agree with the constructivist argument that anti-militaristic norms explain the scope of Japan's deviation from a realist prediction of Japan's national security. But I do not support the constructivists' arguments for the independent, direct causal effect of anti-militarism norms on Japan's security policy-making. Policy-makers' compliance with anti-militaristic norms has not automatically taken place, particularly as elite and public opinions on military security clearly differ. Domestic norms, as such, cannot directly account for Japan's military security policy. It is assumed that elite and public opinions interact with each other. In short, domestic political opportunity structures (or norm compliance mechanisms), such as electoral systems, determine how elite opinions (strategic thinking) respond to societal demands (social norms). In sum, a bridging approach encompassing both realism and constructivism seems to be more appropriate. Constructivists wish to emphasise non-material or ideational factors at work in Japan's military security policy-making, while realists see material resources and power as determinants of policy-making. The view of either elite-led or mass-led processes alone neglects to examine how ideational factors or norms widely shared among the public are converted into political resources and power, which might influence agenda-setting, formation and implementation of government policies. On the theoretical side, this project will thus explore the ways of promising cross-fertilisation between realism and constructivism.

In writing this study, I have accumulated debts of gratitude to the Faculty of International Relations at Ritsumeikan University in Kyoto for the institutional support received there, and especially Hori Masaharu and Nakatsuji Keiji for making my research in Japan productive while I was a visiting professor in 2003–2004. I would also like to thank the Department of Social Sciences at Curtin University of Technology in Perth, Western Australia, for a leave-of-absence that enabled me to continue my research.

I am also particularly grateful for the generous support of the Centre for Advanced Studies in Australia, Asia and the Pacific (CASAAP) at Curtin University of Technology.

The production side of this book would not have proceeded far without the editorial assistance of Jenny Hall at the Monash Asia Institute. Her professional skills at putting complex pieces of my manuscript together contributed to the completion of this book.

Yasuo Takao

Perth, Western Australia

introduction

New developments

A Japanese man wearing a *Shogun*-like helmet appeared on the cover of *Time* magazine on 16 August 1999 holding a folding fan with the Japanese national flag on it under the caption 'Japan Returns to Nationalism'. Traditionally the realm of the right-wing, nationalism in Japan was seen to be entering mainstream culture. Indeed the same month saw the enactment of a law relating to the National Flag and National Anthem, codifying the *hinomaru* (sun-circle)—widely displayed as military insignia in wartime Japan—as the national flag. Even Prime Minister Mori Yoshiro had a slip of the tongue saying, 'Japan is a divine nation, with the Emperor at its core' (*Japan Times* 17.5.2000).

Then, on 23 December 2001 came an incident that appeared to demonstrate Tokyo's willingness to use force; the Japan Coast Guard fired on a boat suspected of being a North Korean spy ship in the East China Sea (*Japan Times* 23 & 24.12.2001). In contrast to Japan's previous refusal to be provoked, for the first time since the end of the Second World War the country's armed forces had violently pursued and sunk a foreign vessel. The uncharacteristic nature of Tokyo's assertive stance towards national security has caused serious concerns and criticisms from both within Japan and outside the country (Matthews 2003:74–91). Some observers worry that such sudden changes in Tokyo's attitudes may indicate a sign of new nationalism with the hidden agenda of a revival of Japanese militarism (see McCormack 2004; Johnson 2005:12).

Recent breaks from Japan's anti-militarism stance

Shortly after 11 September 2001 terrorist attacks on New York and the Pentagon, a diplomatic source in Japan quoted US Deputy Secretary of State Richard Armitage as telling Japanese Ambassador to the United States, Yanai Shunji, '[Japan] show the flag.' Two months later, Yanai referred to this exchange with Armitage,

I had an informal meeting with Mr Armitage on September 15. We discussed the importance of dealing with the matter carefully...I don't remember if he used the phrase 'Show the flag' per se, but it was clear that he was calling on Japan for a visible contribution and to display *hinomaru* (sun circle) flags (*Kyodo News* 6.11.2001).

The Japanese government was extremely wary about repeating past experiences, in particular the diplomatic bungle caused by Japan's failure to dispatch its Self-Defence Force (SDF) to the 1991 Gulf War against Iraq to carry out noncombatant support operations. After 11 September, key government officials and SDF officers were under strong pressure and felt obligated to share risks incurred from the US 'war' on terrorism rather than take a spectator's seat (*Washington Post* 20.9.2001; *Japan Times* 21.9.2001; *The Daily Yomiuri* 22.9.2001). On 19 September, Prime Minister Koizumi Junichiro pledged direct support, such as medical services, intelligence, humanitarian aid and ship supplies, for US action against terrorism. Many American and domestic observers reported that his pledge would be a test to dissolve overseas perceptions of Japan as an indecisive and unreliable ally (*The New York Times* 19.9.2001; *Asahi Shinbun* 20.9.2001; *The Washington Post* 20.9.2001; *The Daily Yomiuri* 22.9.2001).

As soon as the US air attack against the Taliban regime had begun in Afghanistan, Prime Minister Koizumi determined to pass anti-terrorism legislation permitting Japan to dispatch the SDF to the Indian Ocean. For the first time since the Second World War, the SDF would provide rear-area logistical support for US *military combat operations* against al-Qaeda and the Taliban regime. Introduced (as a revised government bill) on 16 October, the *Anti-Terrorism Special Measures Act* was passed in an incredibly fast fashion and enacted on 29 October, despite it being such a major bill.[1] On 4 December 2002 the Japanese government decided to dispatch the *Kirishima*, one of SDF's Aegis destroyers, equipped with intelligence-gathering and air defence systems. The *Kirishima* was to provide rear-area logistical support for the anti-terrorism military activities of the United States and others in the Indian Ocean. Newspapers reported that Armitage was delighted at this decision, remarking, 'The US government thinks this is a splendid example of Prime Minister Koizumi's leadership' (*Japan Times* 6.12.2002).

In March 2003 the United States invaded Iraq in order to topple the Saddam Hussein regime. Although Prime Minister Koizumi announced unconditional support for US military action in Iraq, the deployment of the SDF became feasible only after President George W Bush declared the end of 'major combat operations' on 1 May. In his meeting with President Bush on 23 May, Prime Minister Koizumi stated that Japan would dispatch the Air Self-Defence

Force's (ASDF) C-130 aircrafts for transport of goods in the region (MOFA 2005). He followed through on this pledge, arguing that direct participation in reconstruction efforts in Iraq were crucial for Japan to become a responsible member of international community (PMJC 2003). On 1 August, the Japanese government enacted the *Iraq Humanitarian Reconstruction Assistance Special Measures Law*, which allowed Japan's SDF in Iraq to participate for the first time in foreign territory under the administration of an occupying power. At the same time the law limited the area of SDF activities to 'noncombatant zones'. The proposed Ground Self-Defence Force (GSDF)'s deployment under this law was seen as a sharp break from Japan's past practices within the United Nations Peacekeeping Operations (PKO) framework. However, Koizumi's leadership still faced relentless domestic opposition to Japan's activism outside the UN framework. Meanwhile, as Iraq's security situation remained volatile, Japan was indecisive in the dispatch of SDF to 'noncombatant zones'. A Kyodo News source quoted Armitage as telling Japan's special ambassador to the Middle East, Arima Tatsuo, 'Don't walk away' from support for US military action. At the same time he underlined the real risks, warning that Iraq reconstruction would not be like attending a 'tea party' (*Koydo News* 13.8.2003; *Japan Times* 31.8.2003). Armitage's remarks presented yet further US pressure on Japan to shift security policy towards a strongly alliance-oriented, high-risk strategy.

In January 2004, the Japanese government dispatched 550 GSDF members to the capital of Muthanna, Samawah, a region Prime Minister Koizumi claimed was 'a noncombatant zone'. However, those GSDF members were frequently bombarded by rocket ammunitions as they assisted with water supply, medical care and the construction of schools. On 7 April three Japanese citizens (a NPO volunteer, a student activist and a photojournalist) were taken hostage by an Iraqi group. On 21 July in a meeting with Nakamura Hidenao, chairperson of the Diet Affairs Committee of the governing Liberal Democratic Party (LDP), a somewhat irritated Armitage reportedly stated,

> Article 9 [of Japan's Constitution renouncing the use of force except as a matter of self-defence] is becoming an obstacle to strengthening the Japan–US alliance, and Japan must revise the Constitution and play a greater military role for international peace if it wants to gain a permanent seat on the UN Security Council (*Asahi Shinbun* 23.7.2004; *Japan Times* 23.7.2004; *Daily Yomiuri* 24.7.2004).

Armitage's remark reflected strong US dissatisfaction with Japan as a bilateral alliance partner. In his view, Article 9 was the cause of Japan's constitutional inability to defend the United States from armed attack, although the United States was legally obliged to defend Japan. As Japan was unable to send the SDF on high-risk UN missions, Armitage suggested that Article 9 was not only an impediment to the US–Japan alliance but also to Japan's bid to become a permanent member of the UN Security Council.

The above-mentioned remarks by Armitage were among a series that echoed those held by a bipartisan group of Japan experts in Washington, including Armitage, Assistant Secretary of State James Kelly, and Senior Director for Asian Affairs Torkel Patterson who formulated Bush's policy toward Asia. They argued that Japan should revise Article 9 and lift its prohibition against collective self-defence (or legalise the dispatch of SDF abroad for collective self-defence to support US involvement in conflicts in Asia) (*INSS Special Report* 2000:5). They saw the US–UK security partnership as a model for a future US–Japan alliance, which they wished to call 'Britain of the Far East'. The group concluded, 'It is time for burden-sharing to evolve into power-sharing' (*INSS Special Report* 2000:6).

The American expectation of risk-sharing incurred from military emergencies led to a heated debate in Japan on collective self-defence and emergency contingency legislation. Indeed, the Koizumi Cabinet had appeared responsive to US wishes. On 16 April 2002 it drafted three wartime contingency bills to be sent to the Diet, that specified the powers of the government in mobilising armed forces and adopting emergency measures. On the same day, at a meeting of the US–Japan Security Subcommittee (SSC), senior officials from Japan's Defence Agency and Foreign Affairs Ministry disclosed those drafted bills to the Pentagon and the US State Department. The US side praised Japan for bringing up the 'long-pending' bills for deliberation in the Diet (*Sankei Shinbun* 18.4.2002).

In June 2003 the wartime contingency bills were passed in the National Diet.[2] For the first time since the Second World War, the Japanese government was now equipped with a legal guideline to respond to a military attack. For the past half century, any legislation presupposing a national security emergency had been unthinkable—almost a political taboo under the war-renouncing constitution of Japan. Public support for a pro-active security policy had proven a suitable environment not only for the passage of those bills, but also for the revitalisation of the US–Japan alliance within the framework of new US strategies in world affairs.

In the September 2005 election of the House of Representatives, the LDP gained the largest share of seats (296 out of 480) in postwar politics. Its governing coalition with the New Komeito Party now commanded a two-thirds majority in the lower house. This enabled them to initiate constitutional amendments, before submitting them to the upper house and potentially to a national referendum for ratification. The LDP together with its coalition partner, the New Komeito Party, plus the largest opposition Democratic Party, all agreed to discuss the necessary legislation for holding a national referendum on constitutional revision. On 13 April 2007, the House of Representatives passed a bill to instigate procedures for a national referendum to revise the Constitution.[3] The bill would take effect within three years of its approval by the upper house on 14 May. Prime Minister Abe Shinzo declared, 'Now is the time to clarify [the LDP's] intention to create a new Constitution for a new era', taking one step closer to constitutional revision (*Japan Times* 14.4.2007). In addition, in December 2006 the Abe Cabinet pushed through and enacted landmark laws requiring Japanese schools to encourage patriotism in class and promoting the Defence Agency to the status of a full ministry. Abe's initiatives were reportedly designed to boost Japan's military status and promote national pride among the general public.[4]

In recent years, therefore, the Japanese government has launched a set of sharp breaks from Japan's anti-militarism stance:

- the 2001 anti-terrorism legislation, which allowed Japan, for the first time since the Second World War, to provide rearguard support for *military combat operations*;

- the 2003 Iraq reconstruction assistance legislation, enabling Japan's SDF to participate, for the first time, *outside the UN framework* in an area of foreign territory under the administration of an occupying power;

- the 2003 wartime preparedness legislation, equipping Japan with a legal procedure to respond to a national security emergency or *a military attack*;

- the 2007 constitution referendum legislation that enabled Prime Minister Abe to move onto his ultimate goal—*revising the war-renouncing Constitution*.

Frameworks for assessing Japan's potential remilitarisation

Does any of this constitute evidence of a remilitarising Japan? Is Japan really signalling a fundamental shift in its security policy? Is Japan becoming locked into an American global strategy? As late as 1990, Washington exerted pressure on Japan regarding financial contributions to US forces rather than on building up Japan's independent military capabilities. At the same time the US rhetorically argued that Japan must assume greater responsibility for its own and Asia's security. In fact, in March 1990, Henry C Stackpole III, then commander of US Marine Corps bases in Japan stated: 'No one wants a rearmed, resurgent Japan…so we are the cap in the bottle, if you will' (*Washington Post*, 27.3.1990). Yet since the Gulf Crisis of 1990–1991, the United States has compelled Japan to revise Article 9 of the Constitution and to become a 'normal nation' from the viewpoint of American officials. In their view, military deployment is the only condition preventing Japan from assuming the status of a normal nation and Japan is subsequently expected to become part of America's global military strategy.[5] Some scholars argue that the constraints of Article 9's pacifism have been dismissed and Japan is already set on its remilitarisation path, closely integrated into US military strategy (Hughes 2004:368–9; McCormack 2004). Such conclusive arguments must withstand the scrutiny of empirical analysis. The process of remilitarisation can be seen to involve various steps including:

- increasing military expenditure;
- developing strategically offensive military capabilities;
- a growing acceptance of the use of armed forces as a means of settling international disputes;
- legitimising and legalising the dispatch of armed forces to foreign soil; and
- setting up emergency procedures for a military attack.

Policy changes and continuities embodied in these steps can be explained by linking two different areas of scholarship. The first area points to domestic constraints as a major determinant of policy choice, such as collectively shared beliefs, public opinion, political culture, constitutional and legal institutions, the party system, electoral systems, fiscal pressures, and the decision-making process. The second area, focusing attention at the level of inter-state relations, explains effects on domestic policy choice in the international system, including the regional security environment and foreign pressures.

The following chapters explore how Japan's stances and measures toward remilitarisation have changed over time in order to manage both domestic and international constraints on military security; more specifically, it examines how the Japanese government has been sensitive to the general public's strong aversion to the use of force within the US security guarantee. It ultimately attempts to answer if Japan is remilitarising, within the context of American global strategy, because those collective expectations have evolved to the current acceptance of a more pro-active security policy.

First, external constraints such as US pressure and changes in the regional strategic environment, provide incomplete explanations for Japan's consistent opposition to large-scale rearmament. Second, internal constraints such as the war-renouncing Constitution and public opinion are essential to explaining this anomalous opposition. This book focuses on one of the internal constraints, that is, domestic norms. Collective expectations or social norms, shared among the general public in Japan are the primary source determining the course of policy continuity and shifts toward military security. Such widely shared non-physical forces do not themselves independently determine policy formation of military security, but need to be maintained, invested and converted into physical outcomes of policy decision-making or non-decision-making. In other words, the institutionalised medium through which widely shared expectations transform into actual policy outcomes is necessary in this process. We may call it the compliance mechanism of norms in political processes. Policy-makers' compliance with social norms is crucial for a better understanding of Japan's military security as national leaders and the general public clearly differ in their beliefs regarding public safety and security.

In the process of norm compliance, the medium refers to an institutionalised mechanism that converts collective expectations into political constraints and opportunities for policy-makers. It is institutionalised as policy-makers engage in regular sustained interactions with stakeholders within a set of widely shared briefs or expectations. The first type of institutionalisation can be seen as legal and formal in the sense that the compliance mechanism is incorporated in formal rules and organisations. The legal and formal mediums for norm compliance consist of the following:

- Article 9 of the Japanese Constitution, which renounces the use of armed forces as a means of settling international disputes although its interpretation has deemed that the formation of any armed force for self-defence does not violate this article;
- Article 96 of the Japanese Constitution, which requires a two-thirds majority in both houses for constitutional revision, then to be submitted to a national referendum where a simple majority is required for passage;
- electoral systems (a single non-transferable vote in a multi-member district, 1947–1994, for lower house elections), which provide disincentives for LDP politicians to get military security issues on the national agenda;[6]
- the system of civilian control in which the professional military is under the strict supervision of civilian bureaucrats (Otake 1983; Katsenstein & Okawara 1993:92–97).

The second type of institutionalisation occurs when the compliance mechanism becomes embedded in policy-makers' expectations for a set of temporarily fixed or informally regularised rules. The temporary, informal mediums for norm compliance consist of the following:

- the ban on SDF overseas dispatch, which the upper house adopted as a resolution in 1954 (conditionally lifted under the 1992 peacekeeping operations legislation, the 2001 anti-terrorism legislation, and the 2003 Iraq reconstruction assistance legislation);
- the ban on arms exports, which was first announced by Prime Minister Sato Eisaku in 1967—a ban exporting weapons to communist countries, those under United Nations sanctions and those in international conflicts (adopted in 1976 to ban all arms exports regardless of destination, and allowed in 2004 to export missile defence-related technology to the United States) (HRB 1967a);
- the three non-nuclear principles, to which Prime Minister Sato referred in December 1967, prohibiting Japan from manufacturing, possessing or allowing entry of nuclear weapons into Japan (adopted as a resolution in 1971 by the lower house and in 1976 by committees on foreign affairs in both of the houses) (HRB 1967b);
- the ban on collective self-defence, which became the tacit government understanding of Article 9 in 1972 (stated clearly by the Suzuki Zenko Cabinet in 1981, that Japan has the right of collective self-defence under international law but is constitutionally prohibited from exercising that right) (Asagumo Shinbunsha 2001:576);
- the 1% of GNP ceiling on defence spending, which became a tacit target in the late 1960s within the Defence Agency (by 1974 it was regarded by LDP Diet members as the firm upper limit and in 1976 enunciated by Prime Minister Miki Takeo). (The imposition of the 1% of GNP ceiling on defence expenditures will be examined in the following chapters).

Another fundamental constraint on Japan's military security has been the US security guarantee. Collective expectations, widely shared among the general public, for military security are ultimately capable of constraining Japan's military security policy; however, the norm-induced policy becomes a less compelling option without Japan's continuing dependence on the US security guarantee. The compliance mechanism of social norms has effectively functioned on the assumption that the United States continues to provide its security guarantee to Japan. By the late 1960s, however, the decline of US hegemonic power and increased prosperity in Japan has resulted in the United States being less willing and less able to bear the cost of the one-sided security guarantee to Japan. On 25 July 1969, President Richard Nixon stated at a press briefing in Guam that Asian nations must take primary responsibility for their own security.[7] How did the Japanese government manage the US pressure for Japan to assume more of the defence burden?

Japanese politics expert Susan Pharr describes Japan's response to US pressure as co-operative with the United States but at a minimal cost (Pharr 1993:235–62). In her view, the Japanese government has been consistently defensive and implemented low-risk strategies with a long term view of national interests. In other words, Japan's stance against large-scale militarisation derives from a consistent, strategic doctrine at the national level. Other Japanese politics specialists point out that there has been no such strategic doctrine in Japan's response to US pressure. Joseph Keddell Jr, for example, argues that the Japanese government has responded to US pressure in an incremental way to minimise, but not eliminate its conflicts with the United States (Keddell 1993:4–8). Kent Calder, although agreeing with Keddell that Japan's response is not strategic but reactive to US pressure, contends that the LDP has been more attuned to domestic political crisis even when the United States steps up pressure on Japan (Calder 1988a:21, 32, 413–39). The consequence is the same for all of these arguments: that Japan has not shared comparable costs and risks but the United States has provided a unilateral guarantee of Japanese security. Why the United States is able to condone the marked asymmetries in the US–Japan alliance is yet to be answered. One way of responding to this question is to examine the compatibility between US pressure and Japan's domestic constraints on military security.

Keddell suggests that incremental changes occur in Japan's defence policy to cope with contradictory international and domestic pressures (1993:4). The ruling LDP engages in the task of managing contradictory left-wing opposition and US pressures, however Japan is not merely caught between domestic constraints and US pressure in the absence of any strategy. There was compatibility between domestic and US pressures at a fundamental level at least until the early 1990s.

Since the late 1960s, the US government has continually called for an increase in burden-sharing but has given priority to increasing Japan's foreign aid to strategically important countries, such as Pakistan and Turkey, over large-scale Japanese remilitarisation. In response to the Soviet military build-up, from the mid-1970s the US government almost exclusively directed its pressure on Japan's increased financial support for the US military stationed in Japan rather than developing Japan's own military capabilities. In a similar vein, US Congressional pressure placed greater emphasis on sharing the maintenance costs of US military forces in Japan, acknowledging that Japan's large-scale remilitarisation would destabilise the strategic environment in Northeast Asia.

An independent Japanese military, therefore, should not replace the US military presence in East Asia (USHRIR 1977; USSAS 1979; USHRAS 198). As late as April 1990, the US Department of Defence confirmed the necessity of the 'cap-in-the-bottle' strategy arguing that the US military presence in East Asia would deter the rise of a regional power and prevent Japan's large-scale remilitarisation (US Department of Defence 1990).

Such US strategy was compatible with tenacious developmentalism in which Japanese policy-makers had determined to strengthen the state through economic development. In a low growth environment following the 1973 Oil Crisis, the Japanese government was still obsessed with further enhancement of its trillion dollar economy through trade and productivity gains. US pressure on Japan to increase financial support for the US military stationed in Japan was easily met by Japan's trade and productivity gains. With the continuing US security guarantee, Japan, although incapable of fighting war on a major scale, was able to devote her energies to gaining national welfare and save money through this means.

Equally important, the US government's tendency to evade increasing Japan's independent military capabilities provided a supportive environment for the compliance to anti-militarism norms in Japan. By the late 1970s, the majority of Japanese people endorsed the maintenance of the status quo in which Japan would continue to rely on the existing level of SDF and US–Japan security arrangements to defend the nation (discussed in Chapter 3). They clearly displayed a collective belief against the development of Japan's independent war-making capabilities while neither wishing to repeal the US–Japan Security Treaty nor reduce the influence of the SDF. The compatibility between domestic and US pressures seems to be reflected in the defence budget breakdown of 1975–90. After the late 1970s, the Japanese government expanded its financial contribution rapidly to include the stationing of US forces in Japan, while restricting the resources available for building up its independent military capabilities.[8] The compliance mechanism of the 1% of GNP ceiling on defence spending functioned to ensure the continuing US security guarantee while restricting Japan's independent military capabilities. Even in the 1980s (the Nakasone era of pro-defence and pro-constitutional revision) when Japan was seemingly making a break with the past regarding military capabilities,[9] Prime Minister Nakasone was unable to abolish or alter the norm compliance mechanisms, except for marginal changes including permissions for the transfer of defence-related technology to the United States—an exception to the ban on arms exports (Keddell 1993:126–57). Nakasone's move to break the 1% ceiling, exceeding by the marginal amount of 1.004% in 1987, did not bring a real change in Japan's defence posture. Despite their successful 1986 election,[10] many LDP leaders reacted to this symbolic breaking of the ceiling, fearing the implications for the party in the next election (HRB 1986). There were grave concerns among opposition parties and many LDP leaders over the erosion of domestic constraints on defence. Although Prime Minister Nakasone initially pledged to upgrade the defence force levels defined in the 1976 National Defence Program Outline (NDPO–designed to cope with 'limited, small attacks' under peacetime conditions) after achieving the NDPO goals in 1990, he eventually scuttled this pledge in the face of a storm of criticism (HRB 1986). After all, the lifting of the ceiling did not lead to Japan's defence budget regularly exceeding 1%.

Here, it is important to note, as Calder explains, that in Japan defence spending is 'residual' in the sense that the issues of national defence do not generate 'money and vote' but those of agriculture and small business do. Nonetheless, Calder's argument that constraints on low defence spending derive from indifferent politicians and weak special interest groups does not substantiate (Calder 1988a:413). In the past, Japanese politicians have engaged in extending material benefits to the agriculture and small business sectors and thus this process can be seen as a process of political credit claiming. In contrast, defence budgeting is generally an exercise in blame avoidance rather that credit claiming, basically because the costs rather than the benefits of defence expansion are recognised according to social norms in Japan. Social norms require politicians to avoid unpopular policies related to increases in defence spending and defence build-up. Politicians do not follow the same rules of credit claiming for agriculture or small business policy, but in accordance with social norms, they seek to seriously avoid the scrutiny of voters over national military security issues.

In the early 1990s, however, the structural relationship of compatibility between internal and external constraints began to shake with the aftermath of the first Gulf War. The maintenance of compatibility between domestic and US pressures appeared to become irrelevant to changes in Japan's military security policy. Japan's emerging forces seemed to converge with the following new US pressures:

- an emerging US pressure on military risk sharing rather than on payments for 'strategic foreign aid' and the stationing of US forces in Japan;

- the Japanese government's move towards a 'normal state' demonstrating its active behaviour in the area of military security—actively responding to the North Korean threat and the spread of transnational terrorism; and

- Japanese public awareness that Japan should play a more active role in the maintenance of international peace and security—illustrated by the fact that pro-revisionists of the war-renouncing Constitution, for the first time, outnumbered anti-revisionists in the mid-1990s.

These pressures seemed to converge and move in the same direction: Japan's pro-active security policy and remilitarisation.

The social norm structure of Japan's military security is changing but doing so slowly. This statement challenges the conventional wisdom that Japan is 'remilitarising'. Japan continues to display great restraint in its military security policy. Despite its increased military capabilities, Japan has continued to show a strong aversion to military involvement. The swing in collective beliefs among the public can be seen to favour a pro-active security policy but within the limits of continued anti-militarism, with Japan's international contribution not construed as the use of armed forces. Only 20% of Japanese citizens think that Japan should participate in UN *combatant* peace enforcement operations.[11] In view of this, it is highly unlikely that lifting the prohibition on collective self-defence will be nominated for ratification by Japanese voters.

In postwar Japan, national leaders did not play a militarily assertive role in response to Japan's enhanced economic standing. The anomaly that Japanese security policy poses for existing theories has led to competing issues: the systemic consequences of its utility-focused neo-realism, the institutional benefits of its efficiency-driven neo-liberalism, and the independent effects of its domestic norms and culture. One key area of Japanese security policy, though, is rarely explored: How are norms transformed into corresponding security policy in political processes? What is the driving mechanism of norm acceptance by self-interested political agents? How do policy-makers develop ways of balancing norms and international/external constraints? In postwar Japan, citizens were bitterly reactive to military involvement. This strong reaction led to norm formation against the militarist past. In Japan's national security policy-making, policy-makers take action within norms-embedded domestic structures. This has enabled the norms and social understandings to articulate or reconcile the interests of legislative members who seek re-election. The executive has accordingly accommodated the domestic constraints to the external structure, namely US security guarantees for Japan. This book explores the possibility of a productive cross-fertilisation between material utility-driven positivists and nonmaterial norm-based constructivists. Its ultimate objective is to find out the causal mechanism of policy-makers' compliance with social norms.

In examining the development of Japan's military security and a possibility for Japan's large scale remilitarisation, this study uses Japan's defence expenditure figures as a key index of measurement, along with other indexes: Japan's military capabilities; overseas dispatch of the SDF, permissible uses of

Japan's armed forces, and Japan's wartime preparedness. The importance of budgetary capabilities has been remarked upon: 'the desire of Japan's leaders to play a militarily more assertive role has become apparent, a natural response to Japan's enhanced economic standing' (Waltz 1993:65). Kenneth Waltz predicts that Japan will seek its own military capabilities, independent of the United States, for security (Waltz 1993:44–79; 2000:5–41). However, such a neo-realist prediction does not support the fact that Japan's defence expenditure relative to the size of its economy has continued to be uniquely low among the major industrialised countries. The main problem with neo-realist approaches is that purely systemic explanations do not sufficiently address why similar states in similar situations often do not act the same. Defensive realism is a recent attempt to solve this problem, suggesting that systemic factors, such as the anarchic nature of the state system, determine some types of state behaviour but not others (Walt 1987; Synder 1991; Glaser 1996:122–66; Van Evera 1998:5–43). Defensive realism assumes that security is a matter of choosing certain options rather than of following a destined course of action for survival. One variation based on defensive realism has increasingly used a form of cost-benefit analysis in alliance politics and taken collective goods approaches that make apparent who benefits or loses in terms of a state's relative contribution to shared security (Snyder 1997; Powell 1999). It suggests that the smaller contributors could benefit most while depending on the burden of an alliance borne by the larger contributors. Given that Japan has been accused of getting a 'free ride' on defence, such a defensive realism approach appears to remain compelling for a better explanation of Japan's defence spending. The findings from the analysis of Japan's defence expenditure will be discussed within the framework of the theoretical debate between defensive realism and social constructivism.

The literature on budgeting suggests a number of potential determinants for changes in defence spending: external factors—the external environment (external threats and alliance politics) and internal factors—economic conditions (revenue growth and deficit financing), macro-budgeting (bureaucratic control), party politics (partisan control), special interests (veterans and defence industry), and public opinion (material interests and norms) (Lord 1973; Wildavsky 1975; Eichenberg 1981; Martin 1981). Over the past few decades, the level of defence expenditure has accordingly shown a distinctive fluctuation in major Western states; and, as described in Chapter 2 and indicated in Table 2-1, that level in industrialised Asian states has been heavily influenced by emerging external threats. By contrast Japan's defence expenditure as a percentage of gross domestic product (GDP) or gross national product (GNP), which is referred to as 'defence burden,' has remained virtually unchanged for nearly four decades; it appears to be unresponsive to any potential determinant. Defence expenditure as a percentage of GDP or GNP can be used to reflect a country's capability of paying defence burdens to receive its security benefits. In a comparative perspective, official figures for Japan's defence expenditure are also converted into US dollars (see Lind 2004:112; Hummel 1996:141). These figures began to rise dramatically after the 1985 Plaza agreement and quadrupled within a decade.[12] This seems to support neo-realist arguments, that is, the rise of Japan's military power is due to superpower reduction. This upsurge is primarily caused by the appreciation of the yen; Japan's defence spending in yen has increased steadily in an incremental way since the late 1960s (JDA 2006). The upsurge of Japan's defence spending in US dollars does not literally translate into an increase in military capability, especially since the Japanese government spends over 90% of defence acquisitions on domestic procurement (Green 1995:15)—needless to say, personnel expenses account for nearly 45% of defence expenditures (JDA 2006). By contrast, Japan's defence spending as GNP/GDP has remained almost unchanged since 1967 and thus seems neither to be affected by events in the external environment nor by revenues and economic conditions.

Of course, the defence burden as a percentage of GDP or GNP must be examined in relation to other indexes of measurement for remilitarisation. As discussed in the following Chapters, while admitting that even the 1% of Japan's GNP has developed more military capabilities (especially Japan's naval capabilities) than most observers expect (Twomey 2000:167–205; Lind 2004:94–101), a strong aversion to military involvement lies at the hearty of Japan's security policy. Military capabilities can be seen as stocks which might be utilised to achieve policy goals; however, in Japan, the mechanism of policy-makers' compliance with legal and social norms heavily constrains the full realisation of the potential military capabilities.

Public opinion can be viewed as a mirror to normative constraints, and thus as a key measurement index for assessing the possibility of remilitarisation. The social norms expressed in Japan's changing public opinion interact with elite opinion, which helps shape Japanese military security policy. This policy area has remained a key issue in postwar Japan, where the beliefs of the conservative coalition leaders have not accorded with the widely shared collective expectations of the public. These public attitudes derive from the traumatic experiences of the Second World War. In Japan, public opinion has influenced the conservative coalition-building process among LDP politicians, bureaucrats and big business. Japan's military security policy has been constrained by the institutionalisation of public opinion in the norm compliance mechanism.[13]

To examine the interaction of mass public opinion and elites in the process of military security policy, we need to answer the two key questions of how social norms expressed in public opinion were formed and why they were able to influence Japan's conservative coalition-building process. The first question leads to two interdependent approaches: one approach representing state-centred elitism suggests that mass public opinion is a product of elite leadership and manipulation, (Rosenau 1961; Chomsky & Herman 1988; Margolis & Mauser 1989)[14] and the other representing democratic pluralism argues that it is a product of societal consensus among the masses.[15] Most comparative politics scholars observe a set of collective beliefs as socially constructed but argue that political leaders strategically institutionalise them for their self-interested, utility-based objectives. The Yoshida Doctrine, which has been the main pillar of Japan's foreign policy, is explained as such by these scholars.[16] However, the Japanese public has neither easily been manipulated nor exploited by Japan's conservative leadership over military security. State-centred elitism assumes that public opinion on national security issues is subject to state manipulation, because it's a low-salience, low-visibility policy area as compared with domestic policy areas, and because of the limited knowledge of the general public about security issues involved in policy making. Despite this assumption, the case of military security policy in postwar Japan reveals otherwise. For the Japanese who collectively learned from the traumatic experiences of the Second World War, military national security was not merely a technical matter of how to protect the nation from external threats, but rather a critical issue of how to hold the nation together in building Japan's domestic order. Most Japanese people equated the prevention of any form of militaristic revival with democracy itself. In Japan, military security issues are *negatively* salient in the sense that the scrutiny of Japanese voters essentially creates the politics of blame avoidance rather than credit claiming, as described previously, to avoid unpopular policies related to increases in defence spending and defence build-up. Over these issues, Japanese voters are *subconsciously* knowledgeable through their collective experience of past militaristic governments. In sum, leaders tend to follow the masses in Japan's military security policy.

    This leads to the second question of why social norms expressed in mass public opinion were able to influence Japan's conservative coalition-building process. In military security policy, the beliefs of the Japanese policy elite have not corresponded to the collective social norms of the general public in the postwar period, therefore public norms as such cannot directly account for patterns of decision-making in this policy area. To link social norms with elite decisions, we must examine the compliance mechanism of social norms to understand the impact of mass public opinion on Japan's military security policy. This approach focuses on the institutionalised mechanisms (or processes of interest-representation) in which the LDP-led conservative coalition must link collective expectation (or social norms) to the political systems for political legitimacy. As stated previously, the legal and formal compliance mechanisms, such as Articles 9 and 96 of the constitution and electoral systems, can be seen as the processes of interest-representation governed by explicit rules of interaction between public and elite opinions. The informal compliance mechanisms, such as the ban on SDF overseas dispatch and collective self-defence, signify the processes of interest-representation shaped by policy-makers' tacit expectations based on repeated interaction between public and elite opinions. These compliance mechanisms determine how political systems respond to social norms. This book demonstrates that the collective expectation shared among the public is able to clarify or reconcile the interests of political leaders in the compliance mechanisms, and thus constrains self-interested political leaders. The constitutive power of norms is thus realised in the political opportunity structure to effect change.

chapter one

Existing explanations of Japanese security

Post-Second World War Japan is often described as taking a pacifist path. Indeed, Japan's military security policy seems to have been formed with little regard for changes in the structure of the international system. Given its pacifist path, Japan's lack of response to the regional strategic environment would thus seem to provide a clue to understanding Japan's evolving interests in remilitarisation. Some scholars argue that Japan is responsive but driving defensively (Pharr 1993; Miyashita & Sato 2001; Hook et al 2001; Lind 2004:92–121). Others emphasise the necessity of taking into account the domestic actors and norms for explaining the lack of response (Katzenstein & Okawara 1993:84–118; Katzenstein 1996; Berger 1993:119–50; Berger 1998; Chai 1997:389–412; Soeya 1998). Both the perspectives of defensive realism and constructivism present compelling arguments about the importance of material or structural factors and ideational or normative factors, respectively. However these theoretical foundations are not equipped to explain fully the crucial impact of the interaction of material structures and normative contexts on Japan's military security policy.

Social norms are linked through the experience and action of agents (taxpayers/voters) to domestic structures (the compliance mechanism of domestic norms) and international structures (US security guarantee) for enabling and constraining Japan's military security policy. The intrinsic force of norms is not enough to create new structures by itself; norms-driven agents must respond to these existing structures, accessing political resources and opportunities, to shape Japan's military security policy. Constructive empirical research on these interactive effects illustrates the nature and scope of Japan's military security policy.

Realism in making predictions about Japan's remilitarisation

When the Cold War ended, the rising East Asian nations were prosperous and appeared to convert their economic strength into corresponding military capabilities. Harman Kahn once predicted that Japan would inevitably seek to play a major military role with its economic power and behave like other historical rising powers (Kahn 1970:153). Neo-realist Kenneth Waltz gave systemic explanations to make predictions about Japan's large-scale remilitarisation, arguing that structural incentives in a world of anarchy would induce the capabilities of a great economic power into a great military power for survival (Waltz 1979:69–73; 122–3). Even stronger, John Mearsheimer's theory of offensive realism contends that all great powers tend to behave equally 'aggressively' to maximise their odds of survival in anarchy and seek regional hegemony (Mearsheimer 2001). Since the end of the Cold War, given American regional predominance in East Asia, some neo-realists predict that other great powers, such as Japan, will seek to balance the dominant state (Layne 1993:5–51; Waltz 1993:56, 65; Waltz 2000:5–41). In other words, Japan is destined to end its dependence on the US security guarantee. Christopher Layne has predicted that Japan will pursue its independent military capabilities and even begin balancing against the American dominance in East Asia (Layne 1993:5–51). According to balance-of-power logic, a great power will join the side of weaker powers to balance against a dominant power; it could be interpreted that Japan might form its alliance with China to balance against the presence of dominant US forces in East Asia. However there is simply no credible evidence to support the idea that Japan has ever seriously considered abandoning its alliance with the United States, although Japan's unwillingness to contribute to regional security may weaken the bilateral security arrangements. Indeed, Japan's National Defence Program Guideline (NDPG), approved by the Security Council and the Cabinet on 10 December 2004, explicitly states that Japan will maintain its closer alliance structure with the United States, and 'continue to rely on the US nuclear deterrent' (NDPG 2005).

It might be argued that Japan has not yet sought strategic independence but it will eventually emerge as an independent military power (Waltz 2000:5–41; Mearsheimer 2001:390–1). Nonetheless, according to neo-realist reasoning, Japan should have at least become more assertive militarily in response to its economic standing than two decades of high economic growth have established. As Japan has remained an anti-militaristic nation, this anomaly poses a challenge to balance-of-power realism. In the late 1980s, Kent Calder argued that Japan would not assume the responsibility for hegemonic leadership (Calder 1988b:517–41). He regarded Japan as a 'reactive state' in the sense that the state equipped with the power and reasons to undertake foreign policy initiatives fails to do so and responds only to foreign pressure in a piecemeal fashion. In his view, the inability to play a more assertive role derives from the fragmented character of state authority (Calder 1988b:528). Nonetheless, recent empirical studies demonstrate that such passive immobilism was exaggerated and that in some cases Japan's response to US pressure was not 'reactive' but a result of consciously active decision-making (Pharr 1993:235–62). Susan Pharr embraces these findings and further characterises Japanese foreign policy as strategically defensive. In particular, Pharr emphasises four characteristics of what might be called the 'defensive-state strategy': (1) its activist character; (2) its aversion to risks; (3) its low cost, compared to what other major nations pay; and (4) continuity in the approach over the entire postwar era up to the present (Pharr 1993:236).

Pharr describes the Japanese pattern of behavior as co-operative with the United States but at a minimal cost. Jennifer Lind joins Pharr in expounding a similar view that Japan has actively chosen a defensive strategy of 'buck-passing'; to hold back by shifting the cost of fighting onto an ally (Lind 2004:92–121). This self-interested behavior is a variation of defensive strategies in the sense that defensive states contribute as few resources as possible by depending on the larger members in an alliance. The burden of an alliance is accordingly borne in a disproportional way; the larger members pay more than their proportional share to balance against a threat. In other words, the members do not always seek to maximise their power, since, regardless of their share, they may receive the benefits of alliances anyway. There is an aspect of 'public goods' theory in this context (Olson & Zeckhauser 1966:266–79). The benefits of security activities, which are seen as public goods, are nonexclusive so that any one country has a strong incentive to take a free ride on the efforts of others. According to public goods logic, however, if the larger contributor finds the benefits of a defence activity to be less than the cost involved, and thus withholds these benefits, defence becomes no longer nonexclusive to the free rider.

Given Japan's low defence burden, which is incorporated into the disproportionately large burden borne by the United States within their bilateral relations, Japan appears to have acted as a self-interested cost-minimiser. But military security is the most costly public good. In view of defensive strategies, the tendency of the defensive member state is to free-ride works to the extent that its cost minimisation is in the interest of the larger member. There are certain conditions under which Japan as a self-interested cost-minimiser should have increased its military role in the alliance. To be consistent with the defensive state strategy, four general conditions should have increased the likelihood of substantial growth in Japan's military contributions and, if Japan had been left unprotected by its greater contributions, furthered the likelihood of developing Japan's independent military capabilities: (1) reductions in the larger member's strategic contributions to its allies (Lind 2004:106); (2) immediate security threats to the defensive member state (Snyder 2002:162); (3) the larger member's unaccountability and uncertainty to the defensive member state and; (4) increased economic capabilities of the defensive member state. In view of defensive strategies, under each of those conditions, states should act to preserve an existing distribution of power (balancing) than taking no action by shifting the burden onto the larger members in an alliance (buck-passing) (Snyder 2002:161).

In recent years, a new interpretation of realism has attempted to refine Waltz's neo-realism, in order to explain particular states' behaviour. It embraces the core idea of neo-realism whereby the nature and scope of a state's behaviour is essentially determined by the country's relative material power, but argues further that pressures in the state system must be filtered through intervening variables, especially decision-makers' perceptions (Wohlforth 1993; Christensen 1996; Zakaria 1998). This assumption specifies the links between defence capabilities and states' behaviour; it argues that the relative distribution of defence capabilities influence states' behaviour through the medium of national leaders' perceptions (Jervis 1970).[22] In this view, the perceived defensive advantage leads to buck-passing; a state's credibility as an ally is measured by perceptions within the allied state. US credibility as an ally is the perceived likelihood that the US will carry out its promises. In view of the defensive state strategy, the four general conditions stated above are supposed to lower US credibility and increase the level of Japan's defence spending. In fact, Japanese leaders' perception of US credibility as an ally has fluctuated over time since the 1951 conclusion of the US–Japan Security Treaty. The following section attempts to illustrate that contrary to expectations regarding defensive-state strategies, this weakening of US credibility at critical times neither led to a defensively active stance nor increased the level of defence spending.

Impact of US military reductions on Japan

US commitment to its military presence in East Asia has fluctuated over time. This fluctuation can be used to test the consistency of Japanese security policy with the above defence strategies. Despite the free rider aspect of defensive states, according to the line of this defensive argument, if the larger member significantly decreases a contribution to its alliance, then the defensive member states will try to meet the cost of restoring the balance to their allies. In the case of the US–Japan alliance, if the United States has reduced its military presence in East Asia and consequently caused the loss of its credibility as an ally, then Japan should have increased its military contribution relative to the cost of restoring the balance of credible security.

In the past half century, there were two key phases of severe reduction in US strategic commitment to East Asia: one in the early 1970s and the other in the early 1990s. By the time US leaders realised that the Vietnam War was unwinnable, their economic hegemony was declining. In 1969 the Nixon Doctrine sent a strong message that the United States would expect its Asian allies to take care of their own military defence. Several years of declining US economy combined with the deficit in military spending led to an overall trade deficit in 1971 (for the first time since the 19th century). In 1971 Nixon abandoned the gold standard, aiming at trade deficit reductions with allies, especially Japan. This and the subsequent collapse of the Bretton Woods fixed-rate exchange system, prompted US allies to adjust their security arrangements with the United States. In contrast, US foreign policy had promoted Japan's economic prosperity to boost the country's internal security against communism. This led to the 'Izanami boom' of 1967–69 when the economy grew by 13% each year. The success of US postwar policy for Japan appeared to require a significant adjustment in the extent of evident disproportionality between Japan's benefits received and its defence burdens carried.

In November 1969, immediately after President Nixon's statement in Guam calling on Asian allies to do more for regional security, the US agreed to return Okinawa to Japan.[23] Faced with the greatest change in the international system since the end of the Second World War, Japan appeared to have a strong incentive to develop its reliable capabilities to defend the strategically important location of Okinawa in Asia. Instead, the removal of US nuclear weapons that were believed to be stored on the island became the central issue over formalisation of Okinawa's reversion. This was because most Japanese found it unimaginable that the nation would ever store nuclear weapons on Japan's soil. Japan's anti-nuclear stance, held across the spectrum of Japanese society, was deeply rooted in a Japanese sense of victimisation shaped by the experience of the atomic bombings of Nagasaki and Hiroshima (Berger 1993:134–6).

Since the late 1950s, the Japanese government has officially maintained that Japan chooses not to have nuclear weapons even though its constitution does not prohibit them for defensive purposes.[24] In April 1960, Prime Minister Kishi Nobusuke, one of the most hawkish nationalists, declared, 'Japan won't arm itself with nuclear weapons, nor will it allow entry of nuclear weapons [into Japan]' (HRUSJ 1960). In the following year, the US government requested port calls by its nuclear-powered naval ships, but Prime Minister Ikeda Hayato did not sanction them because of concerns, widely held among the general public, that such ships would carry nuclear weapons into Japanese territory (Keddell 1993:45). In November 1967 when the Japanese government accepted (under pressure from the United States) a visit by the aircraft carrier *Enterprise*, public reaction was immediate. The following month continued public pressure led Prime Minister Sato Eisaku to declare the Three Non-Nuclear Principles: Japan, while relying on the US nuclear umbrella, would 'not possess, produce, or permit entry of nuclear weapons into Japan' (HRB 1967b). The nuclear issue continued as Okinawans appealed for Okinawa's 'reversion without US military bases' as well as 'reversion without nuclear weapons'. The Japanese government attempted to persuade millions of demonstrators across the nation by saying that a reduction of US military bases would be sought at a rate comparable to that experienced on the mainland (*hondonami*). To facilitate the reversion further, the LDP, in alliance with centrist opposition parties, adopted a Diet resolution in November 1971 to apply the Three Non-Nuclear Principles to Okinawa in accordance with the same standards as the *hondonami* (HRPS 1971). Since the debate on Okinawa's nuclear issues, Japan's antinuclear sentiment had become stronger than ever; in opinion polls, the percentage of respondents against the possession of nuclear weapons rose from 72% in 1969, through 74% in 1974, to 82% in 1981 (NHK Broadcasting Poll Research Institute 1982:170–1).

In February 1970, Prime Minister Sato, in response to the Nixon Doctrine on Asia, outlined his new approach to Japan's defence; he stated that it was natural for any nation to defend itself by its own forces (*Japan Times* 15.2.1970).[25] In the same year, as soon as he was appointed Director General of the Defence Agency, Nakasone Yasuhiro initiated a review of the Basic Policy for National Defence (Kokubo no Kihon Hoshin), which had been adopted by the Cabinet in 1957. This policy, which emphasised Japan's exclusive dependence on the US security guarantee, had established the principles for formulating subsequent defence plans. In March 1970, Nakasone suggested a clear departure from this security dependence by moving towards the development of autonomous defence (*jishuboei*), which would allow the SDF to play a primary role in Japan's military security (*Asahi Shinbun* 19.3.1970). On 23 March, he presented his 'five principles of *jishuboei*': territorial defence, peace diplomacy, civilian control, the three non-nuclear principles, all supplemented by the US–Japan security arrangement. It is important to note that Nakasone did not advocate autonomous defence in its literal sense but pursued Japan's territorial defence by Japanese forces under the protection of US nuclear deterrence (*Asagumo Shinbun* 19.3.1970; *Mainichi Shinbun* 29.3.1970). Prime Minister Sato initially gave support for Nakasone's *jishuboei*, the promotion of which would, Sato thought, persuade the United States to smoothly return Okinawa to Japan (*Nihon Keizai Shinbun* 24.3.1970; *Asahi Shinbun* 31.3.1970).[26]

However, Nakasone was so nationalistic that his point of view mattered more to his ideological commitment than responding to changes in the regional strategic environment.[27] His right-idealist beliefs sought a radical change of defence thinking towards a more autonomous defence posture by distancing himself from the established Yoshida Doctrine of passivity and dependence on military defence policy.[28] The domestic base of support for the centrist position that Prime Minister Yoshida Shigeru (1946–47, 1948–54) and his LDP centrists had established was seriously challenged by Nakasone's ideological opposition. The push for autonomous defence capabilities was boosted by Nakasone's alliance with Japan's business interests, such as Mitsubishi and Toshiba, which had been strong lobbyists for developing Japan's domestic technology base (Otake 1986). Sakurada Takeshi of Nikkeiren (Japan Federation of Employers' Association) strongly called for *jishuboei*, and Doko Toshio, the chairperson of Keidanren (Federation of Economic Organisation), likewise echoed the call for Japan's autonomous defence capabilities (Otake 1986:53–6).

In April 1971, Nakasone released a draft of the 'New' Fourth Defence Build-up Plan (the Nakasone Plan), with a budget for the period of 1972–77, focusing on building SDF capabilities to repel conventional armed attacks without US support. This plan was estimated to require ¥5.2 trillion—a budget increase of 2.2 times over the previous defence plan. To increase Japan's capabilities of maritime and air defence, the SDF would be increased to 1050 aircraft and 200 naval vessels (*Yomiuri Shinbun* 28.4.1971). As soon as he had presented *jishuboei* as an actual concrete plan, Nakasone suffered a serious setback. He had to shoulder the burden of immediate pressure and strong criticism not only from opposition parties, but from within the LDP. Secretary General Tanaka Kakuei of the LDP, Foreign Minister Aichi Kiichi (from the Sato faction) and other LDP politicians concertedly expressed their concerns that Nakasone's priority to *jishuboei* would undermine the foundation of US–Japan security arrangements. In March, prior to Nakasone's announcement of the drafted plan, Prime Minister Sato was so apprehensive about the anticipated criticism expressed in Japan and abroad against possible military resurgence that he instructed Nakasone not to refer to Japan as a non-nuclear 'middle power' (Nakasone's words) but instead as a non-nuclear 'exclusively defence-oriented (*senshuboei*) state' (*Mainichi Shinbun* 16.3.1971). When Prime Minister Sato found that reaction from the Japanese public and neighbouring states in Asia was hostile, he personally told Nakasone that he would no longer support the Nakasone Plan and he was most concerned with any adverse effects, attributable to Nakasone's aggressive defence policy, on the upcoming national election for the upper house in June 1971 (*Mainichi Shinbun* 16.3.1971). Indeed, in this election, the LDP failed to retain the same share of upper house seats as in the previous government.

In the summer of 1971, the focus of Washington's policy appeared to be shifting from Tokyo to Beijing. Another 'Nixon shock,' caused by lack of prior consultation between Washington and Tokyo regarding a US foreign policy initiative towards rapprochement with China, was misinterpreted by Prime Minister Sato as potential abandonment by the United States (Ito 2003:chp 4).

Prime Minister Sato's faith in the United States seemed to shatter as President Nixon announced in July 1971 that he would be visiting China in the following year. A news source quoted Prime Minister Sato as telling visiting Australian Labor Leader Gough Whitlam, 'I have done everything they (the Americans) have asked, but they have let me down' (quoted in Welfield 1988:295). Japan's fear of US abandonment was reflected in its quick reaction to recognise China immediately after Nixon's visit to China.[29] US popularity in Japan plummeted to the lowest point since the conclusion of the US–Japan Security Treaty (Kosaka 1973:10). Nixon's reconciliation with China, without prior consultation with Japan, seemed to damage greatly Japanese confidence in the alliance. On the other hand, US rapprochement with China suddenly removed one of the major threats to Japan, and the Japanese thus felt less threatened. This change appeared to allow Japan more room to respond to the threats autonomously and thus led to US military withdrawal in an effective way. However, Nakasone left the Japan Defence Agency (JDA) to become Secretary-General of the LDP on 5 July 1971, and the trends towards *jishuboei* lost all momentum.

By the autumn of 1972, under pressure from the general public, Prime Minister Tanaka Kakuei began to emphasise the importance of setting a clear limit on defence capabilities, and Director General of the Defence Agency, Masuhara Keiichi, accordingly determined to restrict the annual defence spending to 1% of GNP for the Fourth Defence Build-up Plan (Keddell 1990:45). Nakasone' idea of *jishuboei* completely disappeared in the final version of the Fourth Defence Build-up Plan. Therefore, although Japan's policy elite began their effort to raise Japan's independent consciousness to assume responsibility for its own defence in the late 1960s, the readjustment of US global military strategies in the early 1970s did not lead to a visible change in Japan's own military security policy. There is no evidence that Japan's defence burden sharing fluctuated according to changes in the US military presence and political will to respond to the security environment in East Asia. Indeed, between 1969 and 1980, Japan's defence burden remained steady at 0.9% of GDP.

Another testable phase came about in the early 1990s when the US commitment to East Asia appeared to wane. As Cold War tensions were easing in the late 1980s, the basic premise, (that is, threats from the Soviet Union), for the security co-operation between the Unites States and Japan was about to become extinct. The collapse of the Soviet Union in 1991 formally ended the Cold War and raised the issue of how to keep the US–Japan alliance alive and relevant to the drastically changed strategic environment. During the Cold War, the United States relied heavily on US bases in Japan to deter Soviet aggression, proving that Japan was extremely important to US military strategies in the Pacific. So much so, the United State continued to forgive Japan's 'free ride'.

With the end of the Cold War, it was no longer necessary for the United States to bear the bulk of the bilateral security relations burden.

In the spring of 1990 on his visit to Japan, US Secretary of Defence Dick Cheney proposed a reduction of the 5,000 American forces in Japan. In April 1990, the Bush administration outlined a security policy in the post-Cold War Asia–Pacific region (East Asia Strategic Initiative—EASI), which appeared in a US Defence Department report titled *A strategic framework for the Asia Pacific Rim: looking toward the 21st century* (US Department of Defence, 1990). This initiative called for the withdrawal of about 30,000 US troops from the Asia–Pacific region in 1990–92, including all troops from the Philippines. The break-up of the Soviet Union and fiscal restraints on the defence budget led the Bush administration to plan a three-phased withdrawal of its military forces over the coming decade. By then Japanese newspapers had disclosed US plans to completely withdraw the Marine Corps from Okinawa to Hawaii (*Asahi Shinbun* 16.12.1989 & 27.1.1990). In both Asia and Europe, there had been reductions in the numbers of American troops. In the early stage of the Clinton administration, troop reductions continued.

The reduction combined with the collapse of Soviet power would provide Japan with a strong incentive to play a larger role in meeting the cost of credible security in East Asia. After the end of the Cold War, US taxpayers and Congress also expected Japan not only to pay the full costs but also assume military risks in the event of a regional military crisis. The Bush administration considered Japan's potential contribution substantial to preserving regional security and tried to sell a more balanced alliance to Japanese policy-makers (Samuels & Twomey 1999:3–20). In June 1990 when Japan renewed the US–Japan Security Treaty, Prime Minister Kaifu Toshiki, recognising US expectations, declared, 'Japan will go out into the world and if there is a need, if there is a request from another party, we should not hesitate in meeting it' (*Foreign Broadcasting Information Service* 25.6.1990).

But how should Japan meet a request from the rest of the world? The issue of autonomous defence came to the surface again in Japanese politics. Two groups emerged through elite discourse over Japan's autonomous defence. The first supported nationalism-based autonomy, led by politician Ishihara Shintaro, who argued, 'The United States will not fight one [a war with China] to defend Japan. Japan must prepare to be able to defend itself independently in a crisis' (*Sankei Shinbun* 5.12.2005). Unlike media star Ishihara, academic Nakanishi Terumasa offered a more pragmatic nationalism for achieving autonomous defence. He argued that Japan had specialised only in economic power and must regain its balance by developing an independent military capability in world affairs. He acknowledged that Japan's alliance with US unilateralism would be a necessary evil in the shorter term because Japan was not capable of defending itself yet. In his view, the United States would eventually withdraw from Asia, and Japan was destined to stand up on its own (Nakanishi 1990:41–7; Iklé & Nakanishi 1990:81–95). Most mainstream politicians, however, distanced themselves from these straightforward nationalist views, although Nakanishi was one of Prime Minister Abe Shinzo's five close and trusted advisors.

In contrast, the second group, driven by realism-based autonomy, entered the discourse well positioned to lead a strong assault on Japan's stance of passivity towards military security. This group, led by then LDP Secretary-General Ozawa Ichiro and academic Sato Seizaburo, agreed that Japan must 'assume military responsibilities commensurate with its economic power' (Sato 2000). To realistically achieve this goal, they called for more co-operation with the United States on military security; revision of the US–Japan Security Treaty to allow for Japan's broader role in regional security; promotion of defence technology sharing with the United States, including those in Theatre Missile Defence (TMD); and active participation in UN peacekeeping operations. It is important to note that Ozawa considered Japan's use of force, involved in the UN mission, to be constitutional, as long as peacekeeping operations were under UN command (Hirano 1996:36–9).

When Iraq invaded Kuwait in August 1990, Japan's wish to act autonomously and to expand its regional weight was tested. Japan was forced to respond when the major countries unanimously sanctioned the aggressor. Japan failed to share the military risks with the US-led coalition, and instead responded to public opinion as well as intense Asian pressure against sending the SDF overseas. The Gulf War impaired the US–Japan alliance for the first time since the end of the Cold War.

Following the imposition of Japan's economic sanctions against Iraq on 5 August, Japan remained indecisive about how to assist with the crisis as the United States and other countries sent troops to Saudi Arabia. On 29 August, Prime Minister Kaifu announced a $1 billion aid package to help with the crisis. In autumn 1990, once the Gulf War had started, the US Commander of Fleet Activities in Yokosuka bypassed regular diplomatic channels and directly requested Japan's Maritime Staff Office to send its replenishment ships and minesweepers to the Persian Gulf (*Asahi Shinbun* 7.1.2001). Given so little time to consult with the cabinet or the National Diet, Prime Minister Kaifu could not possibly send the SDF abroad for the first time in postwar Japan. As Washington demanded Japan's direct contribution to the defence of the region through the dispatch of the SDF, US resentment mounted over Japan's indecisiveness to assume an active role in the Gulf Crisis (*Daily Yomiuri* 19.8.1990; *New York Times* 30.8.1990). Nearly 80% of Americans felt that Japan's contribution was inadequate (*Asahi Shinbun* 1.10.1990). Japan's initial response to US pressure was led by Ozawa and his allies, who put forward the United Nations Peace Co-operation Corps (UNPCC) bill in the Diet. The proposed law was publicly announced on 9 October. It allowed lightly armed SDF troops to be sent to the Gulf region to provide rearguard support for forces of member nations based on decisions of the UN Security Council.

The proposed law did not gain much support among the general public or even among the LDP members. Senior conciliatory LDP members, such as Gotoda Masaharu, Kujiraoka Hyosuke, then Vice Foreign Minister Kuriyama Takakazu, Miyazawa Kiichi, and former Prime Minister Fukuda Takeo, strongly argued against authorising the SDF's overseas dispatch, in order to reassure Asian nations and to prevent a precedent for sending more SDF troops to other countries (*Mainichi Shinbun* 21.10.1990; Gotoda 1990:40–6, *Asahi Shinbun* 18.12.1990). Despite this opposition, LDP Secretary-General Ozawa rammed it through within the LDP, but was eventually forced to withdraw the bill without a vote when the National Diet bowed to the heavy weight of public pressure. In a Kyodo News poll conducted immediately after the August 1990 announcement of Japan's first aid package to the crisis, over 83% of the respondents opposed sending the SDF to the Gulf region (cited in Purrington & AK 1991:309). Another major opinion poll, taken by the *Asahi Shinbun* in November 1990 immediately after the public announcement of the UNPCC bill, found that 78% of respondents opposed the overseas dispatch of the SDF to the region (*Asahi Shinbun* 6.11.1990). Popular pressure and opinion influenced the centrist party Komeito to oppose the proposed bill (Midford 2006:15). At that Diet session, the LDP did not have a majority in the upper house. The centrist party, Komeito, accordingly played a key role in forcing the LDP to withdraw from this bill, as it possessed the casting-vote, a phrase Japanese journalists referred to as a 'balance tipper' in this attempted legislation. This majority opinion in opposition to the UNPCC also forced a growing number of LDP politicians to change their stance; one of the most influential LDP politicians, Kanemaru Shin, for example, began to argue for the bill's withdrawal in a bid to gain one more seat for the LDP in the special Aichi prefectural election for the upper house (Purrington & AK 1991:321). As the proposed bill faced close public scrutiny, many other LDP politicians began to express their concern about possible punishment by the electorate for supporting the unpopular bill (*Mainichi Shinbun* 21.10.1990; *Yomiuri Shinbun* 25.10.1990; *Asahi Shinbun* 1.11.1990). The UNPCC bill was abandoned in early November 1990.

Soon after the end of the Gulf War in April 1991, over 60% of respondents supported Japan's plan to send a minesweeper flotilla to clear Kuwait waters of Iraqi mines (*Asahi Shinbun* 24.4.1991; *Mainichi Shinbun* 14.6.1991). Ozawa was encouraged by this opinion shift to pursue new legislation to allow the SDF to participate in UN peacekeeping operations (the UN PKO bill). He actively promoted a new constitutional interpretation, arguing that the SDF's participatioin in full combat operations would be constitutional as long as it was under UN command (LDP Special Study Group on Japan's Role in the International Community 1992:49–58). In response, Prime Minister Miyazwa and other conciliatory LDP politicians clearly rejected this re-interpretation. In June 1992, a watered-down bill, the International Peace Co-operation Law (PKO Law) was finally enacted. It banned the SDF from participating in any mission entailing the use of weapons, including cease-fire monitoring, weapon collection and disposal, and the buffer zone patrols. It emphasised the humanitarian and disaster relief operations, which were obviously more acceptable to the Japanese public.

Japan's experience of the Gulf Crisis certainly caused Japanese public opinion to shift in regard to lifting the ban on overseas dispatch of the SDF (something that had not occurred in nearly 40 years), but the old constraints on the use of force remained intact. As will be discussed further in Chapter 5, signs of change in public opinion emerged; the Japanese were increasingly in favour of a pro-active foreign policy. Nonetheless, public opinion established clear outer limits beyond which no party would go if it wished to gain or retain public office. These limits lay in the Japanese people's strong aversion to military involvement. A majority of the Japanese supported the need to revise the ban on overseas dispatch to allow the SDF to participate but only in *noncombatant* missions related to UN peacekeeping and humanitarian relief operations.

The Gulf Crisis of 1990–1991 was Japan's first encounter with the reality that the end of the Cold War did not mean the end of regional disputes. Increased uncertainty in the post-Cold War non-bipolar world also contributed to Japan's activism in multilateral security co-operation; a third group emerged regarding Japan's autonomous defence, led by then Foreign Minister Nakayama Taro and then Prime Minister Miyazawa Kiichi (1991–93). They sought a form of autonomous defence through regional political dialogue.[30] Miyazawa continued to oppose Japan's use of force and proposed the 'two-track approach,' which was designed for Tokyo to engage in conflict management and prevention through multilateral security co-operation with Asian countries as well as through its alliance with the United States (MOFA 1993:404–10). The Miyazawa government regarded a multilateral security dialogue as a means to ensure US military presence and involvement in Asia (Sato 1991:43). Equally significant,

Nakayama emphasised the importance of reassuring Japan's Asian neighbours and pointed out that multilateral security talks would provide transparency and mutual reassurance between Japan and its former war victims in Asia (Midford 2000:367–97).

By the summer of 1993, a shifting body politic in Japan began to influence the US–Japan alliance. In a watershed election held in July 1993 for the lower house, the pro-American LDP lost its majority, for the first time since its 1955 establishment. After 38 years of uninterrupted rule, the LDP was out of power. Ozawa and 35 rebels who left the LDP to bring Prime Minister Miyazawa down, established their own party, the Renewal Party, and formed a coalition government with seven smaller parties. These partners chose as their first prime minister Hosokawa Morihiro, who wished to promote Japan's non-military contributions to international security (Dixon 1999:148–9). Ozawa's call for Japan to become a security-active 'normal nation' was viewed with suspicion by other members of the Hosokawa coalition. This suspicion led to the dissolution of the Hosokawa cabinet.

In 1994 a marriage of convenience between the old left-right forces, which had been unthinkable during the Cold War period, took place. The Social Democratic Party of Japan (SDPJ) formed a coalition government with the LDP and New Party Sakigake, and then SDPJ Chairman Murayama Tomiichi discarded his party's long running unrealistic security stance, stating the SDF were a state apparatus approved by the constitution.[31] The traditional ideological right-left cleavage on defence issues seemed to become less relevant in Japanese politics. In 1994 an advisory council, headed by Higuchi Hirotaro, submitted a report, *Ways of Japan's security and defence: visions for the 21st century*, or the 'Higuchi Report,' to socialist Prime Minister Murayama. This report reflected some fears regarding the withdrawal of US forces from Asia and gave alternative arrangements, that is, multilateral ones, a priority above over-dependence on US security guarantees (Cabinet Secretary 1994). Accordingly, some US government officials began to see this trend as Japan's move toward a more independent stance in world affairs (Green 1995:145–52; Iwata 1997:116). In September 1994, US Assistant Secretary of Defence Joseph Nye visited Japan to start negotiations with the Murayama cabinet over redefinition of US–Japan security ties in a bid to diminish Japanese policy-makers' perception of a declining US defence commitment in Asia. His effort resulted in the 1995 *United States Security for the East Asia–Pacific Region*, which became known as the 'Nye Report'. In this report, the US Department of Defence strongly argued for continued US military presence in East Asia and for its commitment to maintain the existing level of about 100,000 troops (cf about 135,000 deployed US troops in 1990) for the foreseeable future (USDD 1995; also Nye 1995:90–102). In

January 1996, Murayama stepped down as prime minister and was replaced by LDP politician Hashimoto Ryutaro. The establishment of the pro-US Hashimoto cabinet emphasised the relevance of US–Japan security ties in East Asia. The Nye initiative was bilaterally endorsed by the 1996 US–Japan Joint Declaration on Security between President Bill Clinton and Prime Minister Hashimoto (MOFA 1996). The trend of the bilateral alliance seemed to become reversed—the prior focus on the advantages of withdrawal shifting to an emphasis on the benefits of commitment, but in a volatile non-bipolar environment. The United States continued to demand a more balanced alliance from Japan.

The defensive state strategy theory predicts that Japan should have expanded its military role when the Unites States reduced its military presence in East Asia. Despite this prediction, in 1990 the GNP share of Japan's military expenditure had fallen below 1% (0.997%) and continued its downward trend until as late as 2001 (0.952%) (JDA 2001). Between 1990 and 1995, procurement budgets in yen decreased by nearly 40%; personnel budgets in yen remained frozen (JDA 2001). In 1995 the government adopted new defence guidelines (1995 National Defence Progam Outline) calling for a 20% cut in the number of ground SDF troops over the following years. By contrast, during this period, defence budgets for Japan's host nation support for the US forces in Japan continued to rise from ¥168 billion in 1990 to ¥ 271 billion in 1995,[32] while defence spending as a percentage of GDP was kept under 1%.[33] To overcome the fear of the withdrawal of US forces from Asia, Japanese leaders' efforts were almost exclusively directed to increases in financial contributions to US forces in Japan rather than building up Japan's independent military power.

Impact of growing military threats on Japan

Defensive state strategies also predict that Japan should have increased its costly military capabilities if the United States failed to respond to growing threats. Indeed, Japan faced threats with immediate geographical proximity from the Soviet Union in the Cold War period and also experienced new ballistic missile threats arising from the regional disputes in the Post-Cold War Korean peninsula. No matter how little the defensive state seeks to contribute to the alliance, once the larger members fail to balance against immediate dangers to the defensive member state, the defensive member states will pay more to counter these dangers.

In the late 1970s, the resurgent Cold War coincided with Soviet military build-up in the Far East. The Soviets access to the facilities at Da Nang and Cam Ranh Bay areas in Vietnam appeared to be direct threats to sea lanes used for Japan's importation of Middle Eastern oil. In 1977 the Soviets began to deploy the mobile SS-20 missiles (with a range of 3,500–4,500 km) to the Far East and by 1981 one third of approximately 330 SS-20 launchers in the Soviet inventory were deployed in the Far East (USDD 1983:51–2). Their air forces carried out a modernisation program by increasing the bomber force in the Far Eastern Theatre to more than 40 BACKFIRE bombers by 1983, which posed a direct threat to Japan (USDD 1983:53). In 1978 when the Sino–Japanese Friendship Treaty was concluded, the Soviets also began to deploy troops to Japan's disputed Northern (Kurile) Territories—four islands off the northeastern coast of Hokkaido. Occupied by Russia since the end of the Second World War, the Soviets had about 10,000 troops stationed on the islands by 1983 (USDD 1983:51). From the early 1970s to 1982, the tonnage of the Soviet Pacific Fleet increased by 60% to 1.6 million tons; from 1978 to 1979 the out-of-area operations days of deployed Soviet naval ships in the Pacific Ocean suddenly rose by 50% to 10,400 days (Watson 1982:183). The Soviet Pacific Fleet was transiting much more often through the Tsugaru and Tsushima straits in Japanese Waters. The Okean fleet exercises in 1970 and 1975 involved the first co-ordinated Soviet naval operations to demonstrate the level of combat skills in the Pacific, including amphibious landing operations (Watson 1982:29).

In 1977 Director General of the Defence Agency, Mihara Asao directed his agency group to investigate a workable legal system of emergency contingency. Soviet communist threats dominated the investigation material, which was prepared 'within the limits of the current constitution' primarily for contingency plans in the case of Russian Far East forces landing on the northern island of Hokkaido.[34] The main concern was that in the event of a major contingency taking place either in the Middle East or Europe, the Russians would attempt to extract their naval forces from the Sea of Okhotsk, and the only way to do so would be through the Japanese straits. A Russian move to seize control of the Japanese straits and Hokkaido was the most likely scenario in which Japan might be attacked.[35] In the course of this debate, General Kurisu Hiromi, chairman of the Joint Staff Council, stated on 17 July 1978 that the SDF might take 'extralegal' measures in the absence of legal guidelines for exercising the right of Japan's self-defence if the home land ever came under surprise attack (Kurisu Hiromi, interviewed by *Shukan Posuto*, 19.7.1978). Director General of the Defence Agency Kanemaru Shin dismissed General Kurisu for 'making controversial remarks for civilian control'. Yet this incident persuaded Prime Minister Fukuda Takeo to acknowledge the necessity of preparedness for such a crisis, directing the Defence Agency on 27 July 1978 to begin studies on emergency legislation.

How did the United States respond to the Soviet military build-up in East Asia? Immediately after his 1977 inauguration, President Jimmy Carter began to work on his campaign pledge to withdraw all US ground forces (14,600 personnel) from South Korea by 1981. However, he was the only person in the

White House who wished to continue with the troop withdrawal, and in the face of increasing opposition he reluctantly scuttled the plan in 1979 (Oberdorfer 1997:84–103). In June 1977, US Secretary Harold Brown warned that, in the past, the US Navy had been able to preserve the balance of credible security against the Soviet Pacific Fleet, but now with the increased Soviet naval capabilities, urged the SDF to assume the defence of sea lanes to Japan (*Yomiuri Shinbun* 7.7.1977). From 1977 to 1983, the numbers of US military personnel, combat surface ships, combat aircrafts, and bombers, deployed in East Asia remained nearly intact.[36] The Soviet invasion of Afghanistan in 1979 accelerated US pressure for Japan to make more efforts on defence, and the US government became preoccupied with cost-sharing. In May 1980, the US Departments of State and Defence requested Japan's Midterm Defence Program Estimate, 1980–84, (weapons procurement plan) to be completed one year early and Japan's defence burden to be increased to 1% of its GNP within three or four years (*Yomiuri Shinbun* 20.5.1980). When Ronald Reagan took office as US president, he reinforced pressure on Japan to increase weapons procurement for sea-lane defence capabilities. In March 1982, US Secretary of Defence Caspar Weinberger urged Japan to assume defence of the sea lanes for 1,000 nautical miles (*Sankei Shinbun* 28.3.1982). Embracing Weinberger's request, Admiral Robert Long, the commander in chief of US Forces in the Pacific, reported to Japanese defence officials that the 1976 National Defence Program Outline (NDPO) became strategically obsolete in coping with the Soviet military build-up in East Asia (*Asahi Shinbun* 28.4.1982, cited in Keddell 1993:113). Under these circumstances, the United States did not initially counter Soviet military build-up in the Far East, but merely stepped up pressure for an increase in allied defence spending. The Soviet build-up thus heightened key US allies' concerns over its possible military superiority in the Far East.

As Table 1.1 illustrates, South Korea's defence burden dramatically increased from 4.2% of GNP in 1980, to 6.2% in 1981 and 7.6% in 1982 as SS-20 IRBM and BACKFIRE bombers were deployed within the effective range (*The Military Balance* 81–82:113; *The Military Balance* 82–83:125; *The Military Balance* 83–84:127). Taiwan and the Philippines had already begun their upward trends respectively from 6.9% in 1975 to 9.3% in 1976 and from 1.6% in 1973 to 3.4% in 1977 once the US Congress passed the Case-Church Amendment[37] (*The Military Balance* 77–78:83; *The Military Balance* 79–80:95; *The Military Balance* 80–81:97). By contrast, the impact of these developments did not register directly on the levels of Japan's defence burden. After the 1977 inauguration of President Carter with his intent of major US military withdrawal from Asia, Prime Minister Fukuda felt that Japan would be exposed to the possibility of being abandoned by the United States as a key ally (Watanabe

2001:36–7; Murata 1998:165–6; Cha 1999). Fukuda sought to persuade Carter to reaffirm the US commitment to defend South Korea; however, in exchange for this, he was only able to guarantee informally the use of Japan's airspace and facilities by US forces in the case of a Korean Peninsula emergency (Murata 1998:167). The Fukuda government, while trying not to irritate the public sentiment of anti-militarism, was not prepared to offer any sort of SDF military support activities (Watanabe 2001:37).

TABLE 1.1. *Average defence burden as percentage of GDP/GNP, 1969–2003[1]*

	69–75	76–80	81–85	86–90	91–95	96–00	01–03	T/B Ratio[2]
Japan	0.9	0.9	1.0	1.0	1.0	1.0	1.0	1.15
USA	6.9	5.4	6.6	6.0	4.3	3.2	3.4	2.27
S Korea	4.3	5.8	6.0	4.6	3.6	3.0	2.8	2.19
Taiwan	8.4	8.1	6.4[3]	5.6	5.1	5.0	2.6	2.34
Philippines	2.1	2.9	1.8	2.0	1.8	2.0	1.3	2.36
Thailand	3.6	3.9	4.0	3.2	2.6	2.1	1.4	2.45

Sources: Calculated from data provided in Military Balance, various issues, International Institute for Strategic Studies.

1. Calculation based on defence expenditure in local currency as a percentage of GDP. In the absence of GDP figures, GNP figures are used.

2. The 'Top/Bottom Ratio' is the ratio of the average of annual defence spending commanded by the highest 20% of total defence spending as percentage of GNP/GDP, 1969–2003, to the average of annual defence spending commanded by the lowest 20% of total defence spending as percentage of GNP/GDP, 1969–2003.

3. The figure for Taiwan in 1982 is not available; the average of 1981, 1983–1985 is given.

Fukuda's stance was seen not so much as coping with the external threat, but bowing to domestic constraints. In October 1976, the National Defence Program Outline (NDPO) was adopted by the cabinet and later passed in the National Diet without any fuss. The NDPO was based on a new concept, *kiban boeiryoku koso* (standard defence force concept), which rejected the necessity of defence capabilities in proportion to the military capabilities of neighbouring countries, but proposed a balanced defence force to manage a small-scale limited conventional attack. The basic premises behind this concept were as follows:

- the US–Japan security ties would be effectively maintained;
- the United States and Soviet Union would continue to avoid a nuclear war;
- even if there was a partial improvement in Sino–Soviet relations, there would be no fundamental resolution of their conflicts;
- China and the United States would continue to moderate their relationships; and
- no large military conflict would occur on the Korean peninsula (JDA 1976:41–5).

The notion of Japan's defence formulated in the NDPO derived from two key players in the Defence Agency: Kubo Takuya (as then Director General of the Defence Policy Bureau and later as Administrative Vice-Minister) and Sakata Michita (then Director General of the Defence Agency). Kubo's views were initially expressed in the so-called 'KB Personal Paper,' which had been circulated in 1971 within the Defence Agency; it was based on 'no threat arguments' while seeing the international strategic environment as a *détente* in a positive and optimistic way (Otake 1986:114). His perception of Soviet threats was quite different from that of military realists; he regarded the Soviet military build-up not as an expansionist advancement, but as a defensive move, to deter the United States from potential military intervention (Kaihara & Kubo 1979:21). Kubo, as a civilian official, had already suggested quantitative constraints on defence capabilities, that is, the 1% ceiling of GNP on the defence budget, in order to win the goodwill of the general public for limited defence capability in peace time (Kubo 1973:21–4). In 1975 Sakata with his view that Japan's defence capabilities should be held in check, was appointed as new Director General of the Defence Agency. At that time, LDP electoral performance significantly declined, with the LDP's share of the popular vote in lower house elections dropping from a peak of nearly 60% in 1958 to slightly over 40% in 1976 (Curtis 1988:19). Sakata believed that it was important to gain the support of the general public. In his view, no clear limits to defence capabilities, if adopted as in the previous weapons procurement plans, would raise fears held by the Japanese people as well as neighbouring countries (*Asahi Shinbun* Tokyo edition, 6.6.1975; Sakata 1975:29). One week after the NDPO was adopted at a cabinet meeting, the cabinet decided that the defence budget would be limited to less than 1% of Japan's GNP, which did not necessarily correlate with military capabilities but was easily acceptable to the general public.

While the NDPO was passed in the National Diet, the United States continued to pressure Japan to improve its sea and air defence capabilities, and on 9 December 1976 the Miki cabinet decided to purchase 170 F-15 interceptor aircraft (Otake 1986:165-6). Yet Miki resigned following the near defeat of the LDP in the lower house election, and was replaced by Fukuda on 23 December. The Fukuda cabinet postponed the procurement of the F-15s until 1978 (Otake 1986:165-6). US requests for major equipment procurement and for policy changes in Japan's sea-lane defence seemed to be beyond the limits of the NDPO objectives and the 1% ceiling. The Japanese government responded to US burden-sharing pressures by contributing more expenses for US forces in Japan rather than expanding Japan's defence operations.

Détente was fading as the Soviet military build-up continued. In the wake of the Soviet invasion of Afghanistan in July 1980, the United States strongly requested Japan to significantly increase its defence spending. In response to this request, former Director General, and then chairman of the lower house Special Committee on Security, Sakata, reminded the US that rapid increases in defence spending would badly damage the national consensus formed in the mid-1970s on defence (*Nihon Keizai Shinbun* 31.8.1980). Yet the Defence Agency requested the Finance Ministry to increase defence spending by 15% for the fiscal year 1981, and the Finance Ministry initially planned to slash it to a 7.5% increase (*Yomiuri Shinbun* 20.7.1980). Former Directors General of the Defence Agency, such as Sakata and Kanemaru, who had been sent to the United States as part of a LDP defence mission and held discussions with the Reagan administration, advised Prime Minister Zenko Suzuki that the US expected a minimum increase of 9.7%. At the final stage of budgeting, however, Suzuki was more concerned about an upsurge of anti-government feeling among voters and opposition party criticism, and reduced it to 7.61% (*Asahi Shinbun* 8.12.1980). This final figure was comparable to the rate of the Finance Ministry's initial response; the ministry was accordingly able to keep the defence budget under the 1% ceiling (based on Keddell 1993:88).

A combination of the two mechanisms, the notion of limited defence capability in peacetime (outlined in the NDPO) and the 1% ceiling, was a politically acceptable means to solidify the Japanese people's recognition of the SDF rather than a strategically calculated device to achieve the goals of defensive-state strategies' expectations. The NDPO and the 1% ceiling were constructed not so much as a consistently defensive and low-risk strategy against external threats, but to adhere to domestic constraints. As Table 1.2 shows, Japan's defence expenditure in yen had steadily increased in an incremental way since 1976 when the Miki government officially adopted the 1% ceiling, and it was almost unaffected by the dramatic Soviet military build-up of the late 1970s and early 1980s in the Far East. After the basic political decisions made in the NDPO, the annual budgetary constraints combined with the payment system for weapons procurement to lock the Japanese government into a specific level of equipment spending in each fiscal year.

TABLE 1.2. Japan's defence budget, FY1969–FY2006

Fiscal Years		Defence Budget (in ¥100 million)	Rate of Change (from the previous FY)	As % of GDP
The Third Defence Build-up Plan	1969	4,838	14.6	0.84
	1970	5,695	17.7	0.79
	1971	6,709	17.8	0.80
The Fourth Defence Build-up Plan	1972	8,002	19.3	0.88
	1973	9,355	16.9	0.85
	1974	10,930	16.8	0.83
	1975	13,273	21.4	0.84
	1976	15,124	13.9	0.90
The 1976 National Defence Program Outline	1977	16,906	11.8	0.88
	1978	19,010	12.4	0.90
	1979	20,945	10.2	0.90
	1980	22,302	6.5	0.90
	1981	24,000	7.6	0.91
	1982	25,861	7.8	0.93
	1983	27,542	6.5	0.98
	1984	29,346	6.55	0.991
	1985	31,371	6.9	0.997
	1986	33,435	6.58	0.993
	1987	35,174	5.2	1.004
	1988	37,003	5.2	1.013
	1989	39,198	5.9	1.006
	1990	41,593	6.1	0.997
	1991	43,860	5.45	0.954
	1992	45,518	3.8	0.941
	1993	46,406	1.95	0.937
	1994	46,835	0.9	0.948
	1995	47,236	0.855	0.949
The 1995 National Defence Program Outline	1996	48,455	2.58	0.968
	1997	49,475	2.1	0.947
	1998	49,397	-0.2	0.938
	1999	49,322	-0.2	0.978
	2000	49,358	0.1	0.975
	2001	49,553	0.4	0.956
	2002	49,560	0.0	0.999
	2003	49,530	-0.1	0.993
	2004	49,030	-1.0	0.979
The 2004 NDPG	2005	48,564	-1.0	0.949
	2006	48,139	-0.9	0.937

Sources: Compiled from the Ministry of Defence (formerly Defence Agency), *Boei Hakusho* (Defence of Japan), annual reports 1970–2006.

Impact of uncertain US commitments to Japan

The defensive member state seeks to gain benefits while minimising costs. But there is another factor off-limits to the area of cost minimising strategies. To be a cost minimiser or 'a free rider,' the defensive member state must be able to calculate the limits of larger members' tolerance toward these strategies. To this end, it must be well informed about its ally's intentions and motives and continue to receive reassurance from the larger member. If uncertainty arises, the expected reaction of the defensive member state is to reduce the levels of uncertainty by building up its independent military capabilities or acting through multilateral institutions. Another characteristic the defensive state needs to have in its larger ally is trust. The defensive state needs to believe that its ally would prefer not to exploit its co-operation. Mistrust or fear could compel the defensive state to distance itself from its continuing dependence on the larger member's security contribution.[38]

Since the late 1980s, Japan has continued to receive mixed messages from Washington. The American demand for more Japanese military efforts reached new heights in the 1980s when the United States became the world's largest debtor nation. As the United States continued to suffer from budget deficits, trade deficits and unprecedented borrowing, its dealings with Japan became highly charged, sending contradictory messages on US expectations of Japan in the late 1980s. The US Senate and Congress routinely berated Japan for taking a free ride on defence. Undersecretary of Defence, William Taft, echoing this frustration, was quoted as saying, 'it can increase yet more and, indeed, should' (quoted in Chanda 1988:27). Yet Karl Jackson, Deputy Assistant Secretary of Defence for East Asia, contradictorily admitted that Japan's military capability was already 'the best-kept secret in Washington' (quoted in Chanda 1988:26). At that time, the FSX (Fighter Support Experiment) fighter plane strife highlighted the contradictions in Washington's messages to Japan. The FSX was initiated as an exclusively Japanese project to develop an advanced support fighter, but by 1987 the US Congress and American military contractors pressed Japan either to purchase existing American-made fighters or co-develop the plane with American firms. The Japanese government agreed to co-develop the plane. The following year, more pressure applied by the US Congress and trade specialists, forced Japan to revise the earlier memorandum of understanding (MOU) that ensured Japanese contractors would not acquire knowledge of US aerospace technology. Washington urged Japan to spend more on defence yet did not trust Tokyo enough to share their military technology. Even worse, as mentioned before, Major-General Stackpole offended Japanese leaders in March 1990 with his 'cap-in-the-bottle' remark about the US alliance preventing a rearmed, resurgent Japan (*Daily Yomiuri* 20.3.1990; *Washington Post* 27.3.1990). In

September 1990, the US House of Representatives passed a resolution that proposed withdrawing US troops from Japan unless Japan would agree to cover the full cost of maintaining them. Director General of the Defence Agency, Ishikawa Yozo, resented this resolution saying, 'Japan has never asked for the stationing of troops. Let them [the Americans] go home' (Foreign Broadcast Information Service 1.10.1990, cited in Bowen 1992:67). Other Japanese leaders did not publicly state their resentment but possibly felt it when they wondered why Washington asked them to pay more for the US troops who guarded them against themselves.

The poorly managed FSX affair took place as post-Cold War adjustments to defence plans began in Japan. Washington and Tokyo experienced a clash of interests when there was no shared basic premise; a threat from the Soviet Union. The FSX crisis clearly demonstrated that the Cold War phase of one-way technology transfers to Japan ended in US–Japan alliance relations. In 1988 when the Japanese government agreed to co-development of the FSX program, advocates of closer bilateral defence ties in the LDP saw the FSX as a genuine partnership between the two countries, sharing technologies with each other and therefore going well beyond mere defence co-operation to reflect a new stage of mutual trust (HRCS 1988). In the following year, however, when the co-development agreement was claimed to weaken US competitiveness in the aerospace industry (*Washington Post* 29.1.1989), President Bush gave in to domestic pressure and demanded revision of the initial 1988 MOU. The Japanese government pleaded for a separation of trade from security issues, but the US government openly rejected the plea. The Japanese leaders' response was anger at this betrayal. Resentment toward the United States and the US–Japan alliance ran so deep that some Japanese leaders felt Washington did not trust Tokyo enough to share power.

Despite the bluffs and mistrust involved in the FSX bilateral negotiations, the Japanese prime ministers continued to give first priority to maintaining the smooth alliance, rather than responding to their perceived uncertainty of US commitments to the bilateral security ties. The immediate necessity of FSX development was closely linked with Prime Minister Suzuki Zenko's 1981 promise to President Reagan that Japan would assume responsibility for the defence of sea lanes up to 1,000 miles from Japan. To carry out this mission, Japan was expected to share operations with the United States. At Secretary of Defence Caspar Weinberger's request, the Japanese government revised the ban on all exports of weapons in the same year, allowing the transfer of defence-related technology to the United States. Yet Japan's constitutional interpretation would seem to allow no participation in any forms of joint 'military' operations with the United States. Japan's Defence Agency accordingly focused on the needs of Japan's defence or on the Japan-only scenario in sea-lane defence missions, which would allow US forces to operate elsewhere (Smith 1999:82). From the beginning, major Japanese defence contractors, such as Mitsubishi Heavy Industries, Kawasaki Heavy Industries, and Ishikawa Heavy Industries, called for Japan's commitment to autonomous development of the FSX. This group argued that autonomy must remain to the extent that the main contractor and designer would be Japanese, while acknowledging the necessity of US assistance in the form of technology transfer (*Nihon Keizai Shinbun* 15.2.1987; Green 1995:98). As Toshiba Corporation's illegal transfer of US military technology to the Soviet Union caused serious damage to US security, and US congressional politicians strongly objected to Japan's domestic development of the FSX, Prime Minister Nakasone began to take the political nature of the FSX issue seriously. Nakasone, who had attempted to achieve a more autonomous defence posture in the early 1970s, now believed that the FSX issue must not undermine the US–Japan alliance (Otsuki & Honda 1991:106–8). Given Nakasone's instruction to him, in October 1989, Director General of the Defence Agency Kurihara Yuko agreed to co-development with Weinberger. As mentioned above, the ideas of this joint development led to another clash over FSX. Nakasone's successor, Takeshita Noboru, was less prominent in foreign policy and left this second clash to Deputy Chief Cabinet Secretary Ozawa Ichiro, who also expressed his strong commitment to alliance. Ozawa acceded to the US demand for a revised MOU to ensure that Japan's aerospace manufacturing would not gain advantage by acquiring US technology. Nakasone and Takeshita received general support among LDP politicians over Japan's response to the US demand (*AERA* 7.3.1989, cited in Green 1995:120).

In the late 1980s, some argued that uncertainty and mistrust in US commitment to the alliance had lead LDP politicians towards ideas of more independent Japanese security roles in East Asia or at least a shift in Japanese defence budget priorities away from host nation support. However, there is little evidence to support such trends. The steady annual increase in defence expenditure (in yen) came to an end in fiscal year 1992 as the 'bubble' economy (1986–1990) had burst in the previous year. Since 1992 there has been a virtual stagnation in annual defence expenditure. In contrast, as discussed earlier, between 1990 and 1995, expenditure on host nation support for US forces in Japan increased by 61% to ¥271 billion. As the next chapter shows, a majority of the Japanese public has consistently favoured freezing the existing level of defence spending. In response to popular pressure, the Japanese government, while maintaining a traditional commitment to co-operation with the United States by increasing the ratio of defence spending on host nation support, rigidly held the the defence budget in check.

Economic capabilities in the provision of defence

The status of the defensive member state is not static in its reliance on the larger members. As its economic capabilities grow, the defensive member state could pay more in proportion to the size of its economy and make a transition to the status of a larger one. The greater a state's economic capability, the more it can make a difference to the total common effort (Olson & Zeckhauser 1966:266–79). The economically capable state has an incentive to contribute more to the required balance. From the viewpoint of self-interested states, their responsibilities in an alliance can be primarily a question of resources and discretion. States must have sufficient resources, particularly finance, to meet their responsibility; they must have discretionary resources to contribute proportionately in an alliance. The greater size of their state revenue, while maintaining the demand for living infrastructure, provides states with flexibility, probably without the risks of domestic political opposition, to do what they choose in the way they choose. In this sense, as national wealth rises, the defensive member state is expected to increase its share of military responsibility.

From the mid-1950s to the early 1970s, Japan's GNP in relation to the size of world GNP tripled. Japanese government outlays as a percentage of GDP rose steadily from 19.3% in 1970 to 33.5% in 1981.[39] Perhaps the most important single change in government spending patterns was the ever-increasing expenditure for social security; social security transfer payments as a percentage of GDP increased rapidly from 4.8% in 1970 to 10.3% in 1980.[40] This national wealth of Japan could more decisively influence world events in its own interest than ever before. Little sacrifices on the part of the increased economic capability could have greater effect on a balance of power relative to Japan's adversaries. Even from the viewpoint of self-interested cost-minimiser, Japan should have been a larger defence spender in proportional terms.

In the early 1950s when the United States began to maintain a large number of military bases in Japan, Japan's defence expenditure reached a high of 2.8% of GNP, primarily for Japanese contributions to US forces in Japan. From the viewpoint of the US government, the 1954 Mutual Security Assistance (MSA) agreement and the 1954 establishment of the SDF were predicted to be a turning point for Japan's large scale remilitarisation. Secretary of State John Foster Dulles announced that MSA assistance to Japan would stimulate Japan's economy as a way of developing Japanese defence capabilities (Samuels 1994:149–50). Yet Japan was not at all ready to embark on a major armament program. The Japanese public was uneasy about the potential risk of MSA-related obligations dragging Japan into an American war in Asia.[41] At the same time, the passage of the Self-Defence Force Law (SDF Law) to establish the SDF was crucial for receiving more military MSA aid to Japan. In a bid to pass the SDF Law, which was unpopular with the electorate, a ban on overseas dispatch of the SDF was adopted in the National Diet (national legislature) (Keddell 1993:32–5). The SDF was accordingly being built up in the mid-1950s, with about 1.8% of GNP for defence expenditure. In the following years, as Japan enjoyed high economic growth, the defence burden was reduced to 1.2% of GNP in the early 1960s and dropped further below 1% as early as 1967.[42]

Some Japanese policy-makers clearly argued that Japan's greater economic capability should incur more responsibility for its own defence by increasing its independent military capabilities. In the midst of the record-breaking Izanami boom, Arita Kiichi, Director General of the Defence Agency (1968–70), stated (prior to Nixon's statement of US withdrawal from Asia in July 1969), 'It is natural that Japan should do more [to defend itself] as situations allow...As national resources are made readily available to this extent, I suggest the development of autonomous defence (*jishuboei*)' (HRC 1969a). He was preparing Japan's Fourth Defence Plan to build a new level of autonomy for defending Japanese soil. Arita's *jishuboei* placed emphasis on the improvement of Japan's primary role in defending its territory and sought US forces' support to supplement this endeavour. He argued that Japan as a sovereign nation should be able to resist any foreign invasion by conventional forces, securing safety of the seas and air space surrounding Japan (HRC 1969b). His proposed Fourth Defence Plan was aimed at shifting the priorities in Japan's formation of defence forces away from Ground Self-Defence Force (GSDF)—whose build-up was emphasised under the Third Defence Build-up Plan of 1967–71—and toward strengthening the Maritime Self-Defence Force (MSDF) and missile air defence. In September 1969 the Procurement Bureau in the Defence Agency was reorganised into a Development Planning Division and Procurement Demand Division to promote the domestic production of defence equipment as US MSA ceased to provide acquisition funds for Japan's defence (*Nihon Keizai Shinbun* 15.9.1969).

MSA-led aid had been unavoidable during the early postwar period (that is, the First Defence Build-up Plan of 1958–60 and the Second Defence Build-up Plan of 1962–66) because of Japan's physical inability to develop its own defence capabilities. In the late 1960s as Japan topped West Germany's economy to become the third largest in the world, these new movements towards autonomous defence appeared to be the natural course of events. However, LDP parliamentarians anticipated a strong form of public outcry against the proposed defence build-up programme as it was perceived by the public to be a stepping-stone to Japan's rearmament. Throughout the 1960s, the LDP government worked very hard to gain public trust in the SDF by creating an image of the organisation as a non-military organisation for the purpose of disaster relief rather than an armed force for defending the nation (Emmerson 1971:117; Katzenstein & Okawara 1993:101). In 1967, for example, a government opinion poll asked 'which activities should the SDF be devoted to?': only 17% of the respondents voted for national defence and more than three-quarters voted for disaster relief and public safety (Cabinet Office 1967; also Mendel 1975). The centrist LDP politicians, such as Aichi Kiichi and Fukuda Takeo, feared the electoral implications for the LDP and therefore rejected Arita's *jishuboei* proposal (Keddell 1993:46). There is little indication to suggest that Japan was preparing to embark on a major increase in defence expenditure.

In sum, the notions of buck-passing and balancing may appear to be persuasive, yet under close examination, are not consistent with Japan's behavior since 1969. Those notions predict an increase in Japanese defence expenditure when Japan encounters the four general conditions described above. Contrary to the expectations of defensive state strategies, this has not happened. Japan has not consistently followed a defensive state strategy. Its self-interested cost-minimising calculations did not always reflect changes in Japan's external environment. No doubt, Japanese policy-makers are seriously concerned about any weaker or uncertain US commitment to Japan's security. Why then does Japan's low defence contribution persist despite the fluctuations in the international system? Notably, Japan's low defence burden is systemically tied to the disproportionately large burden borne by the United States. Yet, as Table 1.1 indicates, other allies in East Asia are linked with US military contributions in a less disproportionate way and have more decisively responded to changes in their strategic environment. To unravel this puzzle, (1) the relations of variations in domestic structures to the defence burden, which distinguish Japan from other allies, must be examined, and (2) the extent of US motives in continuing to tolerate Japan's deviance must be identified.

Liberalism in making predictions about Japan's security co-operation

After the end of the Cold War, Japan's national security opened up some space for liberal security co-operation as an alternative to bilateral alliances and balance-of-power politics when there was no clear common enemy. So far in the postwar period, the Japanese government has neither tried to cut off its ties with the United States nor to replace them with a multilateral security system. Few truly influential theories of liberalism regarding how Japan can protect itself have dominated the national security agenda. No liberal advocates for Japan's national security are prepared to say that through multilateral security co-operation or institution-building Japan will be completely secured and stable.

Liberal advocates assume that institution-building is a better prescription for ensuring Japan's national security but institutionalism cannot completely replace real-politik approaches as long as counterparts take these approaches in East Asia. The main focus of a liberal approach on Japan's military security seems to seek multilateral security co-operation not as an alternative to the bilateral US–Japan ties, but rather as a means to keep the United States engaged in the unspecific, uncertain security environment of post-Cold War East Asia. A liberal analysis outlines how multilateral security co-operation eases great power rivalry (that is, the United States versus China) and constrains great powers' behaviour toward middle power Japan.

Some liberal analyses explain the effects of multilateral institutions, such as the United Nations and economic international organisations, on Japan's security strategies, which reflected the balance of power between the United States and Japan (see Iriye 1991:38–47). Other liberal theorists emphasise the importance of emerging multilateral institutions for regional peace and security, especially that of American leadership through institutionalised security co-operation (Inoguchi 1986:95–119; Inoguchi & Stillman 1997). One new liberal vision for the US–Japan alliance has been suggested by Michael O'Hanlon and Mike Mochizuki (1998:127–34). They propose that the alliance should be fundamentally based on democratic principles and shared political values, not on a common threat. In their view, the SDF must expand its military role to ensure the longevity of the US–Japan alliance, but collective efforts must be explicitly underpinned in terms of liberal democratic objectives in order to be accepted by other Asian countries. In the long run, they are anxious to see a greater military role played by Japan towards a multilateral collective-security arrangement for East Asia.

As one of the key policy choices in postwar Japan, multilateral security co-operation did not find a place in Japan's military security until the early 1990s. The US Occupation policy for Japan was designed to 'bring about the eventual establishment of a peaceful and responsible government which...will support the objectives of the United States as reflected in the ideals and principles of the Charter of the United Nations' (SWNCC 1945). Japan became a member of the United Nations in 1956; the inaugural issue of *Diplomatic Bluebook*, which was published by Japan's Ministry of Foreign Affairs in 1957, clearly stated UN-focused diplomacy as one of the key principles of Japan's diplomacy. Despite rhetoric about the importance of the United Nations, Japanese leaders, principally Prime Minister Yoshida Shigeru (1946–47, 1948–54), made the decision to create internal security with economic prosperity and to rely on US security guarantees. Yoshida clearly chose bilateralism rather than multilateralism. Japan's bilateral relationship with the United States constituted the fundamental pillar of Japan's security policy. There were some attempts to strike a more independent policy, such as 'resource diplomacy' in the 1970s that aimed at building relations with virtually every resource rich nation, and the so-called Fukuda doctrine in 1977 whereby Japan attempted to serve as a mediator between ASEAN (Association of Southeast Asian Nations) and the Indochinese states (MOFA 1979:326–30; Sudo 1992). However, bilateralism has been the essence of Japan's governing principle of national security since the Yoshida era.

In the early 1990s, some Japanese leaders began to acknowledge the importance of multilateral security co-operation as a way to solve Japan's new security problems for the following reasons:

- given the experience of Japan's response to the Gulf Crisis, the Japanese government wished to take an important part in the process for peace and security in the Asia–Pacific region. Multilateral security co-operation could help to legitimate SDF participation in UN peacekeeping operations (Dixon 1999:147);

- In the past, Japan's activism in foreign policy had always aroused scepticism and anxiety among its neighbouring countries. Multilateral security co-operation could keep the neighbouring countries engaged with Japan and enhance Japan's transparency to neighbouring countries (MOFA 1993:428–9);

- Faced with the reduction of US military forces in Asia in the early 1990s, Japan sought reassurance of the US commitment to East Asia and Japan. Regional security multilateralism could serve as a mechanism to ensure US engagement with, and the sufficient presence of, US military forces in East Asia (Sato 1991:43; Leifer 1996).

The 1995 National Defence Program Outline (NDPO) clearly stated, 'The security arrangements with the United States are indispensable to Japan's security and will also continue to play a key role in achieving peace and stability in the region surrounding Japan and establishing a more stable security environment'. In April 1996 President Clinton and Prime Minister Hashimoto strongly reiterated this fundamental importance in the US–Japan Joint Declaration on Security. Japan's general position was that multilateral security co-operation complemented but did not supplant the bilateral alliance. Japan's interests in multilateral security co-operation were well expressed at the 1994 inaugural meeting of the ASEAN Regional Forum (ARF) held in Bangkok. The ARF was a key place where Japan could set forth its objectives of regional security multilateralism.[43] A liberal LDP politician, then Foreign Minister Kono Yohei participated there as a dialogue partner stating, 'We'll continue to maintain our security ties with the United States and ensure a smooth, effective US involvement in this region, [while] seeking through the ARF the promotion of mutual understanding and mutual trust among nations' (MOFA 1995). The Japanese government did not see the prospects for a rules-based, institutionalised regional security as an independent solution to Japan's military security problems, but rather as a means of ensuring continued US involvement in Asia.

Most liberal theorists admit that multilateral security co-operation cannot completely replace the usefulness of traditional military alliances as they see both NATO's military roles and the European Union as necessary for peace and stability in Europe. Likewise, the US–Japan bilateral alliance worked in the past and still appeared more realistic to Japanese policy-makers than liberal versions of multilateral security arrangements. In Japan, multilateral security co-operation has never been the primary determinant of Japan's military security policy. Even if the ARF will eventually ease tensions or even eradicate the causes of conflicts in Asia, government decision-makers are less likely to take 'short term pain but long term gain' as they seek to prevent the emergence of immediate security threats and protect their domestic political interests.

One variant form of liberal analysis for understanding Japanese security affairs can be found in nonmilitary dimensions of security. This form suggests that the peace-inducing effect of trade as well as the importance of rules and multilateral institutions provide a motive toward co-operation among states. In this view, states become interdependent through economies, and the use or threat of armed forces will disrupt the flow of capital and commodities which therefore becomes very costly (Keohane & Nye 1977). States must co-operate if the wish to promote their prosperity; rules and principles in multilateral arrangements will gain the goodwill of states for international co-operation (Keohane & Martin 1995:39–51). Richard Rosecrance describes postwar Japan as a 'trading state' which recognised that the price of Japan's military expansion in the Second World War had been too costly and the peaceful trading option would be more profitable than invading (Rosecrance 1986). In essence, he argues that higher interdependence promotes peace by making domestic economic development, sustained by an expanding world market, more profitable than territorial expansion.

However, there are clear conditions in order to claim Japan as a trading state in Rosecrance's terms. One of the following three conditions would seem to be necessary for Japan to continue to act as a trading state. First, the benefits that Japan gains from trade can also be realised by others. All other states must recognise that they can do better through trading than by trying to expand their territorial control and that trading is mutually beneficial. Second, given the fact that some states choose to be 'territorial states' obsessed with military expansion, the US security guarantee must continue to deter threats from territorial states. Third, if none of the above conditions are met, Japan may not choose between being a trade state and being a territorial state, but adopt either a trading mode or a territorial game to deal with changes in its external security affairs.

As for the first condition, the shared belief of national leaders that the continuation of trade relations is mutually beneficial and leads to peace probably does not exist even among advanced industrialised nations. Indeed, Japan's trading activity has been viewed as neo-mercantilism, which is considered to be a root cause of trading problems in the global market. Unlike liberal trade policy, Japan's neo-mercantilist policies easily led to trade conflicts and caused political cleavages among the leading economies.[44] The second condition that Japan's continuing dependence on the US security guarantee enables the Japanese government to be a trading state is also not easily met due to fluctuating US commitments to its military presence in East Asia. In fact, as discussed earlier, other US allies in East Asia have developed independent military capabilities in response to these fluctuations. In other words, these East Asian countries seem to manage external security affairs under the third condition. Japan is the only US ally in East Asia that has not clearly responded to the changing level of US engagement in Asia and has continued to avoid major rearmament. Applied to Japan's nonmilitary security policy, Rosecrance's liberal view must focus attention on the domestic factors that help shape Japan's policy options or could explain its unresponsiveness.

Eric Heginbotham and Richard Samuels' understanding of Japan's decision to be a trading state lie in their realist stance; Japan largely ignores regional military threats by enjoying a cheap ride in defence spending and directs its primary attention to achieving technological autonomy and advancement and thus overcoming the vulnerabilities of the resource poor nation in a Hobbesian world (Heginbotham & Samuels 1998:171–203; Hellmann 1989). They call it 'mercantilist realism'. Their approaches to economic rather than military threats seem to appeal to the explanation of Japan as a merchant nation, but neglect to examine other major aspects of Japan's security policy, particularly pacifist policy constraints—the ban on overseas dispatch of the SDF, the ban on arms export, the 1% of GNP ceiling on defence spending and others. To be a cheap, acceptable rider, these policy constraints are the exact areas that Japan should have expediently eased under US pressure for greater Japanese efforts to the alliance. Japan's interests in enjoying a cheap ride off the United States provide incomplete explanation for the anomalous nature of Japan's strong reluctance to moderate those policy constraints. To achieve its autonomy through indigenisation of technology, Japan's mercantilist policy should have increased its defence spending for the future of Japanese industry (Midford 2002:17). A mercantilist strategy of maximising a nation's economic competitiveness can neither account for Japan's small R&D spending on defence industry, nor explain Japan's failure in the aerospace industry. From 1997 to 2006, for example, Japan's defence R&D as a percentage of total defence budgets fluctuated between 2.4% and 3.6%, while those in most OECD countries continued to exceed 10% (MOD 2007). In essence, Heginbotham and Samuels' arguments by themselves cannot explain why Japan's security policies have ended up being quite different from those of other economic powers.

Constructivism's claim over independent impacts of norms

The incompleteness of the above-discussed systemic explanations suggests that domestic factors are the key to understanding the anomalous nature of Japan's military security policy. Constructivism opens up a set of explanations that seem better suited to the question of Japan's reluctance to become a military power commensurate with its economic status. The primary task of constructivists is to establish that domestic norms and other social structures matter in explaining Japan's national security. Thomas Berger, a leading constructivist on Japan's national security policy, acknowledges that Japan's experience contradicts a large body of literature on realism, and argues that a pervasive 'culture of anti-militarism' (political culture), born out of unique historical evolution, accounts for the Japanese anomaly (Berger 1993:119–50; Berger 1998:1). In his view, the horror of war, caused by the Japanese military institution, resulted in a new and uncontested norm; Japan's postwar culture of anti-militarism. Berger suggests that this emerging norm by itself was compelling and became an informal social expectation. Japanese people collectively believe the norm of anti-militarism exists and act accordingly. This is what constructivists refer to as widely shared or 'intersubjective' understandings, which are not reducible to individuals. These shared understandings, rather than material forces such as the exercise of power or coercion, shape actors' interests and behaviour. Berger accordingly demonstrates the independent causal effect of anti-militarism on Japan's national security. He found: 'This negative view of the military is shared all along the political spectrum in postwar Japan, and was held not only by the far left, but by many conservatives and even far right-wing figures as well' (Berger 1993:137) and thus argues, 'in each instance efforts to significantly expand... Japanese defence establishments and international roles foundered on the shoals of domestic opposition' (Berger 1998:6). He notes that large sections of the Japanese elite, while learning the lessons from its troubled past, determined to avoid a repetition of its militarist past (Berger 1998:6–7). In a similar vein, Glenn Hook describes Japan's anti-militarism as a social norm that grew out of

Japanese people's traumatic experience of the Second World War (Hook 1986), and argues that the norm widely shared on the popular level effectively constrains the government's use of military forces as a legitimate instrument of state policy (Hook 1996:8). He also thus emphasises the independently constraining effects of mass attitudes on the normalisation of the military.

Peter Katzenstein and Nobuo Okawara join Berger and Hook in expounding the independent effect of norms yet highlights 'deeply contested norms of military security' in Japan (Katzenstein & Okawara 1993:84–118). Social norms have evolved to reflect Japan's changing public opinion, and interacted with the legal norms that have helped shape Japan's military security policies (Katzenstein & Okawara 1993:101–3). They argue that these contested norms have created rigid policies, such that there has been no major change in the defence burden of postwar Japan. In general, contested norms are more likely to cause disagreements and clashes of interests where norms interact with the exercise of power and coercion. In this respect, Katzenstein and Okawara explain the nature of contestation and policy rigidity by narrowly focusing on the interaction of military security norms and bureaucratic power structures (Katzenstein & Okawara 1993:92–7). In their view, Japan's civilian bureaucracy, in retaining a profound distrust of the professional military, has made it impossible for a military establishment to emerge in Japan and facilitated policy rigidity. In his later work, Katzenstein clearly emphasises the political foundations within which certain norms and ideas emerged not only due to a norm's or idea's intrinsic force but also as a result of political struggles. He argues that Japan's anti-militarist social norms won out and emerged in the nationally divided ideological battle over the course of the 1950s (Katzenstein 1996:30). In other words, those norms began to shape Japan's national security policy, not spontaneously from Japan's disastrous experience of the war, but rather they were politically contested and found their way into policy.

In response to those views of constructivists, Sun-Ki Chai argues that there is a shortage of explanations on how social norms are formed (Chai 1997:403). Chai takes a comparative politics approach by arguing that social norms are shaped or imposed by those with political or economic power (Chai 1997:389–412). Chai highlights the constraining effects of Japan's defence policies, which were institutionalised within a shared set of beliefs. In Chai's view, Japanese political leaders successfully institutionalised their policies (such as the constraints of Article 9 of the Japanese constitution) through direct efforts to influence how social norms were shaped (Chai 1997:403–6). In this sense, the institutionalisation of Japan's anti-militarism is claimed to be a significant barrier to full-scale rearmament. The strength and continuity of Japan's anti-militarist norms certainly depends on the degree to which they become embodied in institutions, but an important part of this argument lies in the question of how norms become institutionalised. Chai's approach tends to be driven by more political concerns of leaders' influence and manipulation (top-down norm formation) rather than by the need to test the degree to which like-minded people outside the state transform their shared norms into institutional purpose (grassroots norm formation). The effectiveness of norms cannot be easily reduced to the interests of powerful political or business leaders, a point Chai's top-down approach does not address.

Katzenstein has recently moved his constructivist approach along in addressing the limits of an ideational ontology and suggested an analytical eclecticism combing realism, liberalism and constructivism in explaining Japan's security policy (Katzenstein & Okawara 2002:153–85). He argues, 'theory and policy are both served better by eclecticism, not parsimony (of a single paradigm)' in the sense that 'scholars and policy-makers try to gain analytical leverage over multilayered and complex *connections between power, interest, and norms* [emphasis mine]' (Katzenstein & Okawara 2002:184–5). The full articulation of how power, interest, and norms interact with one another to shape policies is yet to be seen in the literature.

In the context of Japan's pacifism, potential answers to a set of Japanese security questions could help to disentangle the complex connections between power, interest, and norms. Pacifism is a post-Second World War phenomenon in Japan, and has become institutionalised in the Japanese political system over a short period of time in historical perspective.[45] Many scholars regard the collective experience of Japan's devastating defeat in the Second World War as a direct cause of the sudden shift in Japan's political culture from militarism to pacifism (see Tamamoto 1990:493–520; Kamiya 2002/3:63–75). First, it is undeniable that the collective Japanese memories of aggressive militarism contributed to the rise of pacifism, yet this argument requires a close scrutiny as to why a strong anti-militarist sentiment emerged in postwar Japan but not in the war-torn past of other countries with similar experiences. How, exactly, did Japan's pacifist social norms initially come to matter and how did they come to exist at all? Second, in postwar Japan, a specific form of pacifism, that is, its pragmatic and passive characteristics (as described in the next chapter), eventually prevailed. Why did such a form of pacifism succeed and other forms of pacifism fail to find their way into military security policy? How did the social norm become institutionalised and shape the interests of Japanese policy-makers? Third, the form of social norms is not static but does inevitably evolve over time. How did Japan's new ideas for proactive security policy emerge and rise to popular endorsement in the 1990s? The answers to these questions require a close examination of interaction among power, interests, and norms.

To examine the interaction, I focus on three dimensions of social norms: (1) norm formation, (2) norm compliance, and (3) norm change. Earlier constructivist studies provided little explanation of where norms come from but argue that norms emerge when beliefs are 'inter-subjectively' shared and 'internalised' by social actors (Checkel 1998:338–45). They neglect to examine the process through which beliefs are internalised or fully socialised. What motivated and persuaded the Japanese to internalise pacifism? The process of social learning seems to be crucial for answering the question of where pacifist norms come from. To identify the origins of pacifism in postwar Japan, three factors are key in promoting the process of social learning. First, demilitarisation, one of the fundamental objectives of the Allied Occupation, (1945–1952), was not only to institutionally change Japanese society but also to remould individual values and beliefs, in an attempt to induce the Japanese people to eradicate the Japanese warrior culture and embrace a democratic way of life (see Dower 1979). The spirit of the Occupation authority's determination lay in Article 9 of the 1947 war-renouncing constitution. The Allied Occupation played a causal role in promoting the emergence of pacifist social norms via resocialisation through which the Japanese came to learn the aftermath of their war defeat in constitutional terms. Second, the media, (newspapers, books, magazines and movies in the immediate postwar period), played a central role in the socialisation process whereby the war experience of individual citizens was aggregated into a collective understanding. As discussed in the next chapter, overall, the media collectively reflected the newly emerging values of the society. Third, 'unarmed (*hibuso*) Japan,' which emerged on the agenda of the Japanese intellectual culture immediately after Japan's unconditional surrender, helped to map out the war experience of individual citizens into pacifist postwar values. Even former General Ishihara Kanji in the Kwantung Army began to assert a way of rebuilding an unarmed nation of Japan by January 1946 (Wada 2002:13–4). Many dissidents expressed the necessity of unarmed Japan almost as a reflex action to ensure the independence of postwar Japanese society from the state (Wada 2002:5–26).

Significant differences between national leaders and the general public in their beliefs of military security have remained in postwar Japan. Pacifism-oriented norms are not necessarily shared among conservative LDP politicians or they are often not internalised by these politicians. To this extent, norm compliance by government policy-makers has not spontaneously occurred. Why then do national leaders abide by pacifist social norms? It can be argued that norm compliance occurs in two ways: selfish, utility-based cost/benefit calculations and internalisation/full socialisation. In the former case, norms are not internalised by elites and they are simply one of policy-making constraints.

Elites' decision-making is based on political resources and opportunities, in which they calculate the consequences of alternatives and maximise expected payoffs. Elites comply with norms in terms of strategic calculation, not because of a norm's intrinsic force. In the latter, elites interact with the public and could involve changing elites' attitudes about norms in the absence of material benefits and incentives. The interaction helps elites learn and to be open to argumentative persuasion. This social learning process of norms leads to elites' interest redefinition. In this sense, norms become an independent source of influence in policy-making.

The focal point of norm compliance in Japan's postwar military security policy lies in the Yoshida Doctrine. This doctrine allowed the interests of the Japanese conservative coalition to reconcile with a specific form of pacifism. Yoshida detested the Japanese military who led Japan to disaster, but he was by no means a pacifist. He believed in empire for his country, and had no objection to remilitarisation but gave priority to Japan's recovery and independence (Yoshida 1962; Dower 1979). Yoshida's pragmatic dependence on the US security guarantee promoted the policy of development through low defence spending and maximum investments in economic growth. In many respects, Yoshida's conservative pragmatism, such as low defence spending, was to collaborate with Japanese pacifist sentiments. Yoshida's successors of the conservative coalition utilised the pragmatic Yoshida Doctrine as a main pillar in policy-making while they strategically ensured the development of the doctrine in order to keep up with the strong anti-militarist sentiments of the public. An exercise in the LDP regime costs/benefits calculation led Yoshida's successors to acknowledge or set up a range of norm compliance mechanisms, such as Article 9 of the constitution, the ban on SDF overseas dispatch, the 1% of GNP ceiling on defence spending, and others, and thus to see these mechanisms simply as a policy constraint rather than part of the constitutive power of pacifism-oriented norms.

Perhaps the most important domestic factor in the 1990s was the significant changes in public attitudes towards Japan's security and foreign policy. By the mid-1990s, the Japanese increasingly supported Japan's pro-active security policy stance. In general, then, how do norms change? The constitutive power of norms or the inertial force of normative constructs tells us why their influential patterns persist, but not why they change. Conversely, the sources of change cannot themselves be explained within the logic of norm itself. Changes in social norms occur in response to environmental changes (Eckstein 1988:789–804). New ideas often emerge due to dramatic policy costs, failures, or crises, in which existing government policies have been unable to cope or failed to resolve problems (Kowert & Lego 1996:451–97). The approach to norm change taken in the next chapter examines the causal links between collective expectation for military security and exogenous structural constraints (historical circumstances), such as the post-Cold War strategic environment (the changing nature of Japan's dependence on the US security guarantee, Japan's Gulf Crisis experience, and the Korean Nuclear Crisis). As new structures emerge, normative consensus becomes fluid and divided. Dramatic external shocks or crises undermine citizens' commitments to old norms. Social interaction for problem-solution in the new environment lead to new collective understandings of military security.

chapter two

Norm formation (public expectation)

The effectiveness of social norms is not simply derived from the military and political power of nation states or the financial power of business interests. How did new norms emerge and become standards of legitimate behavior in postwar Japan? Public opinion is a mirror of emerging norms. This chapter examines how public opinion surveys reflected the public discourse and formation of new norms about national military security. For highly charged issues, such as national military security, opinion polls are particularly indicative of and reflect the evolution of social norms. Japan's 'pacifism' is only a postwar phenomenon. If there is such a thing as a social norm of pacifism in Japan, we need to identify the distinguishing features and explain why the shared belief emerged in so short a period of time. We must characterise the existing norms regarding Japan's military security and identify its conceptual underpinnings rather than simply referring to Japan as a 'peace-loving' country. The evolution of Japan's social norms regarding national military security can be traced by analysing changes in and components of public opinion, which has been surveyed by the Japanese government and mass media over time.[46]

In postwar Japan, there emerged a broad public consensus about the form of Japan's pacifism. It is possible to identify three key principles: nonaggression, non-nuclear nation, and anti-militarism. Japan had repeatedly invaded in the name of self-defence but never exercised the right of self-defence to defend Japanese soil against foreign invasion. During the 1946 deliberations on constitutional amendment, Prime Minister Yoshida stated that the new constitution would renounce war regardless of defence or aggression (Otake 1991:138). Yet it is important to note that he did not necessarily mean the prohibition to exercise Japan's right of self-defence. He seemed to deny Japan's invasion under the pretext of exercising the right of self-defence, such as the Manchurian Incident, but not its right of actual self-defence (Otake 1991:149). His real intention probably lay in his denial of aggression. In the deliberations on the new constitution, 'the renouncement of war' showed a strong determination to renounce aggressive war. This determination led to the establishment of a principle in the form of banning SDF's overseas dispatch, which was incorporated into the 1954 defence laws establishing the SDF and the Defence Agency (JDA). The second consensus was formed over a non-nuclear stance, which was based on Japanese people's determination not to initiate nuclear war and not to increase any possibility of nuclear war in the international community. It is true that 'Instead of feeling remorse over Pearl Harbor, most Japanese felt victimised, a sentiment strongly reinforced by the atomic bombings of Nagasaki and Hiroshima' (Berger 1993:135) but also such a sense of victimisation helped the Japanese public to distance themselves from state power. This domestic pressure resulted in the 1967 non-nuclear principles, which prohibited Japan from manufacturing, possessing or allowing entry of nuclear weapons into Japan.

The strong anti-war sentiment in postwar Japan thus derived from Japanese people's response to aggressive war and nuclear war. In this sense, Japan's emerging pacifism was not necessarily an absolute commitment to nonviolence in all actions. From the beginning of pacifism norm formation, ideas of unarmed and nonviolent Japan were not noticeably socialised or internalised among the public. The pacifism was initially shaped by Japan's collective experience of the war rather than religious or individual beliefs. The popular perception was that the wartime military institution itself led armed Japan to disaster or that the disastrous decision had been made by the militarists. Anti-militarism is the third consensus based on the deep-rooted distrust of the military. In the system of postwar civilian control, the professional military came under strict supervision of civilian bureaucrats. As described later, anti-militarism was perceived as a domestic issue to ensure Japan's stability and prosperity, and as postwar Japan entered a phase of high economic growth, this consensus was destined to be depoliticised amid the growing material wealth. The domestic aspect of anti-militarism went along with the conservative coalition of developmentalism.

On 4 September 1945, two days after Japan signed the Instrument of Surrender on the deck of the USS Missouri, Emperor Hirohito declared at the opening session of the Imperial Diet 'the establishment of a peaceful nation' as a slogan for rebuilding Japan (*Yomiuri Hochi* 5.9.1945; *Asahi Shinbun* 5.9.1945; *Osaka Mainichi Shinbun* 5.9.1945). All national newspapers made it front page news. This declaration was followed by that of Prime Minister Prince Higashi-Kuni in his general policy speech: 'I believe that we must make a fresh resolve and strive to build a peaceful, cultural Japan of the future' (*Yomiuri Hochi* 5.9.945; *Asahi Shinbun* 5.9.1945; *Osaka Mainichi Shinbun* 5.9.1945). Two days before first meeting with General Douglas MacArthur, Emperor Hirohito responded to American journalists' questions: 'It is unthinkable that the threat or use of weapons brings permanent peace to us. Harmony among nations, including victors who do not use any force, and the defeated, holds the key to the solution of peace issues' (*Osaka Mainichi Shinbun* 30.9.1945). A series of these statements gave the impression that Emperor Hirohito wished to see Japan unarmed, while being considered by some historians as a pretext for preventing the emperor from being indicted as a war criminal (Wada 2002:11). In any case, the content of the peaceful nation was yet to be created by the Japanese people.

The origins of the Article 9 'No War' clause can be found in the 'MacArthur Notes' of February 1946: 'Japan renounces [war] as an instrumentality for settling its disputes and even for preserving its own security'. However, the prohibition for the right to defend Japanese soil went too far from the viewpoint of international law, and it was removed from the 'GHQ Draft' (General Headquarters of the Supreme Commander of the Allied Powers) of Japan's constitution. The source of the present form of Article 9 is disputed. Some attribute it to Charles Kades, one of MacArthur's closest associates, and MacArthur himself said that the provision was suggested to him by Prime Minister Shidehara Kijuro (*This is Yomiuri* 1997:334; MacArthur 1964:302). The inclusion of Article 9 would seem to be mutually beneficial. MacArthur saw overwhelming advantages in keeping Hirohito on the throne and using him as an advocate of the US Occupation reforms. The Japanese government saw Japan's acceptance of Article 9 would weaken the arguments of Britain and the Soviet Union to abolish the throne. On 6 March 1946, the Japanese government, after negotiating with GHQ, announced the Outline of a Draft for a Revised Constitution.

The first election of April 1946 in postwar Japan was a chaotic event but it served as a de facto national referendum on Japan's new constitution. The drafted Article 9 stated: 'War, as a sovereign right of the nation, and the threat or use of force, is forever renounced as a means of settling disputes with other nations. The maintenance of land, sea, and air forces, as well as other war potential, will never be authorised. The right of belligerency of the state will not be recognised'. Immediately after the election, 70% of voters considered this clause a necessary part of the constitution and only 28% felt it unnecessary (*Mainichi Shinbun* 27.5.1946). The great majority of people endorsed the renouncement of war; however, their perception of Article 9 was quite different from what the Allies had expected. Article 9 was an expression of the initial expectation of the Allied Occupation in Japan to prevent it from becoming an aggressor again in Asia. But the immediate lesson the Japanese had understood from the war was that they also had been a victim of their own military and directed less of their attention to their inability to prevent the military from becoming a danger in the Pacific and other areas. Civilian support for the peace clause was prompted less by Japan's wartime atrocities and aggressions against others than by their own memories of wartime sacrifice, suffering, and hardship (Toshitani 1962:19). Consciousness at the premature level of belief formation directed their attention to their immediate wartime experience. It could be said that the Japanese, while facing the misery of early postwar Japan, were searching for internal stability, rather than confronting the wartime history of Japan's atrocities committed by their military.

American censorship over publications regarding the atomic bomb was phased out by 1948 (Braw 1991) and the 1950s was a decade of aggregating the war experience of the Japanese into a collective understanding. Movies, magazines and exhibitions, based on the war experience and memory, took a crucial part in this socialisation process where the ordinary Japanese were able to share the war memory with one another. In particular, two writings based on individual citizens' diaries became enduring voices of the Japanese war experience. One was a personal note, titled *Nagasaki no kane* (The bells of Nagasaki), written by a radiologist survivor of the atomic bombing, Nagai Takashi, from his sickbed in 1946. In 1950, this book was made into the first movie about nuclear issues in Japan. The other, titled *Kike wadatsumi no koe* (Listen to the voices from the sea), which was a collection of war diaries by Japanese students killed in the war, was first published in 1949 and sold over one million copies, and its film version also became a smash hit in 1950. Ota Yoko's *Shi no machi* (The town of death), and Hara Tamiki, *Natsu no hana* (Summer flowers) also became immediate best-sellers. *The drawings of the atomic bomb*, a series of touring exhibitions, presented by Akamastu Toshiko and Maruki Iri, which spoke with an immediacy of the war's consequences, started in February 1950 and attracted more than one million visitors across the nation. The 6 August 1952 issue of the pictorial magazine *Asahi Gurafu,* which sold nearly one million copies, provided for the first time a comprehensive photographic account of the catastrophic atomic bombing. In a similar way, the atomic bomb special edition news footage, *Asahi Nyusu* (No. 363, August 1952) was screened at movie theatres across the nation and created a visual impact on the ordinary Japanese.

Between 1950 and 1959, 34 movies, which can be categorised as anti-war or anti-nuclear, were produced in Japan.[47] In 1950 many film industry professionals either were dismissed or simply left major film production companies, largely due to the Red Purge, which were carried out by private corporations with the backing of GHQ (Morishita 1995:42). Some of these professionals started a number of independent film productions and produced influential anti-war films, such as *Genbaku no ko* (Children of the atomic bomb) and *Hiroshima*. It was in the early 1950s that a number of independent films began to draw a large number of audiences. Suddenly, major film makers, such as Nikkatsu,

Shochiku and Toei, changed their production policies when they realised that even small independent film makers could attract more audiences with stories about the horrors of the war. Three big hits, made by major film-makers, proved the great public interest. In 1953 Toei released *Himeyuri no to* (Himeyuri lily tower), produced by Imai Tadashi, which was based on personal encounters in the horrific Battle of Okinawa. Shochiku followed Toei with the 1954 production of *Juni no hitomi* (Twenty-four eyes) by Kinoshita Keisuke, which caught a wide audience with its personal accounts of innocent individuals in the war. In 1956 Nikkatsu also released a big hit, *Biruma no tategoto* (The Burmese harp), produced by Ichikawa Kon, which dealt with humanity and personal conscience toward the end of the war. These films had remarkably consistent war stories. If we ignore some differences in the approach of individual producers, a common core does exist. All of the films emphasised the suffering that was inflicted on the Japanese people as war victims. The fact that the films were big hits with the Japanese public reflected emerging perceptions of the war experience. Collective understanding evolved around a sentiment of victim-hood rather than feelings of remorse over their country's aggression in Asia.

It is equally important to note that such a sentiment of victimisation was adapted in response to the emergence of a new regional security threat and changes in domestic politics. The 1950 outbreak of the Korean War suddenly brought a security threat to the Japanese. It had a dramatic impact on the public's perception of national security. In a public opinion poll taken in November 1950, 54% of the respondents considered Japan's armed forces necessary to defend the nation; and this figure was consistent with the result of an opinion poll taken in September 1951 where 76% were in favor of Japan's rearmament.[48] As of December 1950, only 19% believed that Japan would be able to maintain its neutrality in armed conflicts and 48% did not. The idea of Japan's neutrality in international affairs was promoted by the Socialist Party and its affiliated labor unions as well as by left-wing intellectuals, but by this time it generated little enthusiasm among the general public. Therefore, the change in Japan's security threat environment effectively altered the public perception of national security.

In 1952 Japan became independent again. The conservatives were divided over Japan's post-Occupation policy; Hatoyama Ichiro, who hoped to revise the new constitution and then to rearm with independent military capabilities, challenged Prime Minister Yoshida's incremental armed forces build-up with adherence to the American alliance. Yoshida failed to establish a stable party structure; Hatoyama became prime minister in 1954. The national government began to recentralise control over education and police whose functions had been mobilised by wartime governments to create a totalitarian regime during the war. This reverse course of decentralised education and policy, created by the Allied Occupation for demilitarisation and democratisation, caused a great deal of political unrest. As the Korean War ended, public perception of national security had again changed in the mid-1950s. Following the recentralisation drive, new doubts about rearmament arose among the general public. In the 1955 general election and the 1956 upper house election, the Hatoyama-led conservative forces failed to control two-thirds of the National Diet seats, which were constitutionally required to initiate amendments to the constitution. Public opinion polls in 1955 showed that people who were opposed to revision of Article 9 and thus to rearmament continued to increase and exceeded the respondents favoring it.[49]

Nonetheless, it is significant that more than half of the eligible voters supported the 1954 government's decision to establish the Self-Defence Force (SDF) and only 30% were opposed to it. This is consistent with the results of opinion polls taken in 1956 and 1959 where 58% and 65% respectively wished to maintain the existing SDF.[50] It is safe to say that the increased support of Article 9 did not stem from the literal interpretation of unarmed pacifism, but rather from protests against a return to Japan's militarist past. Editorials in major newspapers reflecting public sentiment argued that the ultimate goal of Japan's democratisation would not be a return to the militarist takeover of the 1930s.[51] Article 9 was construed as an inward-looking process, closed at the national level and without any particular concerns for external relations with other states. Pacifist sentiment was developing alongside the domestic debate of constitutional status quo versus revision. In the mid-1950s, pacifism in Japan had bearing in relation to national integration and stability rather than to peace keeping in the Asia Pacific. Therefore, public attitudes, while strongly resisting Hatoyama's initiatives for constitutional changes and rearmament, did not necessarily refuse the development of defence capability.

A massive public campaign against renewal of the US–Japan Security Treaty ended in July 1960 when Prime Minister Kishi Nobusuke gave up the premiership to his Finance Minister, Ikeda Hayato. Ikeda shifted away from the politics of confrontation; Kishi's open advocacy of constitutional revision was replaced by his 'growth-first' stance. In the early 1960s, the Japanese were beginning to feel prosperous and confident for the first time since the war. Japan's economic achievement brought higher living standards and altered their expectations and perception of pacifism. The attitudes of the general public began to shift toward the belief that economic prosperity would be the best way of deterring Japan from returning to its militarist past. After the 1960 security treaty crisis, those who favored the constitutional status quo increased rapidly.[52] In the 1963 general election, Prime Minister Ikeda declared, 'I will never revise the constitution during my term of office'. A major goal of pro-revision LDP conservatives was shifting from unfeasible revision of the constitution to a publicly acceptable tactic of constitutional reinterpretation, which was intended to clarify the constitutionality of the SDF and the stationing of US troops in Japan.[53]

Popular affluence made it possible for the public to reflect on the shared belief of pacifism, especially in relation to others. Ordinary citizens were oriented toward an active attitude of inquiry into war and war casualties. In 1963, for the first time in postwar Japan, the national government held the National Memorial Prayer Services for the War Dead. The affluent middle class began to recognise the atomic bombings of Hiroshima and Nagasaki as a collective experience among the Japanese people rather than as individual experiences. Editorials in major newspapers reflected a sense of collective duty as a sole atomic-bombed nation, but emphasised that Japanese people were the unprecedented victims of irresistible forces.[54] This domestic attribute arising from the experience of collective distinctiveness was shaping the Japanese people's perception of national identity.

Japanese people's identity was emerging in two ways: 'pragmatic' pacifism supported by economic affluence and 'passive' pacifism driven by a sense of victimisation. As the United States was failing in the Vietnam War, the Japanese identity was developing in relation to this changing strategic environment. President Nixon declared that Asian allies should not seek the help of American troops but must do more to defend themselves. For the first time in postwar Japan, there was lively debate about the role of Japan's pacifism in the context of interstate relations. Intellectuals and opinion leaders began to discuss a desirable form of pacifism at the policy level. In the early 1970s, editorials in major newspapers repeatedly regarded pacifism as indispensable to Japan's security policy.[55] By the late 1970s, as described below, a particular form of pacifism seems to become a collective expectation held by the majority of the Japanese and to be established as a norm for Japan's military security policy.

Conducted every three years since 1969, part of the Cabinet Public Relations Office's survey on national security has gauged public sentiment on the likelihood of Japan's involvement in war. Those who clearly answer, 'There is a danger' or 'There is no danger,' have fluctuated according to changes in the strategic environment. As Figure 2.1 indicates, the ratio of those who recognised the likelihood of Japan's involvement in war showed cyclical swings, declining toward the end of the Vietnam War, bouncing back in the mid-1970s during the Soviet military build-up in the Far East, dropping again to the 1988–1997 low plateau of the post-Cold War environment, and peaking in 2003 after the 1998 test-firing by Pyongyang of a suspected Taepodong-1 missile. The 'Taepodong shock,' in which part of the missile flew over Japan's main island of Honshu, reminded Japanese people of their unpreparedness and vulnerability. Japanese people's fear became real as North Korea decided to restart its frozen plutonium-based nuclear program in December 2002 and officially admitted the possession of nuclear weapons in April 2003. Like those in other nations, the 'pacifist' Japanese have been sensitive to security threats.

FIGURE 2.1. Japanese perception of armed conflict involvement, 1969–2003

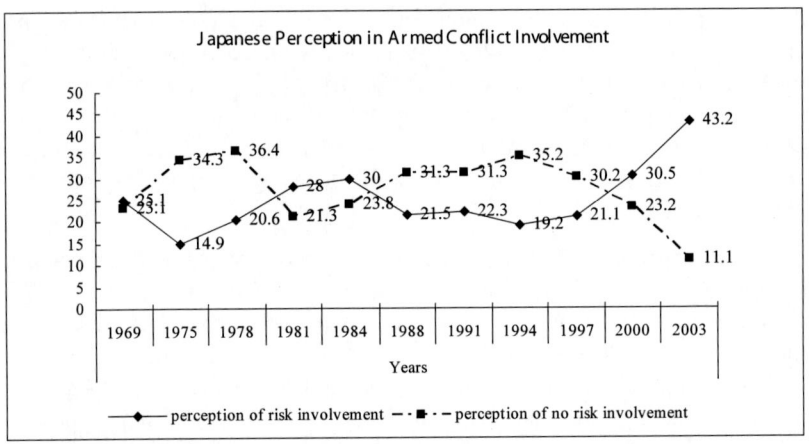

Source: Japan Cabinet Office, 'Jieitai Boei Mondai ni kansuru Yoron Chosa' (Opinion Poll on the Self-Defence Force and Security Problems), three-yearly surveys, 1969–2003.

Note: The opinion poll asks the question, 'The present state of world affairs considered, do you think there is a danger of Japan being forced or becoming involved in armed conflicts?'

It is clear that the Japanese feel vulnerable when they face security threats but how do they pursue freedom from threat? The same survey asks, 'What sorts of national security arrangements should we use to protect Japan?' According to Figure 2.2, those who answered, '(We) protect Japan by means of the Japan–US security regime and the SDF as arranged currently' became the majority in the late 1970s. They wished to implicitly reiterate their opposition to a stance of unarmed neutrality by changing the status quo and to prefer the continuation of the status quo to either reduction or abolition of the SDF. By that time, those who would like both to 'abrogate the Japan–US Security Treaty and to reduce or abolish the SDF,' or who revealed a stance of leftists' pacifism, accounted for a marginal proportion of the respondents. Throughout the 1960s following the US–Japan Security Treaty crisis, the Japanese were concerned about a possibility that 'US bases in Japan will drag us into an American war'. During this period, little over 35% believed that the US–Japan Security Treaty was 'useful' in maintaining Japan's peace and security.[56] Meanwhile, the Japanese government supported the United States on its war in Vietnam yet was not forced to put Japanese boots on the ground. Those who believed it 'useful' reached over 65% in 1970 and remained so continually thereafter. It is safe to say that a majority saw no alternative to the US–Japan security relationship and accepted the existing level of SDF capabilities.

FIGURE 2.2. *Japanese perception of national security, 1969–2003*

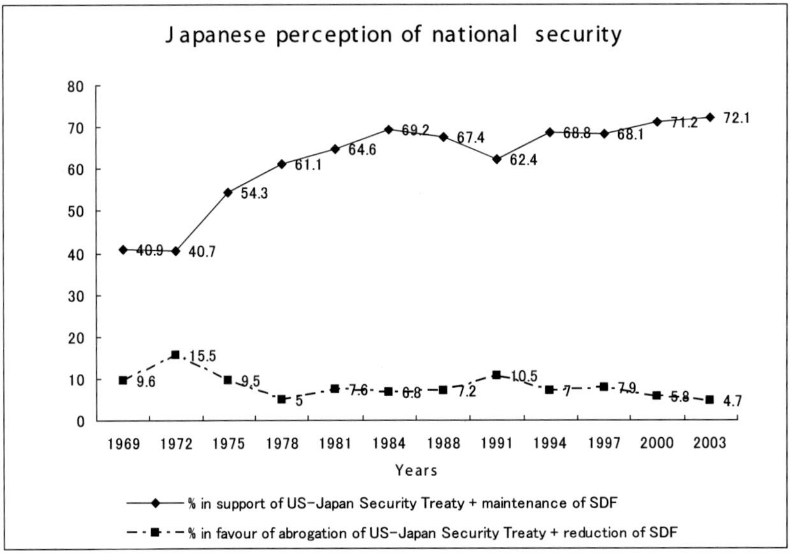

Japanese perception of national security

Years	% in support of US–Japan Security Treaty + maintenance of SDF	% in favour of abrogation of US–Japan Security Treaty + reduction of SDF
1969	40.9	9.6
1972	40.7	15.5
1975	54.3	9.5
1978	61.1	5
1981	64.6	7.6
1984	69.2	6.8
1988	67.4	7.2
1991	62.4	10.5
1994	68.8	7
1997	68.1	7.9
2000	71.2	5.8
2003	72.1	4.7

Source: Japan Cabinet Office, 'Jieitai Boei Mondai ni kansuru Yoron Chosa' (Opinion Poll on the Self-Defence Force and Security Problems), three-yearly surveys, 1969–2003.

In what ways then does the perception of security threats and measures described above reflect the level of defence spending the Japanese public wished to see? The survey conducted by the Cabinet Public Relations Office put a question of defence spending to the respondents allowing them the alternatives 'spend more,' 'spend less,' or 'about the right amount'. As Figure 2.3 shows, the 'spend more' and 'spend less' answers respond significantly to their perceived threats from the external environment, although these responses remain the opinion of the minority. In contrast, the 'about the right amount' responses, which constitute a predominant opinion, do not respond to them at all.

Equally important, the evolution of this predominant opinion highly correlates to the gradual acceptance or legitimisation of the existing US–Japan security arrangement and SDF.

FIGURE 2.3. *Japanese perception of defence spending levels, 1969–2003*

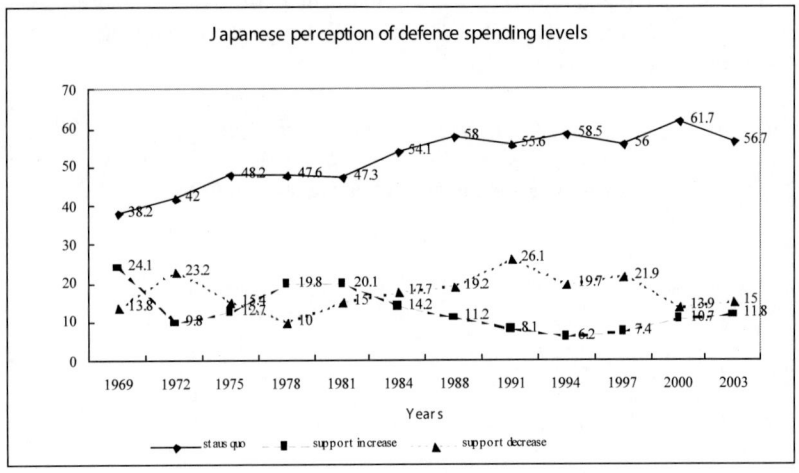

Source: Japan Cabinet Office, 'Jieitai Boei Mondai ni kansuru Yoron Chosa' (Opinion Poll on the Self-Defence Force and Security Problems), three-yearly surveys, 1969–2003.

Changes in citizen support for defence spending are conventionally measured by 'net support for defence spending,' which represents the percentage of those supporting increases in spending minus the percentage of those desiring spending reductions, thus excluding those favouring the neutral response. The net support assumes that the 'increase' and 'decrease' responses can be seen as strong attitudes accounting for change rather than continuity, and that 'about the right amount' is closely associated with the measurement of non-attitude (Asher 1998). The net support for defence spending suggests that Japanese public opinion, like American, French and German public opinion, reflected the external threat environment (Risse-Kappen 1991:494–9). While this observation may fail to identify specific responses by the Japanese people to defence spending, the responses to the category of 'about the right amount' in Japan are disproportionately too large to ignore. An overwhelming majority of Japanese people continued to support the existing level of defence spending while opinion polls continued to show that the American, British and French have never overwhelmingly supported any of the three categories for defence spending.[57] In these countries, the responses to the increase, decrease and neutral categories are proportionally equal and therefore compete with each other. This implies that the high proportion of neutral responses in Japan is not necessarily a reflection of a lack of opinion or low information levels among the respondents.

In the United States and Western Europe, public support for defence spending is largely responsive to changes in the relative growth of defence and social spending (Eichenberg 1989; Wlezien 1995:981–1000). Increases in defence spending, for example, will heighten negative public reaction when there are concurrent decreases in the funding of civilian programs. Thus, defence spending presents a challenge to public priorities when it exceeds the rate of social spending. However, when there is growth in social spending, there is also an expectation and acceptance that defence spending will grow at a similar rate. In the Japanese context, public opinion does not appear to be responsive to the relative growth of defence and social spending priorities. In Japan, public social expenditure as a percentage of GDP rose continuously from 4.3% in 1969 to 16.9% in 2001.[58] Despite increases in social spending, the majority of Japanese continued to support existing levels of defence spending. This is not to suggest that Japanese citizens are not responsive to budgetary priorities, but their neutral responses present a significant indication of their collective expectation of pragmatic pacifism.

During the late 1970s and early 1980s, the collective expectation of national security based on specific forms of pacifism was widely accepted by the Japanese public. There were two aspects of Japanese pacifist sentiment that stood out: (1) the pragmatic approach of the Japanese people who preferred low-cost defence and non-military means to high-cost and risk-involving defence, to serve their economic prosperity; and (2) the passive approach in that the Japanese people had no desire to return to the country's militarist past and were reluctant to change the constitutional status quo of the postwar order. There was also the influence of the historical era. In early postwar Japan, there was a highly politicised locus of ideology-oriented groups, each with competing visions for Japan's security arrangements ranging from unarmed neutrality to independent military capability (see Mochizuki 1983/1984:152–89; Umemoto 1985; Berger 1993:137–40). In the economic prosperity of the 1960s, pacifist sentiment was depoliticised and the collective beliefs of pacifism became tied directly to the daily lives of the Japanese people to protect their increasing level of material affluence.

chapter three

Norm compliance (political representation)

Norms are by themselves the independent source of influence, once norm-consistent behavior is expected. Once adopted, norms can regulate or constrain state policies by specifying what is anticipated to be appropriate to certain matters. Uncontested norms may be accepted partly due to their intrinsic force or constitutive power; they may effectively become a collective expectation because of their goodness and persuasiveness. Otherwise, coercive pressures are initially required to encourage policy-makers to adopt norms as habitual rules or even to force political authorities to adopt them to avoid political costs. Only over time, do norms become accepted and institutionalised within domestic practices. In other words, the adoption of new norms requires the exercise of material leverage in motivating a change in government policies and practices. This chapter will examine how the constitutive power of norms relates to the exercise of material/political leverage to shape a stance about government obligations. It will identify the driving mechanisms behind the acceptance of particular forms of pacifism into Japanese government practices.

Banning the overseas dispatch of the SDF

What then is the domestic structure of political access, constraints and opportunities that have made the collective expectation adopted into political action? How has the collective expectation or idea aligned government policies to its normative commitments through the material structure? The ban on the overseas dispatch of the SDF, which was adopted as a Diet resolution in June 1954, was the first regularised constraint on Japan's military security policy. After the end of the Korean War in 1953, as seen in Chapter 1, Japan was under strong pressure from the United States to sign a framework for US assistance (Mutual Security Assistance), which would strengthen the development of both operational and industrial bases for Japanese defence efforts. Japan saw MSA aid as a means of boosting Japan's economy as the Korean War boom had ended. Yet Japan's MSA negotiations with the United States were accompanied by an obligation to increase Japan's ground forces. In the 1954 Diet deliberations for the MSA agreement, many Diet members expressed their concerns: 'Public fears mounted as Japan's military obligations attached to MSA aid might lead to rearmament' (HCPS 1954a; HCC 1954a). According to the *Asahi Shinbun* opinion poll of January 1953, 43% of the respondents answered that the US forces stationed in Japan 'will draw [Japan] into [an American] war' while only 19% thought that they 'are good for protecting [Japan] from war' (Morishita 1995:38).

In October 1953, the United States pressured Japan's chief negotiator Ikeda Hayato to increase the ground forces to 325,000, but he resisted and successfully offered a compromise of 180,000 to the United States. Prime Minister Yoshida emphasised that constraints, such as Article 9 and public fears, prevented Japan from accepting the initial US request; nonetheless, his ultimate reason in declining was economic (Dower 1979:441–62). The early post-Occupation period did not allow the Japanese economy to stand on its own feet. Even worse, the war procurement boom was about to end as the Korean War cease-fire took effect in July 1953. Yoshida's strategy was to minimise the US demand for rearmament but maximise the US offer of economic aid to Japan. In this way, Yoshida's pragmatism and pacifism-oriented constraints not just coexisted, but collaborated with each other to deal with US pressures.

The SDF were created not only to maintain internal security, but to protect Japanese soil against external aggression. Article 3 of the Self-Defence Force Law stated that the SDF 'shall defend Japan from direct or indirect attack'. In December 1954, to facilitate the establishment of the SDF, the Hatoyama Ichiro cabinet announced the government's view: 'The Constitution does not deny our country the right of self-defence. Thus, it does not violate the Constitution at all to establish real forces within the necessary, adequate requirement for self-defence' (*Asahi Shinbun* Evening edition, 22.12.1954). Constitutional revision was the major issue in the general election for the House of Representatives in February 1955. The anti-revisionist forces, that is, left- and right- Socialist, Labour-Farmer, and Communist Parties, successfully gained more than one-third of the seats needed to block constitutional amendments. In July 1956, these anti-revisionist forces also obtained enough seats in the fourth election for the House of Councillors to veto constitutional revisions. The constraints at work in the required mechanism of constitutional revision squashed Hatoyama's ambition to revise Article 9—revision that would have permitted rearmament.

In March 1949, idealist MacArthur stated that Japan was to become the 'Switzerland of the Far East,' yet one year later the Korean War broke out. Japan began to serve as a primary supply base and US forces in Japan shifted to Korea. In July 1950, General MacArthur ordered Prime Minister Yoshida to establish the National Police Reserve (NPR) of 75,000 personnel to take over the duties of internal security (Otake 1991:426). The establishment of the NPR, Yoshida explained, was only to 'maintain internal security' but 'not to represent any form of rearmament' (HRPS 1950). In the United States' view, the establishment of the NPR was clearly intended to pave the way for rearming Japan (Otake 1991:419–32; Dower 1979:387–8). Yoshida responded to this pressure by saying that a conventionally armed Japan would violate Article 9 and fail to win popular support (Yoshida 1962:266). US presidential advisor John Dulles urged Japan to rearm as the Chinese People's Volunteer Army was drawn into the Korean War.

In February 1951, Prime Minister Yoshida secretly promised Dulles that he would create a National Safety Force (NSF) of 50,000 personnel. In January 1952, Yoshida revealed this plan to the National Diet, saying that the NPR would cease to exist in October and a new defence force, which would not run counter to Article 9, would be established to replace the NPR (HRB 1952; HCB 1952). At the inauguration ceremony of the National Safety Agency in August 1952, however, Yoshida stated, '[Japan] would have immediately possessed armed forces if national resources had allowed' (Otake 1991:449). He recognised, '[Japan] should plan to incrementally increase its self-defence force as the national [economic] power recovers. But it is not time for Japan to rearm yet' (Yoshida 1957:175).

The weight of popular pressure on heavy-handed government practices

Prime Minister Kishi Nobusuke (1957–60), like Hatoyama, hoped to revise the constitution and to expand the SDF. Kishi was clearly aware of the lack of US trust in Japan as an alliance partner. Kishi's memoir quoted Dulles' response in 1955 to Japan's request for revision of the US–Japan Security Treaty as saying,

> It would be impossible to enter a joint-defence agreement between the United States and Japan. It would be impossible for Japan to assume the responsibility for joint-defence since Japan is prohibited from dispatching troops overseas. Why on earth are we talking about revision when your side is not ready yet? (Kishi 1983:195).

To ease US concerns, Kishi pushed the First Defence Build-up Plan (1958–1960) to be announced in June 1957 with Ground SDF (GSDF) manpower of 180,000, Maritime SDF (MSDF) tonnage of 124,000, and Air SDF (ASDF) aircraft of 1,300. In the late 1950s, the tide turned in favour of treaty revision yet protests against US military bases gained momentum and anti-American sentiment was growing.

In 1956 citizens' protests began against the expansion of the Tachikawa Air Base on the outskirts of Tokyo (the Sunagawa struggle), and in the following year a Japanese housewife was shot and killed by an American soldier (the Girard incident). These events attracted widespread media attention, and raised a strong public outcry. As MacArthur's nephew, Douglas MacArthur II, US Ambassador to Japan (1956–61), took office in the midst of anti-US military base movements, he realised that the first priority was to preserve employment of US bases in Japan rather than pursue joint defence arrangements with Japan (Muroyama 1992:194). In September 1958, the United States agreed to negotiate a revision of the US–Japan Security Treaty. After long negotiations, the revised treaty was signed in January 1960.

Prime Minister Kishi saw the new treaty as proof of a new secure relationship, because it, unlike the original treaty, committed the United States to defending Japan in the case of armed attack. The opposition thought otherwise—that the SDF would be used as frontline troops for US military strategies. When the new treaty was about to be ratified by the National Diet, protests resulted in the biggest demonstrations in the history of postwar Japan. This provided national leaders with a powerful lesson about the sensitivity of defence issues in Japan. On 19 May 1960, the LDP, using its majority, made a sudden vote for ratification late at night, while the opposition members were absent. The public was outraged by this act. The *Asahi Shinbun* called for Kishi's immediate resignation (*Asahi Shinbun* 20.5.1960). The Kishi cabinet's undemocratic tactics in the National Diet led to a mass demonstration of over 300,000 protestors surrounding the Diet building. The Kishi cabinet, driven by fears of mass upheaval, assembled some SDF forces in Tokyo. Defence Agency Director General Akagi Munenori strongly opposed the use of the SDF against the protestors and assuaged the crisis (NHK 1995:327–36). President Dwight Eisenhower's visit to set the seal on the new relationship was postponed and eventually cancelled. In July 1960, Kishi resigned, leaving the premiership to his Finance Minister Ikeda Hayato.

Prime Minister Ikeda (1960–64) was an 'honour student' of Yoshida's pragmatism. The lessons learned from the 1960 security crisis led Ikeda to reconcile the weight of anti-militarist popular pressures with the pragmatism of government policies. The Ikeda cabinet conducted 'dialogue politics' and tried to minimise social conflicts in the sprit of 'tolerance and patience'. Ikeda kept a low profile on constitutional and national security issues, while advocating the 'income-doubling plan' for economic development. In his view, it was economic prosperity that would act as an agent of reconciliation between the conservative coalition (LDP-national bureaucracy-big business) and the weight of anti-American sentiment. He declared he had no intention of revising the constitution by saying, 'As constitutional revision is a fundamental issue, I don't think that it is a democratic way of thinking to ram policies through with our majority'. As reported at the time, the Socialist Party said, 'the LDP will revise the constitution once gaining a two-thirds majority. They were startled by a false alarm' (*Asahi Shinbun* Evening edition 22.10.1960).

In 1964 the Constitution Research Council, which was established in 1957 to lay the groundwork for constitutional revision, submitted a final report to Prime Minister Ikeda. Although the majority opinion in the council was in fact pro-revision, Takayanagi Kenzo's revision-is-not-necessary opinion was presented as the council's stance (*This is Yomiuri* 1997:134). This reflected both the public opinion of anti-revision and Ikeda's low-key approach. The implementation of the income-doubling plan doubled personal income in seven years instead of the expected ten years. Although most Japanese people began to feel prosperous for the first time in their lives, rapid economic growth also stimulated public fears that there would be no end to Japan's defence build-up.

Banning arms exports, establishing three non-nuclear principles and renouncing the right of collective self-defence

Ikeda's successor, Sato Eisak (1964–72), also a political protégé of Yoshida, sought to reconcile public fears with the institutionalisation of policy constraints. Between 1950 and 1969, US grants for military assistance to Japan totaled ¥5.8 billion, yet in the 1960s only 21% of those grants were given for the United States to supply Japan's defence equipment (Boei Nenkan Kankokai 1961 & 1971 editions). In 1963, as the Japanese economy was growing rapidly, the United States announced that MSA funding would end in 1967. The end of MSA aid to Japan appeared to work in favour of Japan's defence industry, which represented only 0.5% of total industrial output in the mid-1960s, and called for greater domestic production of defence equipment (Green 1995:18). In the post-Occupation period, Japan had imposed unilateral restrictions on its military-industrial complex, but the Third Defence Build-up Plan (1967–1971), for the first time, provided *kokusanka* (domestic production) of defence equipment as a central feature. In response to this emphasis, Prime Minister Sato confirmed, 'I think it important to domestically produce weapons and others necessary for self-defence, not to purchase them all from overseas. I promote domestic production' (HRA 1967). He added, 'as long as domestic production continues, it is inconceivable [for Japan] to decline orders from overseas for *defensive* weapons' (HRA 1967).

As the United States deepened its military involvement in Vietnam in 1964, Japan became a supply base for US procurement. In 1966 the maintenance and repairs of US military equipment in Japan by Japanese firms increased in value by 146% from the previous year (Havens 1987:99–101, cited in Keddell 1993:43). Japanese anti-Vietnam War groups had been mobilised by both students and the intellectual left, their movements peaking in 1968 when students, workers and housewives united against Japan as the 'merchant of death'. Prime Minister Sato feared that co-operating with the US military in Vietnam to promote Japanese manufacturers' profits would cause a domestic backlash and electoral implications for the LDP. Under continued pressure from popular anti-Vietnam war movements and opposition parties, Sato stated that Japan would not export weapons to (1) 'countries at war and communist countries', (2) 'countries subject to any embargo under the United Nations Security Council resolutions', and (3) 'those involved in or likely to be involved in international conflicts' (HRA 1967). This statement became a government policy known as the so-called 'three non-export principles'. As a member of both the Co-ordinating Committee for Multilateral Export Controls (COCOM) and the United Nations, Japan was obligated to observe COCOM restrictions on arms exports to the Soviet bloc and Security Council resolutions under the UN Charter respectively. To this extent, the government policy may be said to simply reiterate Japan's existing international obligations, but the third condition, the ban on arms sales to 'those involved in or likely to be involved in international conflicts,' obviously reflected the weight of domestic pressures. These established principles served as a key index for holding national leaders accountable for military security policies and practices. In 1976 Prime Minister Miki Takeo (1974–76), leader of the smallest LDP faction, increased restrictions on defence equipment, technologies, and facilities, and extended the export ban to all countries.

The return of Okinawa to Japan was a key task for the Sato government. Japanese public opinion demanded Okinawa be placed under the same conditions as applied to the main lands of Japan (*hondonami*). To deal with the continued strategic need of the United States to unrestricted use of the US bases in Okinawa, Prime Minister Sato decided not to adopt any concrete reversion plans, and stated, '[the Japanese government's] position on this issue will remain *carte blanche* (non-committal) [until the time of actual reversion]' (Okakura & Makise 1969:664). This non-committal stance caused a strong outcry. In February 1969 some 60,000 local demonstrators protested against the stationing of B-52s in the Kadena Air Base of Okinawa, and in spring of that year, more than two million citizens across the nation participated in demonstrations demanding the immediate return of Okinawa. By May 1969, Prime Minister Sato reversed his stance and pursued reversion plans for Okinawa in accord with the principles of nuclear-free mainland status. Yet the left-wing opposition parties and activists continued to demand the immediate unconditional return of Okinawa, and mobilised nearly one million citizens in the national protest rallies of October 1969. On 21 November 1969, 750,000 citizens demonstrated against Sato's departure for the United States to negotiate with President Nixon over the terms of Okinawa reversion. In November 1969, Nixon and Sato agreed Okinawa would be returned to Japan by 1972. The Nixon-Sato Joint Communique stated, 'The Treaty of Mutual Co-operation and Security and its related arrangements would apply to Okinawa without modification thereof' (*New York Times* 22.11.1969). Critics immediately scrutinised the conditions for Okinawa's return to see if they included the removal of US nuclear weapons, which were suspected of being stored on the island. In November 1971, the LDP successfully worked with centrist opposition parties, Komeito and the Democratic Socialist Party (DSP), to pass a Non-Nuclear Weapons Diet Resolution, which was committed to applying the 1967 Three Non-Nuclear Principles to Okinawa (*Asahi Shinbun* 18–25.11.1971). These existing principles applied to the mainland had been employed by citizens' groups to increase the participation of individual citizens in the reversion process. The interest of the Sato government had consequently been reconstituted around the principles.

At the end of Sato's tenure, the national debate on collective self-defence became intensified after the announcement of the 1969 Nixon-Sato Joint Communiqué. In return of the reversion of Okinawa to Japan, the Sato government acknowledged joint responsibility for South Korea's and Taiwan's security; the so called 'Korea clause' and 'Taiwan clause,' which were outlined as follows: 'the security of the Republic of Korea is essential to Japan's own security' and 'maintenance of peace and security in the Taiwan areas is also most important for the security of Japan' (*New York Times*, 22.11.1969). These clauses were accounted for in Foreign Minister Aichi Kiichi's speech:

> Particularly in the case of an armed attack on South Korea, this would seriously influence the security of Japan. That being the case, when the United States carries out a prior consultation based on the US–Japan Security Treaty...it is clearly in Japan's national interest to decide its action. Although an armed attack on Taiwan areas is fortunately not foreseen at the present, it is necessary to fully understand that this, if it occurred, would be most important for the security of Japan' (IOCT 2005).

The Korea and Taiwan clauses were debated in relation to two issues: collective self-defence and overseas dispatch of armed forces.[59] The Sato cabinet was forced to withstand the scrutiny of both opposition Diet members and voters who became seriously concerned about the possibility of dispatching the SDF to Korea or Taiwan to assist the United States. Opposition Diet members asked if SDF troops would be dispatched when an armed attack on South Korea or

Taiwan were considered a threat to the security of Japan (see HCC 1972b & HCA 1972).

Until the Korea and Taiwan clauses' debate, the Japanese government's view of the constitutional ban on collective self-defence had remained vague and inconsistent. There were three different yet interrelated interpretations of Japan's position on collective self-defence:

1 as a sovereign nation, Japan has the right of collective self-defence under international law, but does not exercise it as a matter of its policy choice;

2 it is not permissible for Japan to use the right of collective self-defence, since it exceeds the use of minimum necessary force for self-defence as permitted under Article 9 of the constitution; and

3 all forms of self-defence with armed forces are prohibited under the peace constitution.

Yet these different interpretations led to the same conclusion: the ban on overseas dispatch of the SDF for combatant operations. In reply to a possibility of SDF dispatch to Korea or Taiwan, Treaty Bureau Chief Takashima Masuo stated that the government had no intention of exercising the right of collective defence at all since the constitutional status of collective self-defence remained unsettled (HCC 1972b). His view assumed Japan's inherent right of collective self-defence but emphasised Japan's decision not to exercise it at the policy level. In contrast, Cabinet Legislative Bureau Director-General Sanada Hideo argued that as a sovereign nation Japan has the right of self-defence which allowed it to use the minimum level of armed force needed to exercise that right. He argued further that the constitution allowed Japan to exercise the right of self-defence in case of an armed attack on Japan only when the following three conditions were met: (1) there is an imminent and illegitimate act of aggression against Japan; (2) there is no other appropriate means to deal with such aggression; and (3) the use of armed force is confined to the minimal necessary level. He concluded that the right of collective self-defence exceeded the limit of self-defence authorised under Article 9 and it was not constitutionally permissible. In his view, an armed attack on South Korea would not meet the three conditions (HCC 1972b). Prime Minister Sato and Foreign Minister Fukuda Takeo expressed their LDP politicians' view that the overseas dispatch of armed forces was constitutionally prohibited, and as a result, the right of collective self-defence could not be exercised, although they did not say the exercise of collective self-defence was constitutionally permissible (HCC 1972c).

All in all, the general public and opposition parties ultimately wished to ensure the ban on overseas dispatch while the Sato government also seemed to have no intention of sending the SDF overseas. In a government reply to deliberations in the House of Councillors dated 14 October 1972, the Sato government eventually integrated the different interpretations into a constitutional view of the right of collective self-defence. The essence of the interpretation was as follows:

> Since a state has the right of collective self-defence under international law, Japan naturally has it. Nevertheless, the Japanese government believes that even though Japan has the right of collective self-defence, the exercise exceeds the limits of self-defence [authorised under the constitution] and is not permissible... It is not conceivable that the constitution in which the principle of pacifism is enshrined permits an unlimited level of self-defence, but it should be within a minimum necessary level. Therefore, the use of force is permissible only to stop an armed attack on Japan, and the right of collective self-defence [to stop an armed attack on a foreign country] is not permissible (Asagumo Shinbunsha 2001:576).

From this period the Japanese government began to consistently acknowledge the constitutional ban on the right of collective self-defence, which became a policy consensus among government officials.

Regularising the 1% of GNP ceiling on defence expenditure

The comparative literature on the determinants of government budgeting in general suggests that there are three common factors: the state of the economy, incremental budgeting, and politically viable budgeting (Wildavsky 1975; Keddell 1993). Apart from these factors, the characterisation of defence budgeting seems to suggest two defence-specific factors: changes in the external environment that may strengthen or weaken the hand of budget makers, and collective beliefs and culture that may influence a budget-making process through some mechanisms of institutions, such as electoral and legal systems.

First, the primary determinant of total spending concerns the adjustment of government to the domestic economic conditions. From the mid-1950s to the early 1970s, Japan's GDP rapidly rose with Japanese government expenditure. The high economic growth of the period automatically created a larger tax base and thus produced total revenue without deficit financing. Japan managed to stabilise the size of government budgets as a percentage of GDP. In a low growth environment, however, Japan's fiscal size as a percentage of GDP rose rapidly from 24% in 1974 to 34% in 1980. As a result, social security transfer payments as a percentage of GDP increased accordingly in proportion to the increase in fiscal size. By contrast, defence spending as a percentage of GDP remained unchanged during the low growth environment. The shrinking revenue neither created pressures to increase the GDP-based defence spending nor put downward pressure on defence spending given the importance of social spending. To this extent, Japan's defence spending is less responsive to the state of the economy.[60]

Secondly, like Western industrialised nations, Japan budgets in an incremental way; most expenditure items receive a small increase of funds above what had been received in the previous year. But Japan's defence budgeting created its own internal criterion, the 1% of GNP ceiling, which was unlikely to be responsive to its changing security environment. Since the Cabinet had officially adopted the ceiling policy in 1976, the powerful Ministry of Finance demanded that the defence budget must be within the 1% framework (*Asahi Shinbun* 5.11.1976; Ushio 1986:138). Setting a limit on the defence budget, which was unpopular with the electorate, was not only politically desirable, but also provided the Ministry of Finance with a device to manage macro-economic constraints on fiscal expansion. The 1% framework did not emerge from appropriateness of the amount, which would be balanced with other budget items; the spending level on defence was not of a similar growth rate as that of most budget items. According to an Advisory Committee to Director General of the Defence Agency, there was no clear fiscal basis for the 1% ceiling (Boei o Kangaeru Jimukyoku 1975:36). Ironically, when the Ministry of Finance began to impose the principle of zero growth on budget requests in 1982, defence spending was exempted thanks to the rigid application of the GNP-based ceiling. Despite Japan's fiscal crisis in the early 1980s, the 1% of GNP ceiling allowed defence spending to escape the Finance Ministry's pressure to balance government budgets (see HRFA 1982; HCC 1982).

Thirdly, the process of defence budgeting in Japan was minimally subject to political pressures. Most ministries had drawn up five-year-plan expenditures, which the Ministry of Finance generally did not take seriously. An exception was the defence five-year-plans that were observed most meticulously by the Ministry of Finance (Campbell 1977:213–6). Nonetheless, the final stage of defence budgeting was often politicised; the low defence spending bias of the budgets allowed LDP politicians to press for funding additional civilian projects such as pork-barrel ones rather than unpopular defence 'big-ticket' items (Calder 1988a:425). The defence budget was thus usually facing reductions, not increases, in the relative share of defence in the total budget. At the Cabinet-level negotiations, the role of the prime minister and top officials of the LDP was crucial; however, unpopular defence spending severely limited the scope of their powerful role. Even Prime Minister Nakasone managed to exceed the magic threshold of 1% marginally for only three fiscal years. All in all, the Finance Ministry's draft allocation for defence did have to face political pressures yet its margin of error was rather negligible.

Finally, according to the logic of realists' understanding, the external environment encourages or weakens arguments for further defence spending. Contrary to the expectation of structural realism, as discussed previously, Japan's defence spending does not respond systematically to the external environment. This suggests that it is worth knowing if the remaining domestic factor, social norms, is an important determinant of Japan's military security policy and defence spending.

In 1976, immediately after the National Defence Program Outline (NDPO) was adopted, the Miki government officially announced a 1% limit on defence spending. It was obvious that this announcement was an attempt to win public support for defence spending outlined in the NDPO (Calder 1988a:437). There was a significant history behind the adoption of the 1% ceiling. Defence spending fell below 1% as early as 1967. During the period of the Third Defence Build-up Plan (1967–1971), the 1% ceiling became a tacit target within the internal bureaux of the Defence Agency (HCC 1972a, no. 8). In 1972 Prime Minister Tanaka Kakuei informally directed the Defence Agency to set the quantitative limit of Japanese defence spending. It was reported that Tanaka's initiative was intended not only to defuse China's concern over Japan's increased defence capabilities, but to set up the standard for limits on defence spending, which would be more acceptable to the electorate (HRPS 1972, no. 2; *Nihon Keizai Shinbun*, 7.10.1972). By 1974, LDP Diet members clearly regarded the 1% framework as 'the firm upper limit as domestic politics (allows) in Japan' (HCC 1974). An advisory committee to Director General of the Defence Agency Sakata Michita recommended: 'the limit of defence spending that would gain public support is within 1% of GNP' (Boei o Kangaeru Jimukyoku 1975:36). Sakata confirmed a consensus in the LDP-bureaucracy policy community by saying, 'it is mandatory to keep the defence budget down to less than 1% of GNP as in the past' (*Asahi Shinbun* 6.6.1975). The national bureaucracy had accepted the 1% ceiling by acknowledging that defence spending was to be determined not so much for coping with the external threat, but for considering domestic constraints. The political consideration gained status in the national bureaucracy, although military officials in the Defence Agency questioned setting a rigid limit on expenditure.[61]

The application of the 1% ceiling was regularised further by the *kiban boeiryoku koso* (standard defence force concept), which provided the NDPO with a fundamental basis for Japan's security thinking. As discussed previously, this concept was developed to maintain Japan's balanced forces for effectively dealing with a small-scale limited conventional attack on Japanese soil as well as maintaining a full warning system prepared in peacetime (JDA 1976:41–5). It assumed that large increases in the defence budget would be unfeasible under domestic constraints and that Japan would face no realistic threat in the period of détente (in the case of attacks above the small-scale level, Japan would depend on US forces) (JDA 1976:41–5). There were two crucial consequences of this concept on Japanese military security policy: (1) it was more likely to be influenced by domestic constraints than strategic factors for coping with external threats, and (2) it was more likely to set limits on quantitative defence build-up, which would be easily understood by the public, than setting qualitative limits on the SDF in a strategic way.

Kubo Takuya, Director General of the Defence Policy Bureau, laid the foundation of *kiban boeiryoku koso* in his papers. He developed his ideas of defence capability in peacetime when a realistic threat against Japan was remote. At the same time he recognised that the public increasingly expressed their concerns about a lack of concrete limits on Japan's military capability in a high growth environment. In response to these concerns, he proposed that the level of defence expenditure should be adequately limited to 1% of GNP, which had already existed as a tacit target in defence budgeting within the internal bureaux of the Defence Agency (Kubo 1973:21–4). Nonetheless, he anticipated that defence spending would continue to steadily increase as economic growth would automatically create a larger base for the 1% of GNP. The 1% of GNP ceiling was politically feasible for public acceptance but did not derive from rational calculation of Japan's strategic security needs. The LDP positively responded to this political feasibility while attempting to build consensus for a defence build-up through defence expenditure allocations. By February 1973, the LDP government embraced Kubo's arguments and, at Diet deliberations, explicitly mentioned the necessity of the 1% ceiling in explaining the idea of defence capability in peacetime (HRB 1973). Before its 1976 official announcement by Prime Minister Miki, the 1% limit on defence spending shaped expectations over acceptable levels of defence spending among national politicians and bureaucrats.

Avoidance politics in the electoral system

Civilian control over the SDF is one of the most important constraints that limit the scope of Japan's defence build-up. Article 66 of Japan's constitution states that the prime minister and ministers of state must be civilians. In Katzenstein's view, civilian control over the military is the driving mechanism that has prevented Japan from expanding its commitment to national security (Katzenstein & Okawara, 1993:92–7). Within the JDA (renamed the Defence Ministry in 2007), its 'uniformed' (military) officers are subordinate to the administration of civilian personnel and its top bureaucratic posts are reserved for civilian officials from other powerful ministries. Uniformed officers are thus incapable of initiating any strong voice for rearmament. Katzenstein's argument seems to assume that the JDA, especially its uniformed officers, alone wish to rearm Japan, and thus to argue that the civilian-military arrangements are the primary mechanism for deterring any military interpretation and expansion. However, it is also true that other national ministries may have no objection to rearmament, as long as they can preserve or strengthen their bureaucratic interests.[62] More important is the fact that the LDP, when established in 1955, made constitutional revision for rearmament a high priority. Since then, the majority of LDP politicians have held favorable views of constitutional changes.[63] But the prospects for constitutional revision regarding defence remained remote. Constitutional revision for rearmament clearly required elected officials to pursue unpopular policies that must withstand the voters in national elections and ultimately in a national referendum. There was a clear clash between LDP constitutional preferences and its electoral ambitions.

One of the most important formal-legal constraints on Japan's military defence policy is its electoral system, which provided the electorate with the political opportunity to allow their collective pacifist beliefs to constrain the LDP politicians' desire for rearmament. Accepting electoral rules as the major cause of Japan's military security policy is necessary to answer the question of who ultimately controls or sets a veto on policy-making. To bring it into a broader perspective, 'who governs Japan?' To answer this question, the literature has evolved around the elitist-pluralist debate, which has been joined by the institutional approach. I emphasise the importance of institutions, that is, electoral rules, in shaping incentives or disincentives for voters, politicians, and bureaucrats. The institutional basis of power lies especially in electoral rules, and the electorate ultimately sets outer limits beyond which the LDP would not go if it wished to retain office.

The most influential elite model has been primarily represented by the bureaucracy-dominant one. Their arguments essentially confuse the *act* of policy-making with the ultimate *cause* of policy-making. It is true that bureaucrats in Japan have drafted major legislation and managed the state of national affairs through extra-legislative actions, but it does not necessarily mean that they exercised the power to monitor, police, and, if necessary, veto any formation and implementation of government policy.

Tsuji Kiyoaki traces the origins of bureaucratic power in postwar Japan back to three factors: 'indirect rule' (Occupation authorities' decision to rule Japan indirectly through the hands of the bureaucracy), the acceptance of bureaucrats' 'impartiality' and 'neutrality' by the Japanese public, and the existence of inexperienced political parties (Tsuji 1964:90–1). The Japanese bureaucracy subsequently came to control enormous expertise and information. Some scholars, such as Scott Flanagan, Chalmers Johnson, TJ Pempel, and Bradley Richardson, point out that, despite the fact that the constitution gives legislative power exclusively to the elected Diet members, it is the bureaucrats who draft all important legislation (Pempel 1974:647–64; Johnson 1975:10; Richardson & Flanagan 1984:346–7).[64] They argue that another great power of the Japanese bureaucracy derives from thousands of non-statutory measures, such as ministerial ordinances, rules and regulations to implement policy, and they emphasise the importance of administration rather than the rule of law in Japan (Pempel 1974:647–64; Johnson 1995:11; Richardson & Flanagan 1984:348–50).

To examine the applicability of the bureaucracy-dominant model to Japan's military security policy, we need to address two key questions. Why do politicians leave the task of making and implementing military security policy to the national bureaucracy? How can politicians control bureaucrats? These questions are directly related to the fundamentals of democratic control and performance. Democratic politics in Japan's military security policy-making is easily viewed in terms of the hierarchy of governance. Japanese voters prize and choose politicians who can control bureaucrats, at the starting point of policy-making. Politicians then induce the administration of bureaucrats to comply with their wishes, and civilian bureaucrats place severe constraints on the ability of uniformed officials. Perhaps the most important concern in this hierarchy is the institutional mechanisms that allow voters or politicians to hold politicians or bureaucrats accountable for their decisions respectively. There is such a mechanism central to the politicians-bureaucrats relationship: Japanese legislators do not necessarily enact the programs drafted by bureaucrats—LDP legislators pass the bureaucrat-drafted bills in the Diet only providing that they wish to enact them anyway.[65] For bureaucrats, there is a great deal of incentive to do what LDP leaders want them to do, because LDP leaders control their professional promotion and future. For LDP legislators, it is in their best interests to utilise the already existing bureaucracy of capable staff while retaining a veto over any bills or regulations the bureaucrats might initiate. In this sense, politicians control bureaucrats, and the appearance of bureaucracy-dominant policy-making can be deceptive and misleading. More important, elected legislators view the performance of bureaucrats by means of their constituency's need—the primary measure of the impact of bureaucratic performance on re-election. Accordingly, as discussed below, incentives or disincentives in electoral rules become a key constraint on Japan's military security policy.

Like the rules of civilian control over uniformed officials in Katzenstein's arguments described above, there has been an institutionalised mechanism through which LDP leaders control bureaucrats. Although not all of Japan's military security policy requires legislation, Diet approval is required for specific activities: the conclusion of treaties; the reconstitution of responsibilities, authorities and organisations assigned to the Defence Agency and the SDF; and defence expenditure as general government accounts. The Basic Policy for National Defence, the National Defence Program Outline, and the Mid-Term Defence Estimate do not statutorily require Diet approval, but must receive both Cabinet and Security Council (chaired by the prime minister) approvals. While the LDP and national ministries may initiate, it is the Defence Agency that drafts military defence policy. In the process of drafting policy, the Defence Agency also works under the constraints of informal rules or institutions that delineate the political limits of Japan's military security beyond the above legal-formal requirements. These informal rules, such as the 1% limit of GNP on defence spending, the three non-nuclear principles, and the three principles of weapons export, have become the basis for politicians' expectations about the actions of bureaucrats. Bureaucrats work on their own, but operate to meet the need of politicians, (that is, re-election), as LDP ministers control their promotion and future career as politicians (Pempel 1974:653; Muramatsu & Krauss 1984:143; Park 1986:61–77).

A larger number of LDP legislators will increase the likelihood of large-scale remilitarisation. The most important constraint of constitutional reform was and still is Article 96 of the constitution stating that it,

> shall be initiated by the Diet, through a concurring vote of two-thirds or more of all the members of each House and shall thereupon be submitted to the people for ratification, which shall require the affirmative vote of a majority of all votes cast thereon.

To ensure a two-thirds majority to eliminate Article 9 of the constitution, the Hatoyama Cabinet attempted to change the electoral system by replacing multimember constituencies that sent three to five Diet members to the lower house with single-member constituencies that elected one representative favoring majority party candidates. In May 1956, this proposed bill was killed in the Diet. LDP initiatives for constitutional revision in the 1950s came to a deadlock. In 1963 the Ikeda Cabinet adopted the *kaishaku kaiken* (constitutional reform through reinterpretation), which was intended to legitimise the presence of the SDF and the US–Japan alliance by reinterpreting Article 9 without revising the constitution. This tactic was adopted neither so much as a preferable choice of the LDP nor for coping with the external threat, but for the LDP to make concessions to the public sentiment of pragmatism/passivism toward national security.

However, a greater number of LDP legislators, even if they hold two-thirds or more seats in each house and are all pro-rearmament, will not be sufficient to ensure a pathway for remilitarisation, because specific electoral rules impose constraints on the performance of elected pro-rearmament LDP politicians for re-election. The structural nature of the multimember district system generated a weight of political pressure against unpopular defence spending. Japan adopted this electoral system in 1925 and abolished it after the 1993 lower-house election. Each voter was provided one ballot for only one candidate, although several were elected in the district (a single-entry, nontransferable-vote system). For the LDP to continue to have a Diet majority, they had to endorse multiple candidates in the same district. This necessity turned party colleagues into rivals. LDP candidates understandably pursued their electoral success beyond what was offered by the national party. They extended special interests through personal support networks or *koenkai* to their constituents and thus developed a personal reputation separate from their own party (Curtis 1971; Pempel 1998). This practice created a body of the ever-reliable 'hard votes' for each LDP candidate. In Japan, as discussed below, special interests groups that seek to expand Japan's military capability were hardly represented in political processes. LDP Diet members thus became reluctant to get involved in security policy-making but devoted themselves to bringing material benefits from Tokyo to their local constituency for electoral success against the candidates of their LDP colleagues.

By the early 1970s, however, 'floating voters' who drift from party to party or between turnout and abstention at actual elections represented a third of the eligible voters and they continued to rise. The existence of these voters became crucial in the context of multimember constituencies. Apart from the hard votes, gaining support among floating voters became a necessary condition to re-election, especially in urban districts. Since the special interests of floating voters largely remained unknown to candidates, LDP politicians tended to at least support a sentiment of anti-militarism and avoid unpopular defence spending.

In postwar Japan, no strong special interest groups that pursued expansion of Japan's military capability existed to exert pressure on politicians regarding military security policy. Between 1965 and 2003, industrial production of defence items remained less than 0.5% of total industrial output until 1984, increasing slowly to 0.66% in 2003 (JDA 2005). In 1999 the total military sales of Mitsubishi Heavy Industries, Japan's largest defence contractor, accounted for only 11.4% of its total sales, and the ratio of Japan's top ten defence contractors was less than 5% on average (METI 2000). It is true that, by the early 1960s, the Defence Production Committee of the Keidanren (the Federation of Economic Organisations) became the primary lobbying body (known as 'Japan's private defence ministry') for the defence industry and strongly advocated the 'domestic production' of Japan's arms industry with goals of exportation (Green 1995:31–52; Samuels 1994:130–231);[66] however, the image of a strong committee is misleading. Defence production accounted for a small part of Keidanren's business concerns. In principle, the Keidanren continued to promote economic growth driven by non-defence demand, and distanced itself from political involvement of the defence industry by granting autonomy to the committee (Green 1995:34; Samuels 1994:144–5).

As the Korean War boom ended, the Japanese government paid attention to the huge potential market of Japan itself. The MITI (Ministry of International Trade and Industry) policy was resolute on quickly moving away from a procurement-driven economy. The period of 1952 to the early 1960s became known as the MITI's golden age. MITI officials single-mindedly attempted to turn the Japanese industrial structure from light to heavy industries, from import-substitution to export-led economies, where they clearly encouraged and nurtured the development of civilian aircraft, car and shipping industries rather than defence production. After major defence contractors witnessed the bloody 1974 time-bomb explosion at the Mitsubishi Heavy Industries headquarters in Tokyo, which killed eight people and injured nearly 400, they were unable to overtly promote defence-related production. Big business in Japan specialised in consumer-focused goods and services and feared consumers' labelling them 'merchants of death'. Along with the business sector's cautious attitudes toward defence production, the majority of bureaucrats believed that the pursuit of defence demand-driven growth would threaten to disrupt a healthy growth in civilian markets (Green 1995:20–2; Samuels 1994:169–70). When Japan dealt with the FSX affair in the late 1980s, there were certain bureaucrats such as those in MITI's Aircraft and Ordinance Office who strongly pushed Japan's autonomy in defence production (Keddell 1993:163). However, the MITI as a whole was reluctant to actively promote the arms industry but rather aimed to help develop dual-use technologies which could also be sold in commercial markets. Finance Ministry officials were wary of the adverse impact of higher defence spending on Japan's macro-economy, while extending capital to non-defence industries. The Ministry of Foreign Affairs saw the proposed Japanese autonomy in defence production as an impediment to US–Japan relations (USOTA 1990:67).

Since the establishment of the Defence Agency in 1954, service in the agency posts has remained unpopular and avoided by LDP Diet members. In fact, the controversial post of Defence Agency Director General has turned over frequently. From 1954 to 2007, there were 67 director generals, in comparison with 24 prime ministers for the same period. There was no *kokubou zoku* (national defence policy group) as such within the LDP; but by the late 1970s those who had strong concerns about national defence began to form a small group.[67] As the fiscal austerity of the 1980s continued, US pressure to increase defence spending placed Japanese leaders in the difficult position. As a result, defence policy experts (*kokubou zoku*) in the LDP began to get involved in policy-making, especially in budgeting processes (Keddell 1993:86–8). Genda Minoru, a former Imperial Japanese Navy officer and postwar ASDF chief of staff, who turned into a postwar Diet member of the upper house in 1962, was the first legislator with a uniformed officer background. Serving four terms, he became a strong advocate of greater budgets and independent military capability, yet was largely marginalised in political processes (Inoguchi & Iwai 1987:210).[68] In the late 1970s, fiscal cutbacks combined with US pressure to increase LDP awareness in defence issues, but unlike *zoku* in other policy areas where they concertedly advocated greater budgets for their policy areas, *kokubou zoku* were not all in favour of greater spending on defence. Indeed, many *kokubou zoku* demanded more restraints on defence spending.

Between the mid-1970s and the mid-1980s, the specific nature of *kokubo zoku* interaction in policy-making processes emerged. It became characteristic of the influential LDP *kokubo zoku* that members were primarily former directors-general of the Defence Agency, such as Mihara Asao, Michio Sakata, Omura Joji and Kurihara Yoko. They had nothing to do with the LDP's national security-related committees until they became director-generals.[69] Once they had experienced the director-generalship firsthand, they were seen as experts in the field. The *kokubo zoku* group was a locus where experienced former director-generals discussed problems of national security as they arose. For other LDP legislators, this was the place for avoidance politics, as the proverb says, 'Least said, soonest mended'. It was politically too risky for either hawkish or dovish LDP politicians to become *kokubo zoku* in policy-making, constrained as they were by the overwhelming public opinion of negativity toward military security issues (Inoguchi & Iwai 1987:119–20, 209–10).

Military security expansion involved the enactment of unpopular policies in the underdeveloped special interest-group environment where neither politicians nor civilian bureaucrats wished to withstand the scrutiny of stakeholders. The politics of national military security, marked by pressures to avoid blame for unpopular policies, dictates specific strategies for re-election. In this context, floating voters played a key role in determining LDP strategies for electoral success. Those who 'do not support any party' reached a low of under 10% of the eligible voters in 1965 as the LDP versus Socialist Party system became stabilised. But, by the late 1960s they began to increase, indicating nearly 20% in 1969. The ratio continued to grow from over 30% in 1981 to nearly 50% in 1995.[70] These figures do not directly reflect the actual scale of floating voters, which drifted from party to party or between turnout and abstention at actual elections. Even if voters declare that they do support a specific party at some point, a considerable number of them state otherwise at another time (Miyake

1986:75; Miyake 1995:143). Many potential floating voters may turn out to vote and support a specific party at specific elections. The ratio of floating voters to eligible voters may thus be significantly higher than those figures. Although the turnout rates of those whom 'do not support any party' is lower than party supporters, about half of those non-party supporters turn out to vote at national elections (Miyake 1986:143; Miyake 1995:148). When a survey on voters' party support is conducted twice over a time period, three types of floating voters in a broad sense emerge: non-party voters (who did not support any party at either time), floating voters in a narrow sense (whose support shifted from one party to another), and irregular voters (who supported a specific party at one time but did not support any party at the other). In the late 1980s, party support voters as a percentage of eligible voters were about 50%, irregular voters around 30%, floating voters about 10% and non-party voters nearly 10% (Miyake 1989:117–8). LDP candidates had to win voting support from floating voters (in a broad sense) in elections where the loyal hard votes alone were less likely to ensure the candidate's electoral victory. These voters have distinctive determinants of voting behaviour that are different from party support voters. The determinants of voting behaviour can be categorised into three factors: party loyalties, candidate traits, and policy preferences. LDP candidates had to focus on factors other than party loyalty-related ones to draw floating voters. The existence of floating voters induced LDP candidates to take specific electoral strategies.

A nationwide survey on voters' attitudes at the 1983 simultaneous elections for the lower and upper house reveals unexplored aspects of floating voters.[71] Respondents were asked immediately before the election day if they had already decided who they would vote for. Those who answered in the affirmative were tallied as follows: 62% of party support voters (including abstention voters), 28% of floating voters, 18% of non-party voters, 14% of irregular voters. This implies that a candidate's image and traits are highly unlikely to be primary determinants of the floating vote (in a broad sense).

On the other hand, the survey indicates the importance of policy preferences in defence spending as determinants of voting by floating voters. Those who did not support any party appeared to have fewer interests in the ideology-based or complex bureaucratic policy issues favoured by elites; however, Japan's military security issue in the postwar period was symbolic and bottom-up-directed in the sense that involvement was largely framed by the individual level of attentiveness to the controversy. The military security issue, especially defence spending, seems to approximate one of 'easy' issues rather than hard issues, which were favoured by policy elites only (for the notion of easy issues, see Carmines & Stimson 1989). Voters were asked in the survey if there was any party that was close to their opinion on defence spending. Only 28% of the irregular voters, 29% of the non-party voters, and 46% of the floating voters answered yes. Given the anti-defence spending bias of Japanese voters, these figures demonstrated floating voters' dissatisfaction with political constraints on defence spending.

The voter tends to use his or her voting right to get collective gains for a smaller group rather than for a larger group, since his or her personal gain is greater in a smaller group than a larger group (Olson 1965:33–6). Furthermore, the voter tends to seek accordingly an exclusive collective gain so that the benefits will not be taken away by non-co-operators. Bearing these tendencies in mind, since the early 1960s LDP candidates had secured re-election by mediating with the national ministries to extend locally vested interests, or exclusive goods, to their personal support groups of hard voters (Imamura 1978; Hirose 1981; Muramatsu 1981:3–32).

On the other hand, floating voters tend not to cast a vote until all the candidates are present and have stated what interests they represent, or do not cast at all. The candidate does not know ahead of time what exclusive collective goods the individual floating voter wishes to access for his or her personal gain. It is too time-consuming and costly to identify the specific preference and demand of individual floating voters who may belong to unknown or unidentifiable groups. Therefore, there was not much incentive for LDP candidates to undertake such individualised tasks. Alternatively, for their electoral success, LDP candidates directed attention to the inclusive public good, which would provide beyond a single electoral district or across the nation.

National security is an inclusive public good. In Japan, greater budgets for defence were not only inclusive collective goods but also created the necessity of blame avoidance, not the opportunity of credit claiming, for LDP candidates' electoral success. One would expect that veterans' groups should have a strong incentive to increase defence spending in Japan; and seek their personal gain from the exclusive veterans' benefits. But veterans' pensions are not included in Japan's defence-related expenditures. In the national budget, these pensions have been handled as part of social spending (Otake 1982:24). The Nippon Izokukai (Association for Family Members of Japan's War Dead), which has over one million members, has been a strong support group of the LDP, but not a lobbying group for greater budgets for defence expenditure. Another potential group is the SDF, the largest body of government employees in Japan representing 240,000 personnel. In the past, the SDF personnel and their families have been able to gain only one proportional representation seat at most from the LDP for each upper house election. In the 1970s, LDP politicians said issues of national defence did not generate 'money or votes'. The rigidly-fixed spending outlined in defence five-year-plans did not create room for pork barrel politics. Although there was a National Defence Division in the LDP's Policy Affairs Research Council, in 1976 when the National Defence Program Outline was adopted, for example, only four to five LDP Diet members attended the division meetings (Yuasa 1986:166). An increase in defence spending involved the enactment of unpopular policy in an underdeveloped interest-group environment. In essence, defence-spending expansion required LDP candidates to pursue unpopular policies that must withstand the scrutiny of voters. Defence spending was an inclusive collective good in the sense that the expansion would adversely affect the collective expectation of most voters who preferred the status quo of defence budgeting. Support of the existing spending level by individual LDP candidates was an electoral practice in blame avoidance. In Japan, politicians rarely got credit for increased defence spending. Even in the early 1980s when Nakasone willingly took the political risk of proposing the removal of the 1% of GNP ceiling to achieve the spending targets set by the 1976 NDPO, a majority of LDP Diet members interpreted the state of public opinion in a pessimistic way and exhibited an extreme reluctance to be dragged into any electoral disadvantage (see *Mainichi Shinbun* 20.10.1980; *Asahi Shinbun* 4.11.1980). Politics was marked by the weight of popular pressure to avoid blame for the anti-defence spending bias.

chapter four

External structures (US pressure)

Normative consensus, while being capable of constraining state behavior, conforms to certain structures. As Katzenstein admits, 'If Japan is left unprotected by the United States, the defence option that institutionalised norms have prohibited could become a fallback option' (Katzenstein 1996:208). Berger similarly concedes, 'Japan's anti-militarism in its present form could not survive both a weakening of its alliance with the United States and the emergence of a new regional security threat' (Berger 1993:120). In other words, the effects of norms must conform to certain structures, which are known as the external environment where a state and its citizens are entangled and interact. One such dominant environment in Japan's national security is found in the US–Japan security alliance. Postwar Japan did not share comparable costs and risks, but the United States provided a unilateral guarantee of Japanese security. Japan was not a security partner on equal terms. The puzzle arises from the marked asymmetries in the US–Japan alliance capabilities. Why did the United States continue to provide Japan with 'free-ride'? Why was the United States able to condone the asymmetries, recognising that constitutional constraints and pacifism made it difficult for Japan to do more for its self-defence? What was the structure that had allowed or helped Japan's policy-makers to adopt their norms, model their decision-making and frame their claim around the security burden issue?

In 1945 the Allied Military Occupation quickly prohibited Japan's munitions industry, dismantled weapons and purged wartime leaders. Demilitarised Japan inevitably became dependent on the militarised US for defence. The reliance of Japan's security and economy on a single great power was not only unavoidable, but also beneficial to the physically and mentally collapsed nation during the early postwar period. In 1949 Japan, the recent enemy, became a desirable ally of the United States as China became a communist country. Once given key ally status, over time Japan developed a deep sense of dependency on the US hegemonic umbrella. It is true that the geopolitical position of Japan during the

Cold War period was strategically too important, from the view point of American interests, to be the subject of any bargaining. For the first two decades of the US–Japan alliance, the United States enjoyed a stable balance of trade surplus with Japan, and taking a free ride was not a US concern. In 1950 the United States produced more than 40% of world GNP and accounted for about half of its military expenditure. It was the only permanent protector, strong enough and willing to help Japan rebuild in the early postwar period. Until the early 1960s, the United States successfully supported its allied partners by exporting more than importing goods, and spending trade surplus on foreign military aid and economic assistance.

Another factor that helps explain Japan's free ride was widespread opposition in Japan to the US–Japan security relationship in the early 1960s. In the late 1950s, the initial intention of the US to provide financial assistance for Japan's defence build-up was concisely expressed in a June 1957 memorandum from the Joint Chiefs of Staff to Secretary of Defence Charles Wilson: 'as Japanese strength grows, dependence on the United States will lessen and should be replaced by a new common sense of purpose, mutual interests and a working partnership' (USDS 1957:350 cited in Keddell 1993:36). However, the 1960 crisis over revision of the US–Japan Security Treaty fueled political destabilisation in Japan (Scalapino & Masumi 1962:140; Destler et al 1976:21; Otake 1990:147). In the 1960s, the United States treated Japan with caution on political and trade matters to prevent any further structural damage to the US–Japan security relationship. President Eisenhower's proposed visit to Japan to set the seal on the new US–Japan security relationship was cancelled. Neither of his two successors, John F Kennedy or Lyndon Johnson, visited Japan. The United States managed delicate relationships with Japan to dilute Japan's mass show of opposition to the US–Japan security relationship and thus did not press Japan harder to share the security burden.

One of the reasons behind the assumption that the United States would continue to shoulder the primary military burden of US–Japan security relationships was US economic superiority. It wasn't until the United States was failing in the Vietnam War and faced with its first overall trade deficit, that it began to blame Japan for the free-ride. In 1971 the United States ran a disastrous balance-of-payments deficit; the 1971 deficit soared to $10.6 billion (*International Economic Report of the President* 1975:137). Until the early 1970s, trade and commercial issues were treated as secondary foreign policy priorities and placed as a minor issue on the US–Japan policy agenda (Calder 1988b:527). As the United States began to pressure Japan hard on trade issues, its preoccupation with strategic issues, especially regional stability and the containment of the Soviet Union, had increasingly become intertwined with trade and economics. On the one hand, the security relationships between the United States and Japan affected trade and economic issues over bilateral relations (Wong 1989; Dekle 1989). This aspect of the entanglement was not a new development. In the early 1950s, the development of the Cold War already rendered Japan the economic beneficiary of its postwar alliance with the United States in two ways: ready access to the world's largest market and relatively inexpensive transfers of US technology to Japan. On the other hand, the economic interactions between the United States and Japan began to spill over into the bilateral security relationship. This was something new to the US–Japan defence relationship. In the early 1970s, with the collapse of the Bretton Woods regime of fixed exchange rates, the rise of Japan's economy, and the massive increase in US trade deficits with Japan, US pressures dramatically increased for Japan to do more to defend itself (*JEI Report* 1989). In structural terms, Japan's continuing dependence on the United States for its economic prosperity and military security provided the United States with leverage to pressure Japan for greater defence efforts. Japanese leaders initially considered these US pressures legitimate. The Japanese way of thinking over US–Japan relations was that Japan received benefits or help from the United States and therefore should be ready to offer its services whenever the United States required them. US legitimacy as a demander was well rooted in Japan's hierarchical relationships where aid was something subordinates received from their superiors. However, Japan's response was described as 'piecemeal' or 'incremental,' giving neither an immediate compliance with nor an outright refusal of US pressures (Calder 1991:5–19; Keddell 1993).

US pressures for greater burden-sharing but not for large scale rearmament

The end of the Vietnam War and Washington's subsequent rapprochement with China and détente with the Soviet Union in the mid-1970s, saw a respite for Japan from US pressure to assume more of the defence burden. In 1976 Prime Minister Miki was able to officially take self-containment measures when his cabinet decided that the amount of the defence budget must be maintained within 1% of the GNP. Although the 1976 National Defence Program Outline (NDPO) showed Japan's intent to upgrade Japan's sea and air defence capabilities under pressure from the US (Otake 1986:165–6),[72] Prime Minister Miki and his cabinet were careful to appease the public by setting the limits of defence spending in the new defence build-up plan. The US Congress seemed to implicitly support Japan's self-containment measures as marked in Senator Mike Mansfield's report. He argued that US pressure for Japan's quantitative increase in its defence forces would not be in the best interests of the United States since they would cause both domestic and international criticisms of Japan's increased defence spending and destabilise the region (USSFA 1976:7). Indeed, the US Congress expected Japan to continue to depend on the US security guarantee and did not expect Japan to act independently without US assistance other than against a small-scale attack (USC 1977:5). Congress reported that large scale remilitarisation would have forced the Soviet Union and China to respond with their increased military capabilities, thereby triggering a new arms race in the region (USHRIR 1977:2–3). The US Defence Department embraced and extended this line of argument by stating that the presence of US forces in East Asia would deter the rise of a new military power and serve to minimise the necessity of Japan's destabilising military build-up in Asia (USDD, 1990:17–8). On the one hand, the United States wondered if Japan could be trusted with its own defence; on the other hand, Japanese politicians were extremely reluctant to provoke the anti-military sentiment of voters. Despite their different anxieties and concerns, both sides seemed to find common ground on the need for Japan to avoid large scale rearmament. Japanese government officials were aware of the US congressional reports that argued against Japan's large military build-up, and they considered it a strong rationale for constraining Japan's defence profile (Rifomu Kurabu 1980:137–8).

In the wake of the 1979 Soviet invasion of Afghanistan, US pressure for Japan to make greater defence efforts began to increase significantly. Japan's continued trade surplus with the United States, supported by an undervalued yen, led to one of the most dramatic decisions of the 1980s to affect the US–Japan security relationship. It was taken on 22 September 1985, when the 'Group of Five' rich nations decided to intervene in the foreign exchange markets to bring down the value of the US dollar against major currencies, in particular, the yen. Nonetheless, the devaluation of the US dollar failed to have the effect the Americans had hoped for in reducing Japan's trade surplus quickly. The strong yen quickly made Japan the world's wealthiest nation in terms of foreign exchange reserves and net overseas assets. A fresh round of US claims that Japan was free-riding on defence hit new highs in the late 1980s. By the end of the 1980s, American polls suggested that the public sometimes saw Japan's business practices as a greater threat to United States security than the Soviet Union (*Business Week* 7.8.1989:51). The 1980s was a decade of Japan bashing; there were hyped demands in the media, 'Spend more on defence'. Despite this criticism, officially the US did not necessarily wish to see an immediate increase in expenditure on Japan's independent military capabilities. US Congressional pressure on the executive branch in the 1980s remained evasive over how much Japan should be expected to build its own military capabilities. The US government instead pressured Japan to pay more of the costs associated with maintaining US bases in Japan. In reality, the indices of 'burden-sharing' were almost exclusively directed to increases in Japanese host-nation support for the US military stationed in Japan.[73] It was obvious that spending significant parts (9%–12% between 1978 and 2004) of Japan's defence budget on contributions to US forces in Japan restricted the financial resources available for developing Japan's own military capabilities.[74]

Strategic aid as a broader security burden-sharing measure

Japan's contributions to the cost of maintaining US bases in Japan are one of the ways in which Japan's responsibility is apportioned from the viewpoint of US interests. In the pursuit of public goods for burden sharing, spending on alternative security-promoting activities provided Japan with a safety valve for protection against US pressure. In this regard, other public goods, such as strategically tied foreign aid, debt relief, trade and financial liberalisation measures, also seemed to be easing American tolerance toward Japan's small defence burden. Susan Pharr calls it 'substitution policy' in which 'Japan has sought to gain ground in burden sharing by substituting contributions for nonmilitary public goods in the place of defence concession' (Pharr 1993:243). The origin of Japan's substituting contributions for nonmilitary goods can be found in the Yoshida Doctrine that emphasised the importance of economic measures to deter the rise of communist movements within the US containment policy. Substitution policy was formalised under the notion of *sogo anzen hosho* (comprehensive security) in the late 1970s. A report on comprehensive national security, which was assigned to a policy study group in April 1979 by Prime Minister Ohira Masayoshi, emphasised Japan's effective use of development aid and strategic aid to promote political stability in world affairs, while avoiding a large scale rearmament of Japan (Comprehensive Security Study Group 1980). After all, nonmilitary contributions to the sharing of defence burdens were more acceptable than defence concessions to Japanese voters.

By the late 1970s, Japan's Official Development Assistance (ODA) came to be seen as a burden sharing measure. As President Jimmy Carter attempted to reduce US military responsibility abroad, Japan's ODA was pressed into use for strategic purposes. In February 1976, President Carter requested that Japan increase aid to ASEAN as Japan did not appear to be prepared to increase its military spending (Orr 1990:109–110). In the following year, Prime Minister Fukuda agreed to his request and pledged to double Japan's share of ODA to $1 billion (Yasumoto 1986:111).

In 1981 Secretary of State Alexander Haig urged Foreign Minister Ito Masayoshi to extend Japan's aid to Jamaica in line with the United States'

Caribbean strategy; following discussions between President Ronald Reagan and Prime Minister Suzuki Zenko, the 1981 Joint Communiqué emphasised the value of Japan's 'aid to those areas which are important to the maintenance of peace and stability of the world'.[75] In 1984 the US–Japan Advisory Commission submitted a report to President Reagan and Prime Minister Nakasone recommending Japan's extension of aid specifically for strategic use. At Secretary of State George Shultz' urgings, Foreign Minister Abe Shintaro began to develop strategic aid plans as a substitute for military security burden sharing (HRPS 1985:6). Undersecretary of State Michael Armacost was reported as having insisted on 'extending the beneficiary of aid to the non-Asian regions such as Latin America' at a US–Japan undersecretary-level meeting (HCI 1987:1). The Ministry of Foreign Affairs embarked, for example, on active aid programs in South Pacific countries such as Fiji and Papua New Guinea; its officials explained that it was intended to 'drive in a wedge against the Russian advance, in a (Japanese) effort to indirectly support the United States' (HCI 1987:1). In this way, Foreign Affairs officials in fact sought to redefine nonmilitary measures to fit them within the US military strategy. From the US point of view, concerns over the possibility of Japanese major rearmament persuaded the United States to place more emphasis on Japan's ODA disbursements than Japan's further acquisition of defence capabilities. Indeed, US Secretary of Defence Frank Carlucci commented on this situation in 1988, saying that the United States would request no more than a 5% increase in annual rates of Japan's defence spending so that the SDF could not grow into an undesirable offensive force (cited in Keddell 1990:232). Carlucci's warning against Japan's major rearmament was reflected in President George Bush's agreement with Prime Minister Takeshita Noboru in 1989 that Japan would contribute best by increasing foreign aid to security burdens (Orr 1990:136). Even in the late 1980s when threats from the Soviet Union were diminishing, Japan still depended on the United States more than Washington depended on Tokyo in both economic and security terms (Nye 1991:A10). This asymmetry remained a source of US leverage to pressure Japan for greater defence efforts.

In the 1960s, Japan's bilateral ODA flowed exclusively to Asia, reaching nearly 100% of total aid flows in 1969. As Japanese officials publicly acknowledged that foreign aid was being extended as a means of contributing to burden sharing on security, the share of the other Developing World regions rose significantly and Asia's share dropped rapidly to 59% in 1977. Latin America's allocation increased from 0.6% in 1972 to 7.8% in 1981; Africa's from 1.0% to 9.3% during the same period.[76] Aid to countries such as Sudan, Jamaica, El Salvador and Turkey, accounted for Japan's efforts to meet US strategic needs well beyond the nation's existing scope of interest. Strategic aid thus became

Japan's burden sharing alternative to military contributions, and was legitimised under the notion of comprehensive security. Nearly half of Japanese voters were willing to endorse Japan's greater role in ODA.[77]

Concessions to trade relations in the place of defence concessions

Apart from strategic aid, Japan's trade concessions with the United States are another important aspect of Japan's contributions to burden sharing. Japan's security reliance on the US military presence turned to US economic advantage. The Japanese government made concessions in their commercial relations in order to deflect an outpouring of criticism away from the US–Japan security arrangements. Japan's response to the American demand for burden sharing was patterned and ritualised in the economic sphere. In essence, by deflecting US pressures, Japan managed to avoid any radical change of burden sharing for its defence and the defence of Asia. US pressures were closely associated with a comparative decline of the US economy vis-à-vis Japan's economy. Especially from 1969 when the Nixon Doctrine was announced, these patterns became clearly marked. Tokyo's government officials understood that Nixon's reassessment had been caused in part by the harmful impact of disproportionate burden sharing on the ailing US economy. Japan agreed to make a concession, the implementation of its 1972 Seven Point Program, advocating the reduction of the nation's trade surplus, the encouragement of imports and the slowdown of exports, and to floating the yen. Despite the yen revaluation, Japan still had a huge trade surplus with the United States. The Nixon administration continued to strong-arm Japan for further concessions. In 1972 Japan was running a US $4 billion trade surplus with the United States, and by 1987 the figure peaked at over US $52 billion. All of Nixon's successors attacked Japan's commercial practice as unfair, and demanded that Japan must do more for its own and regional security. In response, Japan routinely minimised concessions by requests, not complying immediately to US pressure. Overall, these ritualised patterns indicated that the greater the US trade deficit with Japan, the stronger and more often were US pressures imposed on Japan to assume its defence burden.

The origin of the ritualisation of conflict in US–Japan relations can be traced back to the 1968 US presidential election. The declining US economy led Richard Nixon to highly politicise US–Japan trade disputes in this election (Destler, Fukui & Sato 1979). Nixon promised the US textile industry he would limit Japan's textile exports to the United States. Nixon then offered Prime Minister Sato repatriation of a portion of Okinawa in return for curtailment of Japanese textile exports. Nixon told former Prime Minister Kishi that he feared a protectionist backlash in Congress and that the 'textile wrangle' with Japan might make the Okinawa reversion plan difficult.[78] Under heavy-handed US pressure, the Japanese government eventually conceded the implementation of export restraints in 1971 and Okinawa was reverted to Japanese control in 1972. The textile wrangle with Japan during the Nixon years marked a new phase of recurring confrontations in US–Japan economic relations. After the dispute, these recurring confrontations became routine to the extent that (1) US Congress exerted intense pressure on the administration to get tough with Japan's 'unfair' trading practices, (2) Japan's dependence on the US security guarantee provided the administration with leverage to deal with Japan over trade, (3) Nixon and his successors tried to extract concessions from Japan through import surcharges,[79] anti-dumping sanctions,[80] voluntary export restraints,[81] and a Structural Impediments Initiative (SII negotiations), (4) Washington resented having to allow minimal concessions by Japan to these pressures, and (5) after all, no matter how serious US–Japan trade disputes might become, neither Nixon nor his successors could afford to use the threat of withdrawal of the US security commitment to Japan.

By the end of the 1980s, the Soviet Union's threat, the basic premise for maintaining the US–Japan security relationship, was diminishing. This weakened arguments used for forgiving Japan's contentious trade policies and again opened the door to trade disputes. The most significant case of Japan's commercial concessions was the so-called Structural Impediment Initiative (SII) of the 1990 US–Japan negotiation framework, which was designed to redirect Japan's economic priorities to benefit the US position.[82] After many years of dealing with the Japanese government, American negotiators were infuriated by Japan's evasiveness toward sector-specific problem solving. The Bush administration instead sought Japanese structural reforms, such as those for macroeconomic policies, big business groupings, distribution systems, and bidding practices for public works, which would enhance the chance to open the Japanese market to further US exports. Equally important, in the negotiations the Japanese government also put forward their grievances about America, such as the lack of savings and a deficient educational system. The SII negotiations provided both sides with the opportunity to put issues on the table that they believed to be structural barriers in the other country. The trade negotiations showed a possibility for reciprocal concessions in the future.

Despite his emphasis on a 'result oriented trades strategy,' President Bush essentially failed to get 'results' from Japan that Congress and the business community had pressed hard to attain. When Bill Clinton took office, the first post-Cold War US president free of an external superpower-imposed threat of conflict, he placed trade issues with Japan as a high priority over other foreign policy areas. President Clinton and his advisors maintained a tough stance toward Japan to 'rebalance' US–Japan relations. As President Clinton saw trade as a key security issue, a new pattern of US–Japan economic relations emerged in the early 1990s. Several characteristics of these dealings stand out: (1) the limits of US tolerance began to show to the extent that US pressures on Japan were no longer considered with threats from the Soviet Union in mind, (2) US willingness to pressure Japan increased accordingly (initiatives for action against Japan now derived not only from congressional and business demands and bureaucracy's interests but from presidential leadership),[83] (3) yet US economic leverage over Japan declined significantly (as measured by Japan's dependence on the United States for market access, capital fund raising and investment, and technology transfer) (see Cronin 1994:1–26), (4) increased production and investments that Japan had made in the United States also limited the US capacity to impose sanctions on Japan (Bayard & Elliot 1994:343–6), (5) Japan's one-way concessions, as a reminder of its vulnerable status, were gradually losing legitimacy, and reciprocal concessions were now on the agenda at the negotiation table between the United States and Japan, and (6) despite all the new characteristics, Japan still depended on the United States far more than Washington on Tokyo. This asymmetry remained substantial in both economic and security terms and required Japanese leaders to withstand US pressures (Green & Samuels 1994:13–5).

Defence technology as part of the burden-sharing agenda

By the mid-1970s, the United States had become interested in Japan's advanced commercial technologies with defence application (known as 'dual-use technologies'). Japan's dual-use technologies, particularly in the fields of fiber optics, new composite material, semiconductors, and sensor devices, were considered to be an important contribution to burden-sharing (Tow 1983:4–6) and during the 1980s, defence technology became a key part of burden-sharing negotiations (Keddell 1993:119–20; Green 1995:82–5; Rubinstein 1999:275–6). In 1981 US Secretary of Defence Caspar Weinberger urged the Japanese government to allow the transfer of those technologies to the United States (Green 1995:84). In the early 1980s, a series of meetings, known as the Systems and Technology Forum (S&TF), were held between Washington and Tokyo officials. It became obvious that the implementation of defence technology co-operation would be impossible without revising Japan's restrictions on arms exports. Suzuki Zenko's cabinet was initially very reluctant to risk a public outcry over any attempt to revise Japan's ban on arms exports while the MITI warned that any such transfer would wind up being used by the US to take the industrial lead (Kesavan 1984:29; Green 1995:84–5). Yet as soon as Nakasone Yasuhiro took office as prime minister, his administration was able to defuse the controversy over defence technology co-operation by arguing that it was extremely important for Japan to reciprocate in the exchange of defence technology. In 1983 the Japanese government announced that transfer of military technologies to the United States would be exempted from its ban on arms exports. In the same year, the two governments concluded an Exchange of Notes confirming that commercial technologies with defence application would be freely available to the United States. Nonetheless, throughout the 1980s, such defence technology transfer remained minimal and collaboration on defence technology issues did not take off (Keddell 1993:120; Rubinstein 1999:276).[84]

The 1983 agreement for defence-related technology exchange at the government policy level illustrated that domestic priorities conformed to the predominant structure, that is, the sanctity of the US–Japan alliance. Japan's business sector and bureaucratic missions were unable to persuade LDP politicians to protect the industry's autonomous capabilities because it came into conflict with Japan's broader structural commitment to stable security relationships with the United States. Tokyo's agreement for joint military technology transfers avoided conflict with Washington, but the LDP pursued gradual, but limited, defence technology co-operation to meet domestic demands for constraints on defence. The limited number of transfers in the 1980s also demonstrated the Japanese government's implementation of the agreement in an incremental way that, where possible, protected the industry's autonomous capabilities.[85] Japanese industry remained committed to following the lead of the government.

In regard to other developed countries, Japan was relatively late to industrialise. Japan's early phase of industrialisation was driven by military industries to 'catch up and surpass the West' (a typical government slogan of the period). The Meiji government sought to reduce its reliance on foreign technology, which was considered a threat to Japan's sovereignty, and promote the growth of Japan's national power. In the postwar period, under the US security guarantee, Japanese industrial interests were driven by purely commercial aims. However, the determination to reduce the reliance on foreign technology remained a government policy with the emphasis on *kokusanka* (domestic production of technology) in postwar Japan. Richard Samuels explains this drive for domestic production as a function of 'technonationalism,' which is 'a set of coherent, even laudable ideas' in 'the belief that technology is a fundamental element of national security' in Japan (Samuels 1994:ix–x, 34).

Domestic pressures for autonomy in defence R&D and production fluctuated in postwar Japan, reflecting the trade-offs between domestic production of technology and purchases of US defence systems, production licensed by the US, and R&D collaboration (Samuels 1994:30–318; Green 1995). In post-FSX developments, perhaps the strongest US pressure against domestic production was the Clinton administration's request for access to Japanese dual-use technologies under the 'Technology-for-Technology' (TfT) initiative. The Clinton administration called for Japan's collaboration on Theater Missile Defence (TMD) in 1993 and prepared to use TMD to persuade Japan to provide access to its advanced areas of technology (Green 1995:139). The Japanese government was under heavy TfT pressure from the United States against domestic production of technology and asked to integrate Japan's technological innovations into the industry base of national defence in the United States.

From the viewpoint of the Clinton administration, Japan had used defence as a pretext to gain technology from the United States for promoting its own economic success. The TfT initiative's aim was to win US industry's access to Japan's commercially-based dual-use technologies to expand reciprocity in technology transfer (Green 1995; Rubinstein 1999:276–7). In this respect, TfT was not really intended to contribute to defence technology co-operation, but rather emphasise technology acquisition in itself (Green 1995; Rubinstein 1999:277). This TfT approach seemed to reflect a 'managed trade' agenda in the early Clinton years. Promotion of the initial TfT approach was destined to fail. While the MITI and the Ministry of Foreign Affairs stressed the necessity of joint development and greater collaboration,[86] the Japanese defence industry and the SDF resented and mistrusted the American position on the FSX affair and pushed for defence industry autonomy. The TfT used the channels between the US Defence Department and Japan's Defence Agency to access commercial technologies. Not surprisingly, the Defence Agency had no control over technologies developed and owned by Japanese industry and they were unable to deliver commercial technologies from unconvinced companies (Green 1995:141; Rubinstein 1999:276–7).

The revitalisation of US–Japan security relations was underway by the mid-1990s as described in the next chapter. Both countries attempted to reinvent the relevance of close US–Japan security relations. In this process, the trend toward 'partnerships' emerged in the development of defence equipment and technology as well as for the promotion of defence co-operation in general (USDD 1996). The initial TfT approach was altered by the US Defence Department's policy initiative that would promote 'Japan as not only a customer of US products, but a partner in the development of future equipment and technology' (Rubinstein 1999:277). Japanese officials at S&TF meetings became interested not only in basic research, but in system development projects, which were to integrate technology co-operation as a strategic way of bringing the two countries together (Rubinstein 1999:284n30). Given shrinking defence budgets and technology limitations, Defence Agency and MITI officials acknowledged their stake in being a partner in the development of future equipment and technology with the United States. Pathways to more reciprocal 'partnerships' would eventually require moving beyond mere monetary or nonmilitary contributions towards information and military risk sharing based on mutual trust. More reciprocal security arrangements between the United States and Japan would run counter to social norms, which were widely shared among the Japanese public, although Japanese voters became increasingly in favour of Japan's pro-active security policy by the mid-1990s.

In the 1980s and the early 1990s, defence technology became an important part of burden-sharing negotiations between the United States and Japan. Japan's commitment to its security ties with the United States structurally superseded its commitment to autonomy through domestic production of technology. Yet the more the United States shifted away from its commitment to the alliance, the more Japan attempted to pursue its autonomous defence technology. Japan continued to maintain and nurture an independent defence technology base, while persuading the United States to remain committed to Japan. Japan's technological direction, which would occupy a crucial part of its strategic thinking, essentially depended on the US commitment to Japan. There seemed to be three scenarios in which defence technology management would take place in Japan: (1) a full partner in the development of future equipment and technology within the alliance with the United States, (2) a stronger independent technology to work with US leadership in multilateral security arrangements (if the United States chose to co-operate with actions of other nations), and (3) a full independent technology to provide for self-defence (given the possibility of US withdrawal from its commitment to Japan) (Advisory Group on Defence Issues 1994). Whichever approach Japan would adopt, all three options initially would require a stronger independent defence technology. The significant changes in US approach toward the management of the US–Japan alliance emerged in the mid-1990s, which will be examined in the next chapter. These changes would narrow the scope of the three scenarios and constrain Japan's autonomy in defence technology.

chapter five

Norm changes (transitional structures)

Norms or collective expectations are not always static and fixed products, but rather are constantly in a process of construction and reconstruction. Norms may be recreated through the interaction of agents and structures. As new structures emerge, normative consensus may become fluid. More specifically, dramatic external shocks or crises can weaken commitments to existing norms. Citizens react to the changing environment and may begin to adopt new ideas for problem solving. Social interaction may lead to new collective understandings. Political change is more likely when the collective understandings are successfully implemented and consolidated in the domestic structure of political access, constraints and opportunities. The strength of new collective beliefs relies on the extent to which they become institutionalised and subsequently the independent source of influence for regulating or constraining state policies without coercive pressure.

In the 1990s, the debate on Japan's pacifism entered a new phase as a result of the post-Cold War environment. Japan's reputation for public security was dramatically deteriorating due to a series of crises: the long-lasting trauma of the economic boom bust (1991), the Korean Nuclear Crisis (1993–1994), the Great Hanshin earthquake (1995), the Aum Shinrikyo's sarin gas attack (1995), the 'Taepodong shock' (1998), and the nuclear accident at the Tokai plant (1999). Those who 'have worries and feel anxiety in everyday life' rose from 47% in 1991 to 67% in 2003; by contrast, those who 'neither have worries nor feel anxiety' dropped from 51% in 1991 to 31% in 2003.[87] Following the Gulf Crisis of 1990–1991, Japan's encounter with the rise of potential regional disputes ignited a hot debate on its security preparedness. The debate centred on whether Japan's self-imposed inward-looking pacifism could or should survive, or if Japan should become a 'normal nation'—one willing to take part in international security measures. The pacifism sentiment of pragmatism and passivity began to show a great degree of disintegration in the early 1990s. This disintegration reflected divisions among major national newspaper editorials. The *Yomiuri*

Shinbun (15.8.1992) ridiculed Article 9-based security as 'one country pacifism' and proposed Japan adopt a 'normal nation'-for-active-security policy while the *Asahi Shinbun* (15.8.1991) urged the preservation of the spirit of Article 9 as Japan's 'essential attribute'. The *Mainichi Shinbun* (15.8.1991; 15.8.1995) also emphasised the importance of Japan's peace-oriented security policy, not undertaken in the form of 'inward-looking pacifism' but rather as going beyond national borders in order to be accepted by the international community. In the 1990s, major national newspapers rarely expressed the view that the Japanese had been victimised by the atomic bombings or their own military. The *Asahi Shinbun* (15.8.1990; 15.8.1995) and the *Mainichi Shinbun* (15.8.1992; 15.8.1997) overwhelmingly acknowledged their role as aggressors against foreigners and foreign countries, and recognised the rise of peace consciousness beyond the limits of the self-centred 'one-country' perception.

Little consideration for contributions to the resolution of international conflict, which was significantly caused by the legal and constitutional constraints, generated a sense of contradiction and incongruity among the Japanese. From 1995 to early 1996, Japan's peace consciousness that had been expressed in anti-revision opinions of the existing 'peace' constitution began to shake. Around 1995 public opinion polling data, provided by major national newspapers, showed for the first time since the early 1950s that the number of those who believed it necessary to revise the constitution exceeded those who opposed it (*Yomiuri Shinbun* 6.4.1995; *Nihon Keizai Shinbun* 15.8.1995; *Mainichi Shinbun* 5.1.1996). Between 2000 and 2004, major national newspapers and the Japan Broadcasting Corporation conducted over 20 such opinion surveys ; pro-revision respondents represented 46–65% and anti-revision ones accounted for only 14–36%.[88] The primary reason why they thought 'it necessary to revise' was because they felt it necessary for Japan to 'assume a role in the international community.'[89] However, it is very important to note here that pro-revision respondents did not necessarily wish to revise Article 9 completely. Indeed, during the same period, those who wished to eliminate Article 9, Clause 1—the 'renunciation of war'—represented only 30–36% of the total respondents, while those who wished to revise Article 9, Clause 2—'prohibition on the maintenance of armed forces'—reached 70% in 2005 (*Asahi Shinbun* 3.5.2005). There still seemed to be much appreciation for aversion to military involvement, which is expressed in support of Clause 1, and, at the same time, much apprehension of the need to explicitly recognise the existing SDF, which is seen as its contradiction with Clause 2. In short, the majority of Japanese acknowledged the contradictory reality between the armed forces and the constitution, and thus were in favour of revision to accept the existing SDF; however, they preferred to see the constitutionally recognised SDF's position only as defending Japan's soil and participating in UN noncombatant peacekeeping operations.[90]

The swing in public opinion certainly encouraged the government's effort on active defence policy. Former Prime Minister Nakasone Yasuhiro stated: 'As things are, every survey is in favour (of revision)...After all, we politicians must keep in mind this big change in the national view' (HRCRC 2001). The attempted revision seemed to be more feasible at this time with a dramatic change in the current public opinion. Other senior LDP politicians sent a strong message to Prime Minister Koizumi Jun'ichiro by asking: 'Prime Minister, now will you address this change in national consciousness?' (HRECB 2003). Prime Minister Koizumi admitted: 'I see (Japan's) Self-Defence Force essentially as military forces. It is not natural that we aren't allowed to say it' (HRECB 2003). The prime minister thus directly emphasised the necessity of revising the so-called 'peace clause,' Article 9 of the constitution. However, Diet members' perception of national security kept some distance from the changing collective expectation held by the general public. In 2004 those lower-house members who believed Japan should be able to invoke the right of collective self-defence reached 66%.[91] A high of 96% of LDP Diet members thought it necessary to revise the constitution; and 84% of those members were in favour of invoking the right of collective self-defence.[92] Over one-third of the Diet members believed 'collective self-defence' referred not only to participating in UN noncombatant peacekeeping operations but also to UN combatant peace enforcement operations, yet only 8% supported joint military operations with allies (*Mainichi Shinbun* 3.5.2004). It is safe to say that only some Cabinet members and hawkish LDP politicians argued that Japan should lift its prohibition against collective self-defence, in order to promote US–Japan joint military operations on an extended scale.

On the domestic political level, the LDP lost its parliamentary majority in July 1993, and its 38 years of uninterrupted rule ended. Following this LDP defeat, the Renewal Party, which was established by about 30 former LDP members, formed a coalition government with smaller parties.[93] Party realignment continued to take place thereafter. Between 1993 and 1997 alone, eleven different political parties shared power and four prime ministers held office. In 1994 a new electoral system for the House of Representatives was introduced with intentions aimed primarily at stopping money politics.[94] Party politics was in the midst of a massive overhaul. Shifts in public opinion coincided with this political volatility.

Hosokawa Morihiro, chosen as the 'reformist' prime minister by the new coalition partners, took defence issues as well as electoral reforms, seriously, yet understood that defence issues would be divisive among coalition partners that ranged from former LDP members to the Socialists. In February 1994, he commissioned a special advisory committee, known as the Defence Affairs Study Council, to deliberate on revising the 1976 National Defence Program Outline. Higuchi Hirotaro, then Asahi Beer president, was chosen to chair the committee and submitted the completed report in August 1994 to Socialist Murayama Tomiichi who had replaced Hosokawa as prime minister under a new LDP-Socialist coalition. Murayama announced his party's (the Japan Socialist Party—now called the Social Democratic Party of Japan) support for the US–Japan alliance and the constitutionality of the SDF in order to become a coalition partner with the LDP in the same period. The Cold-War-driven ideological divisions on defence issues continued to diminish within Japan's party politics (Hook & McCormack 2001:29). However, the 'Higuchi Commission Report' (The Modality of the Security and Defence Capabilities of Japan—The Outlook for the 21st Century) asked if Washington would continue to make a commitment to the maintenance of US military presence in East Asia (Advisory Group on Defence Issues 1994). It proposed, in anticipation of declining US commitment to the region, that Japan's multilateral initiatives would serve to *complement* the US–Japan bilateral alliance (Advisory Group on Defence Issues 1994:13–6). In other words, it was still within the framework of the US–Japan alliance that the Higuchi Report explored the possibility of Japan's participation in multilateral activities. But some Tokyo observers, such as Tsuru Shigeto (economist) and Sakamoto Yoshikazu (historian), embraced this idea and wished to go one step further by giving multilateral arrangements a priority over the US–Japan bilateral relationships (Dixon 1999:166n24). Multilateralism seemed to become a fashionable form of rhetoric to promote Japan's participation in regional affairs and to assert the SDF's new role in peacekeeping operations. Foreign Minister Kono Yohei in the Murayama cabinet was seen as the leading multilateralist within the LDP. Despite the diminishing ideological division, these different positions had not yet really neutralised the debate on defence issues in Japan.

Under these circumstances, reports surfaced in Japan that the Pentagon feared Japan might drift away from the United States (*Asahi Shinbun* 28.2.1995). Some Japan specialists, such as Patrick Cronin and Michael Green, of the National Defence University (a subcontractor to the Pentagon) were reported to take the Higuchi Report reactively as a serous sign of Japan's drift from the United States (Johnson 1996). In September 1994, as soon as the Higuchi Report had been released, Assistant Secretary of Defence Joseph Nye visited Tokyo to reassure Japan about the primacy and credibility of the US–Japan alliance. On this visit, he started negotiations with the Murayama administration to update the relevance of the alliance. Joseph Nye and his advisors on Japan, such as Ezra

Vogel (National Intelligence Officer for East Asia) and Paul Giarra (Japan Desk Officer at the Pentagon), made a concerted effort to eliminate Japan's fear of the imminent withdrawal of the United States from Asia and to remove the damaging image of a declining US commitment in Asia. This effort led to the release of the 'United States Security Strategy for the East Asia-Pacific Region,' *East Asian Strategy Report 1995*, which became known as the 'Nye Report'. Unlike the first and second East Asian Strategy Reports in 1990 and 1992 that anticipated reductions in US deployed forces, in this 1995 report the US Department of Defence stated its continued commitment to 'maintain...at the existing level of about 100,000 troops, for the foreseeable future,' while increasing US efforts to strengthen its bilateral alliance with Japan (USDD 1995).

In his negotiations with Tokyo, Nye demanded that the upcoming reformulation of Japan's 1976 NDPO must consistently work with the Nye initiative. In response to this demand, when it was released under the Murayama cabinet in November 1995, the new NDPO used the phrase 'Japan–US security system' 13 times in the text, as compared with only once in the old NDPO, to emphasise the importance of the US–Japan alliance (Murata 2007:133). However, it is important to note that despite the Nye initiative to keep US ground forces in Japan, the Murayama cabinet decided to cut its own forces in the new NDPO. The 1995 NDPO proposed reductions in Japan's overall troop level from 180,000 to 160,000 men (demobilising four army divisions), tanks from 1,200 to 900 units, surface ships from 60 to 50, and interceptors/fighters from 430 to 400. It set itself apart from the 1976 NDPO by proposing that Japan should defend itself not only through strengthening its bilateral alliance with the United States but also contributing to a more stable international security environment (MOFA 1995b).

In January 1996, Murayama resigned as prime minister and was replaced by a hawkish, pro-US LDP leader, Hashimoto Ryutaro. The momentum for updating US–Japan security ties was then accelerating. At the April 1996 Clinton-Hashimoto summit, both agreed to review the 1978 Guidelines for US–Japan Defence Co-operation. The United States and Japan had accordingly worked to update the relevance of the US–Japan alliance in the post-Cold War environment. This effort resulted in the 1997 Guidelines for US–Japan Defence Co-operation, which superseded the 1978 guidelines. Perhaps the most important change of the new 1997 guidelines affecting Japan's military security policy was in the introduction of a new notion of military response to 'areas surrounding Japan.' The 1978 guidelines brought US and Japanese forces together for the first time to propose the mechanism of joint operations but did not make much progress in building a credible mechanism beyond the narrow mission of defending Japan. The initial US–Japan alliance was established to defend Japan against the Soviet threat during the Cold War (Article 5 of the US–Japan Security Treaty), but the US perception of threat was broadened to include threats from regional disputes in the post-Cold War environment. US–Japan security co-operation in the 1997 guidelines was extended beyond the limits of defending Japan to 'co-operation in situations in areas surrounding Japan', whose concept 'is not geographic but situational' (MOFA 1997).[95]

The 1997 guidelines proposed Japan's commitment to supporting US forces in 'areas surrounding Japan,' although not obligating Japan to take any legislative and administrative measures for defence co-operation. Such a commitment would amount to no more than logistical support under Japan's existing policies. As discussed below, however, the guidelines, rather than seeking merely Japan's logistical support, seemed to be an indication of US desires for Japan to invoke the right of collective self-defence and to be equipped with emergency contingency laws. By 2000 when the so-called Armitage Report was released,[96] the United States clearly expected Japan not only to share financial costs, but to share risks incurred from military emergencies. Indeed, Deputy Secretary of Defence Paul Wolfowitz requested that Japan provide 'boots on the ground' to Iraq (HRPS 2003a). The US military's Joint Vision 2020, a blue print to 'establish the ability of operating alone or with allies, to defeat any adversary', indicated a shift in the importance of Japan's expected contributions from indirect and non-military sharing to direct and military sharing. The focus of how to measure the public good of the alliance was now on military risk sharing rather than on money paid for 'strategic aid' and the stationing of US forces in Japan. United States' willingness to tolerate Japan's free ride was at a crossroads. To expand Japan's role in the alliance, the Armitage Report stated: 'Japan's prohibition against collective self-defence is a constraint on alliance co-operation. Lifting this prohibition would allow for closer and more efficient security co-operation' (INSS 2000:5). The pressing US need for Japan to lift its prohibition against collective self-defence was strongly marked in this report. The recommendations in the report were not made for cases of direct armed attacks on Japanese soil, but exclusively for regional disputes in areas such as the Korean peninsula, the Taiwan Strait, and the Indian subcontinent. The real intent or motives behind the recommendations did not seem to update the US guarantee to defend Japan in case of armed attack, but rather to heighten pressures on Japan to support US military operations in regional conflicts. The report looked to the US–UK security partnership as a model for a new US–Japan alliance, and emphasised 'power-sharing' rather than 'burden-sharing' (INSS 2000:6). US pressures for greater Japanese defence efforts clearly shifted emphasis from burden-sharing in budgetary terms to power-sharing in military risk strategies. The Bush administration put yet another pressure on the Koizumi cabinet to shift Japan's policy toward a strongly alliance-oriented, high-risk strategy with the United States; the 11 September terrorist attacks unexpectedly led to Bush's 'war on terror' and Prime Minister Koizumi was put on the critical spot to respond to Bush's call to act together against terrorism.

In the new, post-Cold War environment, it seemed that as the public attitudes shifted toward pro-active security policy, so did US pressures toward power sharing. It appeared more feasible than ever before that Japan would become a more 'normal nation' through the use of military, where Japanese soldiers would fight for the country's national interests. Japan's influential ruling conservatives are either realists or neo-conservatives. In Richard Samuels' view, LDP neo-conservatives, such as Koizumi Jun'ichiro, Abe Shinzo, and Aso Taro, have been less apologetic about Japan's wartime record of aggression, compared with LDP realists such as Nakasone Yasuhiro and Ishiba Shigeru, who see the neo-conservative position on historical issues as unnecessarily provocative (Samuels 2007:142–6). Nonetheless, a common core does exist and is shared by both Japan's realists and neo-conservatives; they agree on the need to revise the constitution, emphasise the importance of the US–Japan alliance and collective self-defence, are willing to deploy the SDF for 'power-sharing', and wish to become a great power again (Samuels 2007:129, 145). Indeed, there seems to be a number of recent government measures that may signal a shift on Japan's military security policy and facilitate a significant move towards becoming a militarily 'normal nation.' These measures, as mentioned in the introduction, include: (1) the 1999 passage of guideline laws allowing the SDF to provide US forces rear area support, (2) the 2002 passage of anti-terrorism legislation,[97] (3) the 2003 passage of emergency defence bills, (4) the 2004 dispatch of the SDF to Iraq, and (5) the 2007 passage of national referendum legislation to set the procedures for constitutional revision. Is Japan really preparing to become a militarily normal nation that can use armed forces as a means of settling international disputes? If so, is Japan being locked structurally into the US global strategy? In the following sections, I will examine the possibility of this transformation by linking it with changes in Japan's social norms.

The indirect effects of social norms on government policy are difficult to trace and thus are easily neglected. The Japanese people's deep scepticism about the utility of armed forces deserves to be mapped out and still fundamentally affects security-related government measures by influencing the coalition-building process among national elites. Japan's collective expectation of foreign policies is the most stable and consistent of all industrialised democracies (Bobrow 1989:571–603; Stockwin 1987:111–34). Despite public opinion's shift toward a pro-active security policy in the mid-1990s, the stable and immovable nature of social norms regarding the Japanese public's strong aversion to military involvement has remained intact in the post-Cold War environment. This strong underlying aversion is still effectively embedded in the norm compliance mechanism and sets outer limits beyond which no political party will go if it wishes to gain or retain office. A close examination indicates that the limits of Japan's recent moves toward becoming a militarily 'normal nation' reflect this immovable part of social norms. The Japanese government's measures taken after the 11 September attacks have legally widened the scope of what the SDF can do, but two immovable constraints—the ban on the overseas deployment of the SDF for combat operations and a stringent set of statutory restrictions on the use of weapons by the SDF—have remained intact. Neither the norm-induced political climate nor statutory measures will allow the dispatch of the SDF to play a direct role in the US war on terror.

Public response to Japan's deployments in support of the war on terrorism

Immediately after the 11 September attacks, Prime Minister Koizumi was keen to show prompt support for the United States and seemed to demonstrate his decisive leadership in the antiterrorism legislation of the 2001 *Anti-Terrorism Special Measures Law*, which allowed the dispatch of SDF ships to the Indian Ocean to help the US operations for intelligence services, fueling, medical services and humanitarian relief (Shinoda 2003:19–34). In the past, the SDF had neither been dispatched abroad without a UN mandate nor sent on a mission under wartime conditions. The antiterrorism legislation created a significant precedent for SDF participation in non-UN-led multinational operations while combat operations were underway. Can it be seen as 'a sharp break from Japan's pacifism'? (Shinoda 2003:19). Some observers see the SDF dispatch as part of American global strategy (see Hughes 2004:368–9). Others bluntly state that Japan is emerging as a key ally that will join US military operations on an extended scale (Miller 2002:1–4). Japan's response to the Bush administration-led war on terrorism represents a critical case for testing whether Japan is becoming a militarily 'normal nation' that can go to war as the 'Britain of Asia' as the Armitage Report suggested (INSS 2000:6).

The anti-terrorism legislation was swift and proved a top-down leadership success for Prime Minister Koizumi. On 25 September, the ruling coalition of the LDP agreed on the legislation, and by the end of October, the bills were enacted. There seemed to be a number of factors that facilitated Koizumi's top-down style of leadership. First, the new 1994 electoral system weakened factional influence over the prime minister and thus helped Koizumi avoid the resistance of faction leaders (Shinoda 2003:21–4). Second, the 2001 administrative reform strengthened the role of policy initiatives from the prime minister and the Cabinet Secretariat and weakened the bureaucracy's influence (Shinoda 2003:25–8). Third, in the post-Cold War environment, ideological differences on defence issues among political parties were smaller and the proposed measures were negotiable (Pekkanen & Krauss 2005:440). Fourth, unusually strong public approval for Koizumi's leadership enabled the major bills to be passed quickly.

Public support for the Koizumi cabinet certainly facilitated Japan's unusually quick responses to the 11 September attacks but limited the scope of the SDF deployment in order not to go beyond the parameters for the use of force. In late September 2001, opinion polls conducted by major newspapers indicated that respondents representing 60%–70% supported Japan's co-operation with the United States to respond to the 11 September atttacks.[98] However, only 40% approved of Prime Minister Koizumi's initial proposal for bills allowing the SDF to provide 'rear-area support' for US military action while 46% disapproved of it (*Asahi Shinbun* 1.10.2001). Given the record high approval rating for the Koizumi cabinet, for example, 71% on 1 October 2001 (*Asahi Shinbun*'s poll), ignoring public opinion for this unpopular initiative could have had negative effects on Koizumi's populist leadership. Koizumi then pledged to help the US military operations within Japan's constitutional framework. Under the Koizumi administration, the overseas mission of the SDF received significant public support, yet public mistrust of the state ability to use armed forces remained intact. The Cabinet Public Relations Office survey showed popular endorsement of a pro-active security policy, with those who supported Japan's participation in UN noncombatant peacekeeping operations continuing to increase from 46% in 1991 to 80% in 2000.[99] By the mid-1990s, a solid majority of the Japanese people for the first time accepted the dispatch of the SDF overseas. However, only 23–24% thought that Japan should also participate in UN combatant peace enforcement operations (*Asahi Shinbun* 2.5.2001).[100] The overwhelming majority of Japanese firmly opposed the SDF becoming involved in overseas combat, even within a UN peacekeeping framework.

In a telephone opinion poll conducted by the *Yomiuri Shinbun* on 24–25 September 2001, 24.7% of respondents agreed that Japan should actively support US operations against the terror attacks and 62.4% agreed to some extent; by contrast, only 12% did not agree (Yomiuri Shinbunsha 24–25.9.2001). Among those who agreed to Japan's co-operation with the United States against the terror attacks, 86.5% of the respondents identified rear-area support as one of Japan's desirable contributions, 54.9% were for financial support, and 8.2% for participation in combatant operations. A month later, a nationwide interview survey, conducted by the *Yomiuri Shinbun* during 20–21 October 2001, found that the support for a rear-area role had declined to 57.1% and for participation in combatant operations, had dropped sharply to 3.6% (Yomiuri Shinbunsha 20–21.9.2001). Although the 24–25 September poll revealed the Japanese people's *great* concern about the 11 September attacks (82.5% of respondents), this short-term anxiety never led the Japanese public to permit the use of force by the SDF on foreign soil. Even public support for Japan's noncombatant logistical role in the rear-area remained a sensitive issue. The *Anti-Terrorism Special Measures Law* indeed reflects the collective expectation among Japanese people, authorising SDF participation in extending material assistance and other support services to the multinational forces, and in engaging in search-and-rescue activities. It strictly itemises the permissible activities: provision of fuel, food, and water; transport of personnel; maintenance of machinery; medical services; support of telecommunication; support activities at airports and seaports; and administrative services.[101] This list of activities comes with clear strings attached: no combat should be present in the area in which the SDF will be deployed; the SDF is to operate only on the high seas and the airspace above it; the SDF cannot operate on foreign soil without explicit consent from the host country. The law derives the legitimacy of these SDF activities from the UN Security Council Resolution 1368 that declared the 11 September attacks to be a threat to peace and security (PMJC 2007).

In 1991 the Japanese government decided to dispatch MSDF minesweepers to the Persian Gulf, and argued that the mission of minesweeping in the high seas would be to ensure the safe passage of vessels and thus should not be interpreted as a use of force. However, it reinterpreted Article 99 of the SDF Law by authorising the high seas operations outside of the 'vicinity of Japan' (for the initial interpretation, see HRFA 1972). The legal conditions under which the SDF should be dispatched overseas were moderated significantly between 1991 and 2001, including the 1991 Five Principles on SDF participation in UN-related peacekeeping operations,[102] the 1992 amendment of the International Disaster Relief Law,[103] and the 1999 enactment of the Law to Ensure Japan's Peace and Security in Situations in the Areas Surrounding Japan (Regional Crisis Law).[104] The scope of what the SDF could do legally certainly has expanded over time; however, two explicit constraints, which reflect the immovable components of Japan's social norms—the ban on SDF participation in overseas combat and overwhelming restrictions on the use of force—remained intact and unchallenged. The *1999 Regional Crisis Law* limited SDF activities strictly to the area of rear support to Japanese territory and the sea and airspace surrounding Japan, yet the *Anti-Terrorism Special Measures Law* extended their activities to the high seas and the airspace above it (the Indian Ocean area) and further to foreign soil with explicit consent from the host country. Nonetheless, those two constraints were firmly entrenched in the antiterrorism legislation.

The successful enactment of the *Anti-Terrorism Special Measures Law* did not end the debate on the definition of noncombatant areas and the extent of rear-area support allowed for the SDF deployed to the Indian Ocean. The Japanese government strongly argued that the designated areas for SDF operations would be regarded as noncombatant zones. Although the new law limited the area of SDF activities to 'noncombatant zones,' a noncombatant area could easily become a battle zone. Even Prime Minister Koizumi once confessed, 'It does not make sense if the SDF are not allowed to be dispatched to dangerous areas' (*Daily Yomiuri* 25.10.2001). This appeared to indicate the real risks involved in the SDF operations. Nearly 50% of Japanese expressed their opposition to the SDF dispatches proposed under the *Anti-Terrorism Special Measures Law*, even to 'noncombatant zones' for rear-area support to the US military (*Asahi Shinbun* 27.11.2001).

At an early stage of the antiterrorism legislation, in alliance with public concern about the risk of combat, the Japanese government had argued that the constitution did not allow Japan to provide military aid to allies under attack (*Kyodo News* 1.10.2001). Nonetheless, the Koizumi cabinet initially planned to dispatch an Aegis destroyer (equipped with state-of-the-art surveillance and information-gathering capabilities), P-3C marine patrol planes, and AWACS (Airborne Warning and Control System) planes to the Indian Ocean for rear-area support of US military operations (*Yomiuri Shinbun* 21.9.2001). Despite Koizumi's enthusiasm for these proposed dispatches, strong opposition emerged within the LDP, as the impact was already showing up in public opinion polls. Prime Minister Koizumi gave in to pressure within the LDP, withdrawing dispatches of the P-3C and AWACS, yet he still determined to send an Aegis destroyer to the Indian Ocean (*Kyodo News* 28.9.2001).[105] Anti-Koizumi LDP politicians, such as former LDP Secretary General Nonaka Hiromu, LDP General Council chairman Horiuchi Mitsuo, and lower house Counter-terrorism Committee chairman Kato Koichi, concertedly expressed their fears about the electoral implications for the party (*Yomiuri Shinbun* 18.11.2001; *Daily Yomiuri* 19.11.2001). Koizumi's close ally LDP Secretary General Yamazaki Taku eventually admitted that defying public opinion would impede the progress of Koizumi's structural reform (*Yomiuri Shinbun* 18.11.2001). Public pressure consequently tabled the dispatch.

However, the US government put additional pressure on the Koizumi cabinet; on 29 April 2002, during a meeting with visiting Japanese Diet members in Washington, Deputy Secretary of Defence Paul Wolfowitz requested the deployment of the Aegis ships and P-3C anti-submarine patrol aircraft to the Indian Ocean. In response, Nukaga Fukushiro who headed the non-partisan delegation of the Diet members to Washington, cautiously explained that the unpopular dispatch, if implemented, would be politically damaging (*Yomiuri Shinbun* 4.5.2002). Prime Minister Koizumi was also careful to emphasise that the deployment of Aegis destroyers was still not an option for Japan's rear-area support to US military operations. On 1 December 2002, however, it was reported that the Aegis equipped ship was most likely to be dispatched at the end of the month (*Yomiuri Shinbun* 1.12.2002). A news source quoted Kaji Misako, spokeswoman for Prime Minister Koizumi, as saying, 'no new laws would be required to send the Aegis, so logically it is possible' (*Reuters* 30.11.2002). On 4 December the Japanese government announced the dispatch of the Aegis equipped *Kirishima* to the Indian Ocean, and on the same day Deputy Secretary Richard Armitage immediately stated that the US government appreciated Japan's decision to dispatch the Aegis. When Armitage visited Japan on 8 December, the United States had already shifted its focus from Afghanistan to Iraq. The unprecedented decision to send Japan's Aegis was seen as a move that would relieve a US Aegis destroyer from US operations in Afghanistan and thus give support for a possible US attack on Iraq (*The Associated Press* 6.12.2002; *Singapore Straits Times* 6.12.2002). The Koizumi cabinet worked hard to minimise the anticipated public outcry. It justified the move by arguing that the primary purpose of the dispatch was to improve sailors' onboard quality of life,[106] while emphasising the security that the Aegis ship would provide during ocean refuelling (*Asahi Shinbun* 3.12.2002). In its view, MSDF ships were vulnerable to attack during refuelling and the Aegis guard, whose radar could detect such a possibility, was crucial for their safety. The Japanese public remained sceptical. A telephone opinion poll conducted by the *Asahi Shinbun* on 14–15 December 2002 showed that 48% of respondents opposed the dispatch, while 40% approved (*Asahi Shinbun* 16.12.2002). Scepticism remained even within the LDP; some LDP leaders, such as Nonaka and Horiuchi, explicitly warned that the dispatch could trigger US pressure to drive Japan in a dangerous direction, including the deployment of the SDF against Iraq (*Asia Times Online* 19.12.2002). Under these circumstances, the Koizumi cabinet was forced to ensure that the Japan's Aegis would never get involved in the March 2003 US attack on Iraq.

Japan was still far from seeing the invocation of collective self-defence, explicitly including its joint military operations with US forces. The Japanese government provided only 'rearguard support' for the war on terrorism by dispatching the Aegis destroyer to the Indian Ocean, which would 'not result in an exercise of Japan's collective self-defence' (HRECB 2002). Japan sought a policy change within the easily acceptable limits of continuity of its activities that were not construed as the use of armed forces. It was a long way from growing into the 'Britain of East Asia'. In its effort to meet this, the *2001 Anti-Terrorism Special Measures Law*, for example, covertly stipulated that the SDF were able to use their weapons not only to protect themselves, but also to protect 'those who are with them on the scene and have come under their control while conducting their duties' (Article 12–1). In this way, the Japanese government might have been able to modify national security policy by making changes around the edges but were unable to make a fundamental shift.

Public response to the dispatch of the SDF for Iraqi reconstruction

On 20 March 2003, President Bush launched the pre-emptive war against Iraq. On 17 March, Prime Minister Koizumi had already stated that Japan would support US military action, even without a UN resolution to authorise the use of force against Iraq (*Japan Times* 18.3.2003). However, the Japanese government was not able to move as swiftly as it did in the case of US military operations against al-Qaeda and the Taliban regime in Afghanistan. The Koizumi cabinet initially shelved the option of SDF dispatch for certain reasons: (1) before and during the US attack on Iraq, a majority of Japanese voters consistently saw the war as wrong; and (2) it was difficult to justify the deployment of the SDF, to provide rear-area support for the coalition forces, within the existing legal framework (including the PKO Co-operation Law and the Regional Crisis Law); in other words, Prime Minister Koizumi needed to struggle to pass another special measures law for the SDF overseas dispatch. *Asahi Shinbun* polls on the anticipated US attack on Iraq were conducted four times between August 2002 and February 2003. As the Bush administration demonstrated its willingness to co-operate with the United Nations, Japanese opposition to the Iraq War dropped from 77% in August 2002 to 65% in December 2002 (*Asahi Shinbun* 4.9.2002 & 16.12.2002). However, Washington was reported to be preparing for the attack on Iraq without UN endorsement, causing opposition to rise again quickly from 69% in January 2003 to 79% in February 2003 (*Asahi Shinbun* 27.1.2003 & 25.2.2003). Once started, the Iraq War showed disapproval ratings of 59% on 20 March 2003 (*Asahi Shinbun* 22.3.2003). It seemed that 10 to 20% of Japanese voters who had initially opposed the war felt that Japan could not avoid offering some support to the key ally's war involvement. Nonetheless, as causalities continued to be reported visually in the media, disapproval ratings increased significantly to 65% on 29 March 2003 (*Asahi Shinbun* 31.3.2003). In essence, a majority of Japanese voters did not regard Japan's commitment to the key ally as enough of a reason for approving the Iraq War, and disapproved of the US military operations as unjustified (*Asahi Shinbun* 30.3.2003).

FIGURE 5.1. Japanese support for the US attack on Iraq, August 2002–March 2003 (%)

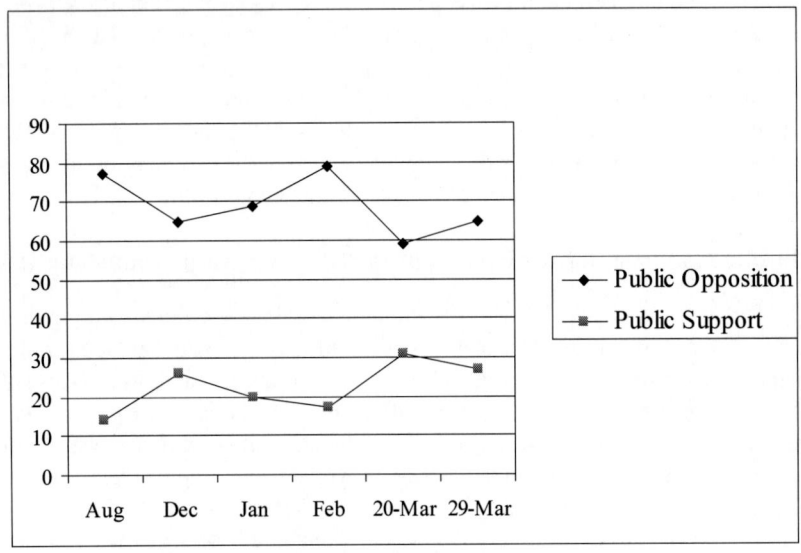

Sources: *Asahi Shinbun* 4.9.2002; 16.12.2002; 27.1.2003; 25.2.2003; 22.3.2003; 31.3.2003. Note: On 20 March 2003, the United States began its attack on Iraq.

As soon as President Bush had declared the end of 'major combat operations' in Iraq, Japan's opportunity to deploy the SDF in Iraq's reconstruction assistance efforts arose as a realistic contribution. The Koizumi cabinet drafted a bill, the *Iraq Humanitarian Reconstruction Assistance Special Measures Law*, which would allow the dispatch of the SDF to Iraq. Prior to the July 2003 passage of this law in the National Diet, the public was divided on whether to dispatch the SDF to Iraq for reconstruction assistance, with 46% of respondents expressing support for the dispatch and 43% expressing opposition (*Asahi Shinbun* 30.6.2003:evening edition; 1.7.2003). Despite this divisive issue, Japanese voters seemed to be more supportive of Koizumi's determination to help the US war efforts than of 'Bush's war' itself. Significantly the support derived from the Japanese people's desire to make an international contribution; the largest ratio, 29%, of respondents identified *kokusai koken* (international contributions) as the primary reason to support dispatch while only 6% thought the importance of relations with the United States as such (*Asahi Shinbun* 30.6.2003:evening edition). As previously discussed, the collective expectation of Japanese people regarding international contributions remained firmly within the limits of non-military and noncombatant operations. By this token, those who opposed dispatch were sceptical about the safety of SDF operations; 16% of the respondents cited the dangerous conditions in Iraq as the primary reason to oppose dispatch and 13% saw the availability of non-SDF support as such (*Asahi Shinbun* 30.6.2003:evening edition).

FIGURE 5.2. Japanese public support for dispatching the SDF, June 2003–April 2004 (%)

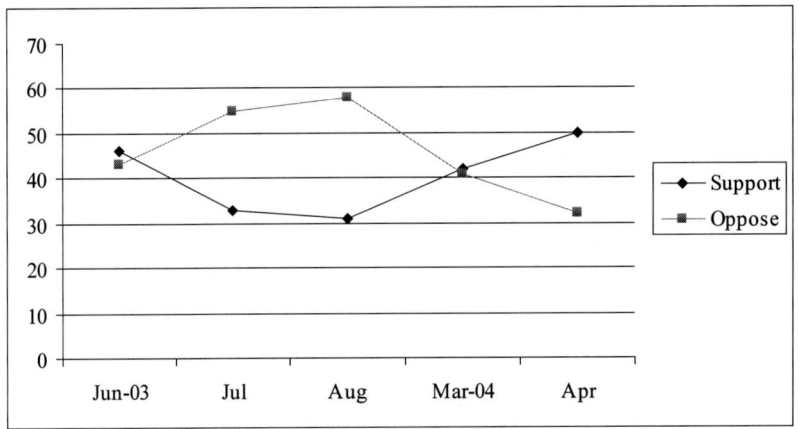

Sources: *Asahi Shinbun* 30.6.2003; 22.7.2003; 25.8.2003; 16.3.2004; 17.4.2004.

Note: By the end of March 2004, the final group of the GSDF contingent joined the Samawah mission, completing the 550-member contingent.

As the Diet deliberations revealed the real risk involved in the proposed SDF operations, by the middle of July, those who opposed dispatch increased quickly and represented a solid majority with 55%, while those who supported dispatch dropped to 33% (*Asahi Shinbun* 22.7.2003).[107] Both the ruling coalition and the opposition questioned whether the SDF would be expected to transport ammunition and weapons, whether Iraq would be too volatile to designate noncombatant zones, and whether SDF operations could conflict with Japan's constitutional ban on exercising the right of collective self-defence (HRPS 2003b; HRCI 2003a; HRCI 2003b; *Asahi Shinbun* 25 & 26.6.2003). To ease pressure from outspoken critics within the LDP, such as former party secretary generals Nonaka Hiromu and Koga Makoto, Koizumi stipulated that the SDF would not be involved in activities in Iraq under the command of other countries (*Asahi Shinbun* 26.6.2003). Koizumi responded to the opposing majority, agreeing to turn the proposed law into an emasculated instrument. The law imposed severe restrictions on SDF operations in Iraq: in case fighting broke out near the noncombatant area of SDF operations, their activities would be suspended and the personnel would be evacuated (Article 8); the SDF would be prohibited from providing fuel and maintenance to aircraft on stand-by prior to departing to engage in combat (Article 8); and their use of weapons would be authorised only for self-defence (Article 17). In essence, the Koizumi cabinet responded to public opposition by trying not to contradict past precedents of SDF involvement.

Koizumi seemed to overcome the legal hurdles for Japan's dispatch of the SDF to Iraq when he successfully rammed the unpopular bill through the National Diet in July. Despite Koizumi's compromises, however, the anticipated dispatch of SDF troops for the first time since the Second World War to a country where fighting was still taking place was not acceptable to the majority of Japanese voters. Immediately after the enactment of the *Iraq Humanitarian Reconstruction Assistance Special Measures Law* in August, those who opposed dispatch increased further to 58% of the respondents and those who supported dispatch continued to decline to 31% (*Asahi Shinbun* 25.8.2003:evening edition).

As US soldiers were being killed almost every day in Iraq, Koizumi remained indecisive about SDF dispatch to an area under the administration of an occupying power. There was no way for the Koizumi cabinet to implement the unpopular dispatch before the lower house election scheduled on 9 November 2003. In this election, the Democratic Party of Japan (DPJ) effectively challenged the LDP-centred governing coalition, making it the largest opposition party. The LDP lost its single-party majority, requiring it to ally with coalition partners. Not surprisingly, the election was not fought over the issue of SDF dispatch to Iraq; Japanese voters focused on economic stimulus measures and state pension reform and took the Iraq issue as secondary (*Yomiuri Shinbun* 24.10.2003; *Asahi Shinbun* 2.11.2003; *Mainichi Shinbun* 3.11.2003).

There was a fundamental difference between such domestic issues and foreign policy issues. Domestic issues called for extending benefits to large numbers of people, yet the SDF dispatch proposition would be made in return for diffuse and uncertain gains and at the cost of tax payers. The voters tended to react to tangible gains in popular policies, such as economic stimulus and state pensions. Nonetheless, *unpopular* policies must also withstand the scrutiny of voters. Besides material gains or losses, the collective beliefs of national military security remained a potent determinant of voting in Japanese politics. LDP leaders continued to take voters' strong aversion to military involvement in a serious way. The LDP's failure to maintain a single-party majority required a delicate effort to minimise the political costs involved in the SDF dispatch to Iraq and to transform the dispatch into an electorally attractive proposition for the upcoming upper house election of July 2004. The Koizumi cabinet cautiously responded to public conerns, illustrated by its decision to send 550 GSDF (Ground Self-Defence Force) troops to Iraq where they were housed in the isolated Samawah fortress, secure behind its own moat and barricades.

In the upper house election of July 2004, the prospect of the SDF becoming involved in armed clashes was reported as one of the top five determinants of voting, along with economic stimulus measures, state pension reforms, employment measures, and the North Korean abduction issue (*Mainichi Shinbun* 15.6.2004; *Asahi Shinbun* 22.6.2004; *Yomiuri Shinbun* 28.6.2004). Voters' strong aversion to military involvement, which had been a key component of anti-militarist social norms in postwar Japan, was transformed into one of the determinants of voting in the upper house election. The LDP was only able to win 49 of the 121 seats, failing to achieve its own target of 51.

Although the 150-member ASDF (Air Self-Defence Force) team, based in Kuwait, began to assist the US-led coalition forces in transport operations by mid-January 2004, the GSDF contingent in Samawah captured enormous public attention within Japan. This was primarily because their reconstruction mission in Samawah might easily have become a target of terrorist attacks and put the safety of GSDF members at risk. By the end of March 2004, the final group of the GSDF contingent joined the Samawah mission, completing the 550-member contingent tasked with supplying water, rebuilding community infrastructure, and offering medical services. By early 2004, as the media enthusiastically televised men (and some women) in boots bidding farewell to their tearful families and reported positive feedback that the reconstruction mission continued to receive from the local population in Samawah, those who supported the dispatch achieved a small majority. In a March 2004 poll, conducted by the *Asahi Shinbun* 42% of respondents supported the dispatch of the SDF to Iraq, while 41% were opposed (*Asahi Shinbun* 16.3.2004). A month later, *Asahi Shinbun* polls reported support for dispatch increasing further to 50%, with opposition falling to 32% (*Asahi Shinbun* 17.4.2004).[108] This overall trend was seen also in *Mainichi Shinbun* polls, which found 50% pro-dispatch versus 43% anti-dispatch in March, and 47% pro-dispatch versus 46% anti-dispatch in April (*Mainichi Shinbun* 8.3.2004; 19.4.2004). Even the *Asahi Shinbun* which had been highly critical of the SDF dispatch to Iraq, released the results of opinion polls on Samawah's residents, jointly conducted with local newspapers, reporting 'approval by 85% of Samawah's citizens [of the SDF reconstruction assistance]' (*Asahi Shinbun* 29.6.2004). However, this political climate was transient. The negative public view of SDF deployment to Iraq remained deep-rooted and pervasive, and public opposition to continued SDF deployment began to increase rapidly by May 2004.

On 12 February 2004, two mortars were fired into downtown Samawah, breaking a few windows but causing no casualties (*Japan Times* 13.2.2004). This was a minor attack but the first one in the city since the arrival of the GSDF. After that, these minor incidents continued and captured enormous public attention in Japan, and SDF officials dutifully pledged to improve security measures. On 31 October 2004, a rocket shell landed inside the Japanese troop camp for the first time, harmlessly hitting a steel container (*Yomiuri Shinbun* 2.11.2004). Director General of the Defence Agency, Ono Yoshinori apologised for failing to make the incident public until 19 hours after the attack, saying, 'It is quite expected that the government make public the safety of the (GSDF) members as it is of enormous public interest' (*Kyodo News* 2.11.2004). Prime Minister Koizumi subsequently admitted, 'I recognise that the security situation in Samawah is unpredictable' (HRPS 2004). The Japanese government was then under pressure to decide whether to extend the deployment of the GSF contingent beyond the mission expiration date of 14 December 2004. Koizumi emphasised, 'The government will make a decision taking into account debate in the Diet and public opinion, as well as the reconstruction and local security conditions in Iraq' (HRPS 2004). On 9 December, the Koizumi cabinet announced that the deployment of the SDF in Iraq would be extended for another year.

By May 2004, monthly polls, conducted by Nippon Television Network Corporation, found a solid majority opposed the continued deployment of the SDF in Iraq. From January to April 2004, public opinion was very much evenly split on the continued deployment, with 42.5–46.5% in favour and 43.2–47.0% opposed; however, the May 2004 result showed a sharp increase in opposition to the continued deployment with 52.2% while indicating a corresponding decline in support with 39.6%.[109]

There seemed to be three fundamental factors that contributed to this: (1) many Japanese voters began to feel that the security in Samawah had deteriorated so much as to threaten the troops' lives; (2) they anticipated that the mission of the SDF in Iraq, which would expire on 14 December 2004, required some extension if the government continued to deploy; and (3) they believed that Prime Minister Koizumi would not be held accountable if he made the decision to extend the deployment of the SDF beyond the mission expiration date. Public opposition to the continued deployment continued to grow after the July 2004 upper house election. After the end of October when the rocket shell landed in the Japanese camp, major opinion polls indicated that opposition to the extension of deployment beyond the 14 December expiration date had consistently exceeded 60% of respondents. An *Asahi Shinbun* poll conducted on 23 and 24 October found that 63% opposed the extension of the deployment and only 29% were in favour (*Asahi Shinbun* 26.10.2004). A Japan Broadcasting Corporation poll, conducted from 3 to 5 November, had a similar result: 63% opposed and 26% in favour of the extension of deployment. In a similarly worded poll taken from 21 to 24 November, *Nihon Keizai Shinbun* found that 61% expressed opposition to and 25% expressed support for the extension of deployment (*Nihon Keizai Shinbun* 25.11.2004). Koizumi's announcement to extend the deployment of the SDF in Iraq for another year had an immediate impact on public opinion; in an *Asahi Shinbun* poll, conducted on 18 and 19 December, 76% of respondents questioned Prime Minister Koizumi's accountability in his decision to extend it (*Asahi Shinbun* 21.12.2004). In this poll, approval ratings for the Koizumi cabinet, which was as high as 87% in April 2001, plunged to an all-time low of 37%. Koizumi had certainly established strong authority for policy initiatives and decision making from the prime ministerial position. However, Koizumi's top-down style of leadership, initially supported by strong public approval, was destined to eventually fail once he grossly ignored public opinion on the Iraq deployment.

FIGURE 5.3. Japanese public support for continuing SDF deployment, January 2004–November 2005 (%)

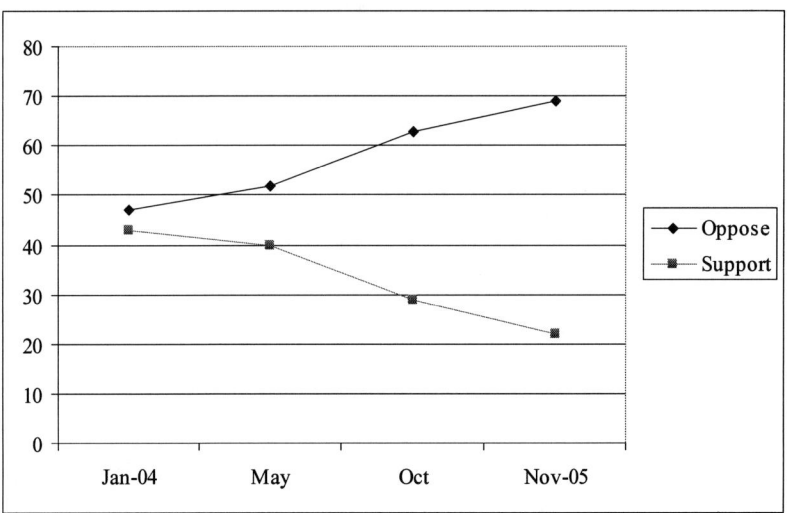

Sources: Nippon Television Network Corporation, *Nippon Terebi Yoron Chosa* (NTV Public Opinion Polls), available at http://www.ntv.co.jp/yoron/, last accessed July 2007; *Asahi Shinbun* 26 October 2004, 30 November 2005. Note: Figures for January and May 2004 adopted from NTV sources.

In August 2005, Prime Minister Koizumi called for snap elections after bills to privatise the Japanese Postal Service were rejected in the upper house. The lower house election of 11 September brought a stunning victory to Koizumi's

LDP. Despite this landslide victory, as the deployment expiration approached once again, public opposition to the extension of the deployment rose much higher than in the previous year. A *Mainichi Shinbun* poll, carried out on 8 and 9 October, showed a record high of 77% opposed and only 18% in favour of the extension of the deployment (*Mainichi Shinbun* 10.10.2005). A high disapproval rating was also found in an *Asahi Shinbun* poll conducted on 26 and 27 November, with 69% in opposition over 22% in support (*Asahi Shinbun* 30.11.2005). This poll reported that even nearly 60% of LDP supporters opposed the extension of SDF deployment in Iraq. Amid much public criticism, a lot of speculation emerged about when the GSDF would withdraw from Iraq. On 20 June 2006, Prime Minister Koizumi announced, 'the government has decided to withdraw GSDF troops from Samawah,' as British and Australian forces were scheduled to withdraw from Muthanna province (whose capital city is Samawah) (*Japan Times* 21.6.2006). Koizumi's decision allowed the GSDF members, whom he had dispatched to Iraq, to come home in summer before he stepped down at the end of September. This was an honourable way of ending both his defiance against public expectation and his premiership.

Public response to constitutional revision

In the September 2005 nationwide election for the House of Representatives, the LDP won only 47.8% of the total votes, yet gained the largest share of seats (296 out of 480 seats) in postwar politics. This landslide win may indeed be attributed to the switch of the election system from the multimember constituencies to the single 'winner-takes-all'. As a result, the governing coalition now commanded a two-thirds majority in the lower house, which enabled them to initiate constitutional amendments, then submit them to the upper house and on to a national referendum for ratification. The LDP, its coalition partner New Komeito Party and the largest opposition Democratic Party agreed to discuss necessary legislation for holding a referendum on constitutional revision. On 14 May 2007, a new referendum law was passed in the National Diet. The law requires that the proposals for a revision to the constitution must be submitted item-by-item rather than as a package of amendments (*Japan Times* 12.5.2007). The legislation will come into effect in May 2010. This certainly takes the LDP one step closer to constitutional revision. But there is little to suggest that the Japanese political mainstream will contemplate constitutional endorsement of Japan's military participation in the US global strategy. The new collective belief that Japan should assume a greater responsibility in the international community accommodates constitutional revision, yet within the scope of the existing norm, that is, a strong aversion to military involvement.

The new collective understandings of international responsibility have not loosened commitments to the existing norm. LDP politicians cannot afford to operate outside of the normative structures in political action. The key domestic structure of political constraints through which the collective expectation brings LDP politicians to normative commitments is that constitutional amendments require the affirmative vote of a majority of all votes cast at a national referendum. Less than a third of Japanese think that Japan should lift its prohibition against collective self-defence. A *Yomiuri Shinbun* survey based on interviews, conducted on 20 and 21 March 2004, found that only 30.1% of the 1,823 respondents believed Japan should revise the constitution to lift its ban on the exercise of the right of collective self-defence (*Yomiuri Shinbun* 2.4.2004). When Prime Minister Abe Shinzo decided on 5 April 2007 that the government would establish an advisory panel to examine if Japan should *revise the current interpretation* of the constitution in order to allow Japan to engage in specific cases of collective self-defence operations, the controversial use of force to defend an ally's troops drew close attention from the general public.[110] According to the 12/13 May 2007 results of a *Kyodo News* poll, 62.0% of respondents continued to support the current constitutional interpretation of collective self-defence, whereas only 13.3% believed Japan should revise the current interpretation to permit the exercise of the right of its collective self-defence (cited in *Tokyo Shinbun* 14.5.2007). These results suggest that a strong sense of fundamental mistrust among Japanese people remained over the state's ability to wield the sword. In a similar vein, a *Mainich Shinbun* poll, conducted on 28 and 29 April 2007, found that 51% of respondents believed Japan should remain prohibited from exercising its right of collective self-defence and only 11% of the respondents accepted the SDF's use of force under specified circumstances in its overseas deployment (*Mainichi Shinbun* 2–3.5.2007). It is highly unlikely that lifting the constitutional prohibition on collective self-defence of allies will be submitted to voters for ratification. The collective expectation among Japanese people is at most that the constitution should be amended to explicitly recognise Japan's right to self-defence, to legitimise the SDF with the existing level of defence spending, and to enable use of the SDF in UN-backed peacekeeping operations and humanitarian aid.

On 12 September 2007, Prime Minister Abe unexpectedly announced his resignation, immediately after his pledge to renew the anti-terrorism measures legislation, throwing Japanese politics into turmoil. Constitutional revision, if any, would not take place until the 2010 enforcement of the new referendum law, but Abe initially wished to reinterpret the constitution to allow Japan to exercise the right to collective self-defence far earlier. With his resignation, the planned reinterpretation was most likely to be delayed or abandoned. Given the LDP's defeat in the July 2007 upper house election when the LDP coalition lost its majority, Abe's successor, Fukuda Yasuo, was forced to give priority to pressing domestic issues, such as pensions and health care, rather than aggravate public sentiment about the proposed reinterpretation. About 45% of the 'floating voters' who were not affiliated with any party were expected to be a key determinant of Fukuda's successful initiative in the run-up to the upcoming lower house election. Fukuda cautiously avoided declaring his stance toward Abe's proposal to change the government's constitutional interpretation (*Yomiuri Shinbun* 23.9.2007). In his first policy speech to the National Diet on 1 October 2007, Prime Minister Fukuda unmistakably shied away from Abe's policy initiatives, making no mention of either constitutional revision or collective self-defence (*Asahi Shinbun* 3.10.2007). The political climate would seem to prevent Japan from exercising the right to collective self-defence in the foreseeable future. It is more likely the constitution will provide the Japanese government only with an opportunity for covert remilitarisation to meet US demand for power-sharing. In its effort to meet this, the *2001 Anti-Terrorism Special Measure Law*, for example, covertly stipulates that the SDF is able to use their weapons not only to protect themselves, but also to protect 'those who are with them on the scene and have come under their control while conducting their duties' (Article 12–1). In this way, the Japanese government may be able to modify national security policy by making changes around the edges but is unable to make a fundamental shift.

Candidates' response to the new 1994 electoral system

In 1994 Japan introduced the new mixed-member electoral system replacing the old medium-sized constituency system, which was initially adopted in 1925 to allow voters one non-transferable vote for three to five representatives per electoral district. As discussed earlier, the main problem of the old system existed to the extent that candidates from the LDP ran against each other within the same electoral district but LDP candidates from the same party were not able to carry out campaigns against each other over party-based policy differences. To be elected or re-elected, they were forced to solidify their local turf beyond the national party support and develop their own support groups. LDP politicians thus tended to compete over special interests, personal favours, or money, not over policies. The new 1994 electoral reform was intended to change such candidate-centred campaigns leading to political corruption and create incentives for party-centred elections. It was expected to develop a competitive two-party system with both policy-centred and party-centred elections.[111]

Under the new 1994 electoral system, each voter must cast one ballot for an individual candidate running for the SMD (Single Member Districts) and another ballot for a political party that registers a list of candidates in the regional district, which is one of 11 PR (Proportional Representation) blocs.[112] The single-member system, which permits only one party to win in each electoral district, was to work in favour of major parties whereas the PR system was to give minor parties a chance to gain seats (Duverger 1954; Rae 1971; Lijphart 1994). Yet both SMD and PR systems were expected to concertedly lead to the establishment of policy-centred and party-centred elections. Is the new electoral system producing the expected outcomes in Japanese politics? The 1996 election was the first one held under the new system. Japan had three more elections for the lower house in 2000, 2003 and 2005. Over time, the Democratic Party of Japan (DPJ) has grown into the only party alternative to the LDP. Some scholars claim that Japan has been a two-party system since at least 2003 (Reed 2007:96–106). As Prime Minister Koizumi refused to nominate anyone who opposed his postal reform, in the 2005 election, the process seemed also to become centralised and party-centred (Hiwatari 2006:22–36). Nonetheless, no one argues yet that the extensively candidate-centred elections in Japan have been fundamentally transformed into policy-centred elections.

Various indicators suggest significant changes in the nature of electoral competition under the 1994 system. In the 1996 election, Shinshinto (New Frontier Party) was the primary challenger, but the DPJ was only the secondary challenger to the LDP, accounting for 15% of the SMDs where DPJ candidates were the first place or the second place finisher. Since the 2000 election, however, the DPJ has become the sole, serious challenger to the LDP. The number of SMD candidates from the DPJ continued to increase and reached 96% of 300 SMDs in the 2005 election. Competition in the SMDs became 'bipolar' between the only two serious candidates (Reed 2007:96–106). The number of SMDs where a LDP candidate and a DPJ candidate occupied the first and second place increased steadily from 197 in 2000 through 235 in 2003 to 251 in 2005. The DJP had not only become a serious contender against the LDP in the SMDs, but also, by the 2000 election, the DPJ was able to gain first place in nearly half of the PR blocs. The results of party shares of the votes in the PR system showed that the LDP and the DPJ were neck-and-neck in: the 2000 election with 28.3–25.2%; the 2003 election with 35.0–37.4%; and the 2005 election with 38.2–31.0%. It is safe to say that Japan is likely to become a two-party system where alternation in power could take place in the foreseeable future.[113]

Despite this trend toward a two-party system in Japan, the new 1994 electoral system has only produced a mixed result in providing incentives for candidates to make their election campaigns policy-centred. It has not clearly materialised policy-centred election campaigns in which candidates primarily sell the policies of their parties to the voters, who then cast ballots while drawing on the party policies. LDP candidates have even recently followed old habits of candidate-centred election campaigns, and once elected, they still try hard to bring local benefits from Tokyo to their home districts to gain re-election.

After conducting a statistical analysis of the 1996 election, Miyake Ichiro concludes, 'the effect of candidate-centred factors [on voting behaviour in the SMDs] was equally important as in the [old] medium-sized constituency system or even more important [than the effect of those factors in the old system]' (Miyake 2001:55). There are several structural reasons that the 1994 SMD system can still create incentives for candidate-centred competition.

- Each single-member district creates only one incumbent, and the increased effect of his or her personal reputation on re-election strengthens the incumbent's position. His or her repeated electoral success helps the incumbent create stable supporters and allows him or her to become more self-reliant for electoral success, requiring the incumbent to be less party-centred or policy-centred in his or her election campaigns. In the case of the LDP, the electoral advantage of incumbency is critically important since the incumbent LDP Diet members almost automatically win their party endorsements for re-election in the same district.

- As the size of the SMDs (300 districts) becomes much smaller than that of the medium-sized districts (130 districts), a candidate's image is projected to represent locally specific benefits. In particular, under the new system the core supporters of the LDP in rural districts continued to vote for LDP candidates who had worked hard to bring locally specific benefits from Tokyo and meet the 'individualised' need of local communities (Miyake 2001:57). For those LDP candidates, running party-policy-centred campaigns, as opposed to campaigns based on their personal appeal, can be an unnecessary risk.

- The candidate's *sekihairitsu* (the ratio of a candidate's vote to the district winner's vote), which is used to break or re-rank ties among dual SMD/PR candidates ranked in the same position on the party's PR list, provide those candidates with incentive to make their election campaigns autonomous and candidate-centred so that they are ranked higher in the finalised list (Suzuki 1999:32–51; Kawato et al 2001).

- The larger the number of prefectural assembly seats that exist in the SMD, the less the importance SMD candidates' appeal to party policies becomes (Maeda 2007:67–83). LDP candidates still compete against each other at a prefectural assembly election within the same multi-seat district, which ranges up to 15 seats or more, and the SMD national election is thus likely to reflect their rivalry within the same party rather than national party leadership.

- Those who participate in social networks still tend to value candidates rather than party policies. Gerald Curtis emphasises the importance of social-obligation voting in Japan as a vote based on social networks to which voters belong (Curtis 1971:38). Voting is described as a group phenomenon coming from obligation rather than individual decision-making. To this extent, the new electoral system has not affected the cultural phenomenon arising from social obligations.

These findings suggest that the post-reform elections are neither solidly policy-centred nor party-centred. Particularly, the results of the 2000 election clearly demonstrate that the SMD votes were heavily affected by non-party factors. In this election, the LDP's vote shares in PR dropped by 4.3%, but the LDP's vote shares in SMD increased by 4.3% (MIAC 2007). The decline in the PR portion was understandable due to the unpopular tenure of Prime Minister Mori Yoshiro (his cabinet approval ratings dropped to as low as 14%), but the increase in the SMD portion seemed to be explained only by non-party factors. All in all, changes in the nature of electoral competition require further studies over a long period of time, especially because it takes a while for candidates to learn and adapt to a new electoral system. In other words, there can be a time lag between the introduction and the expected effect of a new electoral system (Reed 1991:335–56). Those incumbents who developed their reputation under the old electoral system may not immediately receive incentives from the SMD system to make their electoral campaigns policy-centred (Miyake 1995:3–4).

The electoral system as a norm compliance mechanism

The new 1994 electoral system functions as a norm compliance mechanism for constraining new developments in Japan's military security. Two dimensions can be identified to assess the impact of the new system on national military security policy-making. The first dimension involves the impact of electoral competition at the level of personalisation of elections. A local body of the ever-reliable 'hard votes' for LDP incumbents in rural districts has little interest in national policy issues but directs attention to candidates and local contexts so that the core supporters of LDP incumbents will continue to receive particular benefits (Miyake 2001:57). For those incumbents, making their electoral campaigns policy-centred (or advertising the party's national defence policy) as opposed to their personal reputation can be an impediment to their electoral success. The locally connected LDP incumbents have no strong incentive to become a defence policy expert or *zoku* or represent the vested interests of the national security issue in policy formation.

The second and emerging dimension is found at the national level where the new system opens up avenues for more unified, top-down national security policy initiatives. The new system promotes party control, at the expense of factions, over individual candidates. Factions within the LDP have faced their loss of control over nominations in SMDs, and top LDP executives have more control over nominations in both SMDs and PR. These executives have gained authority in both candidate selection and campaign funding.[114] The new system encourages the patterns of intra-party cleavage within the LDP to shift from decentralised, factionalised to centralised, top-down leadership. Policy-making is likely to be strengthened at the level of top LDP executives. This means that the new system gives the president of the LDP, that is, the prime minister, more centralised power to initiate security policy-making (Shinoda 2003:19–34; Pekkanen & Krauss 2005:429–44).

In relative terms, the new system seems to gradually change the nature of voting behaviour from candidate-centred to party-centred. The Akarui Senkyo Suishin Kyokai (Association for the Promotion of Clean Elections) survey, conducted in the 1996, 2000, 2003 and 2005 elections, asked respondents whether they 'voted in a party-centred way or a candidate-centred way in [their] single-member districts'. As can be seen from Figure 5.1, party-centred voters have increased and candidate-centred voters have decreased since the introduction of the new system.

TABLE 5.1: Voting behaviour in single-member districts under the new electoral system

	1996	2000	2003	2005
Party-centred	43.8%	46.1%	47.0%	50.3%
Candidate-centred	43.8%	42.8%	36.5%	35.0%

Source: Akarui Senkyo Suishin Kyokai 2006:49.

Nonetheless, voters' perception of the importance of parties versus candidates has not necessarily developed in favour of parties in a linear, straightforward way. From 1996 to 2005, the voting determinants for DPJ candidates in SMDs was becoming increasingly party-centred, yet those who voted for LDP candidates in SMDs, especially in rural districts, reversed the trend in the 2005 election (Tsutsumi 2007). The core of LDP voters in rural districts are still less likely to vote directly on national policy issues and shape the policy agenda, while other voters and candidates are gradually adjusting their behaviour to the new electoral system.

Equally important, there are also emerging factors that may structurally force LDP candidates in rural districts to encounter difficulties in candidate-centred campaigns, and LDP voters in these districts to exhibit little interest in candidate-centred voting. In recent years, the government has substantially decreased particular benefits to local communities, which had previously allowed candidates to maintain the candidate-centred, pork-driven campaigns (Takao 1999:265–92). Recent reductions in public works (deregulation) and government subsidies (decentralisation) suggest that candidates will find difficulty in ensuring benefits delivered to their electoral districts. Although the previous arguments on the structural impact of SMDs in Japan demonstrate that candidate-centred factors in election campaigning and voting would not wither away, these new factors seem to produce incentives for candidates to take national policy issues seriously. However, it is extremely important to note in this regard that once taken seriously, national policy issues in Japan will be likely to reveal Japan's military security as heretical in policy areas, due to Japan's anti-defence spending bias and strong aversion to military involvement. These candidates will be less likely to pursue *unpopular* military security policy that must withstand the scrutiny of voters.

Despite unpopular policies at the local level, the office of the prime minister must respond to US pressure. The new electoral system combined with the 2001 administrative reform to facilitate an increase in the centralisation of power in the office of the prime minister and allowed for the adoption of a faster response to US requests (Shinoda 2003:19–24).[115] The top-down leadership of Prime Minister Koizumi between 2001 and 2004 enabled him to constrain the vested interests of faction leaders under the new electoral system and, as described earlier, enact a series of new security initiatives based on legislation (Pekkanen & Krauss 2005:437–43).[116] Prime Minister Koizumi was aiming for strong leadership and a responsible government that could deliver on promises made to the alliance partner. This phenomenon can be seen as part of a move toward a pattern of security policy-making where the office of the prime minister becomes a more autonomous political force. But making Japan more responsive to its allies was not an easy task. Koizumi's top-down policy-making failed to have the effect the Americans had hoped for; that is, a shift in Japan's focus from indirect, non-military sharing to direct and military sharing. As discussed below, the norm-embedded electoral system seemed to become an effective political limit to top-down military security policy-making.

A mass of non-party-affiliated voters and voters with weak party identification, who maintain a keen interest in and remain critical about politics, presented the LDP with a great challenge. In 1993 when the LDP lost its majority in the lower house, 45% of voters with no party affiliation greatly outnumbered the mere 23% of LDP supporters.[117] Persuading floating voters became crucial for the LDP's electoral success. Whenever Koizumi's populism made concessions to public concerns about risking the SDF in overseas combat, the effect the Koizumi cabinet had hoped for in receiving more public support was to materialise in an increase in LDP votes from non-party-affiliated voters and voters with weak party identification. In this context, the norm compliance mechanism was in place to prevent the popular Koizumi cabinet from stepping out of the normative limits.

Surveys, conducted by the Association for the Promotion of Clean Elections in 1996, 2000, 2003, and 2005, show that 32% to 39% of respondents 'usually' supported the LDP (a margin of 7%) while 32% to 35% of respondents usually did not support any party (a margin of 3%) (Akarui Senkyo Suishin Kyokai 2006:56). These surveys held immediately after each election, posed the question 'Which party do you *usually* support?' whereas the *Asahi Shinbun* polls asked 'Which party do you support *now*?' The wording of the association's survey reflected a much smaller representation of respondents with no party affiliation than those in the *Asahi Shinbun* polls, with 32% versus 44% in 1996 and 33% versus 50% in 2000.[118] The association's survey helps us find the distribution of party supporters immediately after elections, identify changes in the distribution, trace changes in the core body of non-affiliated voters, and understand the impact of party support on actual voting.

In the lower house election of 2005, the association's survey found that 26% of the respondents who 'usually support' the LDP did not vote for the LDP in SMDs, and correspondingly 29% in PR. It also asked the party supporters if they 'strongly support' their chosen parties or 'not so much' support them. What it found was that only 26% of these respondents identified themselves as strong supporters and 72% considered themselves weak supporters. Interesting enough, the association's survey indicated that 40% of respondents had switched their votes to other parties over the past ten years or since gaining the right to vote. Considering the continued decline of LDP votes from 45% in 1990 to 32% in 2000 (although recovering to 39% in 2005), the existence of a large proportion of LDP supporters who might switch their votes to other political parties creates fluid electoral results and swinging-voter support plays a critical role in determining the electoral fortunes of the LDP.[119]

The core supporters of the LDP, 45% of LDP votes in the 2005 election, had continued to vote for the LDP over the past ten years regardless of individual LDP candidates. In 2005, some core supporters of the LDP still belonged to personal support groups (*koenkai*) for locally elected politicians, and 15% of voters in villages and towns (the percentage of LDP voters alone is expected to be higher but the figure is not available) were members of *koenkai*.[120] These core supporters of the LDP in rural areas tended to care less about national policy issues but firmly supported their local LDP candidates that continued to bring specific local benefits to their communities. Otherwise, a large proportion, nearly three quarters of LDP supporters, considered themselves weak supporters and had the potential to be swinging voters depending on parties and national issues rather than local issues.

Equally important, a large number of eligible non-party-affiliated voters, who have a keen interest in politics, tend to cast votes rather than eligible non-affiliated voters who are indifferent to politics. The association's survey found that 58% of non-affiliated respondents did vote in the 2005 lower house election. The breakdown of the non-affiliated respondents' votes supports the claim that these votes played a key role in leading to the LDP's landslide victory in the 2005 election. In the SMDs, 23% of non-affiliated respondents voted for the LDP in 2005 (as compared with 13% for the LDP in 2003) whereas 19% of those respondents voted for the DPJ in 2005 (as compared with 26% for the DPJ in 2003). In the PR where voting and support for political parties closely correlate with each other, 21% of non-affiliated respondents voted for the LDP in 2005 (as compared with only 9% for the LDP in 2003) while 17% of those respondents voted for the DPJ in 2005 (compared with 26% for the DPJ in 2003).[121]

The extent to which the LDP depends on a huge mass of voters with no party affiliation and weak party identification for its electoral success would seem to transform the whole electoral structure and make the elections party-centred and national policy-centred. To this extent, LDP candidates need to appeal to those voters in regard to LDP policies on national issues. There are two types of national issues in Japan's military security policy: continuous disputes and discrete disputes. The national issue over defence spending can be seen as a continuous dispute as all political parties concede that they need to avoid a large-scale increase in defence spending for electoral consideration. The difference between party policies over defence expenditure is a matter of degree. The politics of avoiding blame for unpopular defence spending dictates specific strategies for re-election. In contrast, the SDF dispatch to Iraq can be regarded as a discrete dispute since political parties split bitterly over whether Japan should send the SDF to Iraq at all. The mechanism of norm compliance tends to occupy a strategic position in the discrete security disputes as the LDP leaders deem it necessary to make concessions to majority voters. As described above, even the popular Koizumi cabinet was unable to go beyond the outer limits set by the norm that overwhelming majorities of Japanese firmly opposed the SDF becoming involved in overseas combat, even within a UN peacekeeping framework.

Political leadership in the implementation of the 2004 National Defence Program Guideline (NDPG)

As described in Chapter 2, the public perception of threats to national security indicates that the Japanese have increasingly been affected by new developments in the security environment, especially following the 1998 Taepodong missile launch by North Korea. In more recent years, a Chinese nuclear submarine was reported to have entered Japanese waters in November 2004, and in April 2005, large-scale anti-Japanese demonstrations erupted in Beijing, Shanghai and other urban areas in China. Even worse, in October 2006 North Korea announced that it had successfully conducted a nuclear test for the first time. To reinforce the legal framework for responding to security emergencies, the Japanese government introduced seven new laws and amended three laws during 2003–2004. To tackle the emerging issues involved in these new developments, the Japanese government set about revising its NDPO once again. In October 2004, Prime Minister Koizumi's Defence Advisory panel presented its final report, known as the *Araki Commission Report*, to provide the blueprint for a revised NDPG. The report suggested two major goals of Japan's military security policy: (1) preventing Japan from facing a direct threat; and (2) reducing the chances of threats emerging in other parts of the world that would threaten Japan's interests. It identified three fundamental approaches available to Japan's 'integrative' defence strategy: (1) developing Japan's own defence capability; (2) co-operating with the United States; and (3) working with the international community (Council on Security and Defence Capabilities 2004).

The Araki Commission worked hard to produce a blueprint to adapt the SDF's capability to the post-11 September security environment. It proposed a range of concrete measures for reorganising the structure of the GSDF to transform into a more mobile force, the MSDF to shift its force to more maritime security and ballistic missile defence, and the ASDF to develop its long-range air transport capability (Council on Security and Defence Capabilities 2004:28–30). Nonetheless, the Araki Commission Report failed to address the two crucial issues that underlay its proposals: financial and constitutional issues, although the commission was never designed to respond to such issues (Tatsumi 2004). The report did not articulate realistic measures of how the costly new defence systems and equipment would be procured in the political climate of anti-defence spending bias and national budget squeeze. Nor did the report discuss Japan's right of collective self-defence closely. This is extremely important because the future direction of national military security policy will rely largely on Japan's decisions regarding constitutional revision and the constitutional status of collective self-defence. The debate on the financial and constitutional issues was left to the public forums and the National Diet. The pressing need to decide on these issues opened up possibilities for political leadership.

However, with their strategic guide for the implementation of the 2004 NDPG, political leadership in Japan once again failed to provide financial measures and constitutional renewal. This revised NDPG, released in December 2004, was primarily influenced by the *Araki Commission Report*. In the 2004 NDPG, special emphasis was placed on responses to 'new threats': ballistic missiles, terrorist attacks, invasions of offshore islands, and large-scale natural disasters (MOD 2004). The conventional capabilities, which could be mobilised only in homeland defence, were accordingly to be reduced, while a new approach, which could enhance the required capabilities of flexibility, mobility, and timeliness, was to be taken to respond to new threats. The 2004 NDPG argued strongly that Japan should develop a multi-functional force equipped with state-of-the-art technologies and intelligence capabilities (MOD 2004). Washington mindfully negotiated with Tokyo to make Japan's commitment to the 2004 NDPG more alliance-oriented, and at the conclusion of the Security Consultative Committee (SCC) announced an October 2005 joint document, the *US–Japan Alliance: Transformation and Realignment for the Future*.[122] This document identified the missions in which Japan could co-operate with the United States: air defence, ballistic missile defence, counter-proliferation, maritime minesweeping, intelligence, humanitarian relief, reconstruction assistance, peacekeeping operations, counter-WMD attacks, logistical support, noncombatant evacuation operations, and use of facilities (SCC 2005). Although not obligating Japan to take legislative or budgetary measures, Japan's complementary roles in these missions can be seen as American demands for Japan to form a strategic alliance with the United States beyond the Asia Pacific region.

FIGURE 5.4. Trends in midterm defence program estimates

1976 National Defence Program Outline		1995 National Defence Program Outline		2004 National Defence Program Guideline
1985 Midterm Defence Program 1986–1990	1990 Midterm Defence Program 1991–1995	1995 Midterm Defence Program 1996–2000	2000 Midterm Defence Program 2001–2005	New Midterm Defence Program 2005–2009
Budget estimates: 18,400 billion yen	Budget estimates: 22,750 billion yen	Budget estimates: 25,150 billion yen	Budget estimates: 25,010 billion yen	Budget estimates: 24,240 billion yen
Battle tanks: 246 Destroyers: 9 Interceptors & fighters: 63	Battle tanks: 132 Destroyers: 10 Interceptors & fighters: 42	Battle tanks: 96 Destroyers: 8 Interceptors & fighters: 51	Battle tanks: 91 Destroyers: 5 Interceptors & fighters: 59	Battle tanks: 49 Destroyers: 5 Interceptors & fighters: 55
	Midterm Defence Program Revision 1993–1995	Midterm Defence Program Revision 1998–2000		
	Budget estimates: -580 billion yen	Budget estimates: -920 billion yen		
	Battle tanks: -24 Destroyers: -2 Interceptors & fighters: -13	Battle tanks: -6 Destroyers: -1 Interceptors & fighters: -2		

Sources: Compiled from *Boei Hakusho* (Defence of Japan), annual reports, 1986–2006.

Like the 1976 and 1995 NDPOs, the 2004 NDPG was implemented not so much to transform the SDF in a rational, strategic way and thus enable the SDF to respond to new threats, but primarily because of the government's domestic decision-making constraints with regard to short term fiscal and political possibilities. Negative growth in defence spending occurred for four consecutive years from 2003 to 2006. During this period, acquisition represented about 18% of the dwindling defence budget (peaking at nearly 20% in 1999 after the end of the Cold War), whereas personnel expenditure has remained constant at about 45% of the defence budget since 1998 (JDA 2006:350). This downward trend coincided with Japan's 2003 decision to introduce its BMD (Ballistic Missile Defence) system. Fiscal year 2007 expects Japan's missile defence expenditures to increase by 31% from the previous year to ¥182.6 billion, yet overall defence spending to decrease by 0.3% from the previous year to ¥4.8 trillion (Matsuura 2007:7). In other words, by the very nature of the stagnant defence budget, the government can call for a rise in missile-defence expenditures only when other defence budget items are squeezed. The lower investment in other defence items has delayed and undermined the implementation of the 2004 NDPG. Even worse, the May 2006 agreement between Washington and Tokyo to relocate US forces in Japan has further increased the need for fiscal restraints on the SDF transformation (SCC 2006). It was reported that the Japanese government pledged to share the cost of US$20 billion for the relocation of US forces, including the Marine's relocation to Guam (*Yomiuri Shinbun*, 26.4.2006). The fiscal stress caused by the dual factors—BMD and US force relocation—has already forced the Defence Agency to scale down the new Midterm Defence Program 2005–2009 (*Nihon Keizai Shinbun*, 31.5.2006).[123]

Political leadership is a crucial ingredient in Japan's ability to deal with military security policy. Few prime ministers in postwar Japan have had enough popularity or other resources to deal with Japan's issues over national security. In this respect, Prime Minister Koizumi displayed a style of strong leadership that represents a clear break from Japan's 'leadership deficit' in the past. Koizumi's top-down leadership was the strongest attempt to further his security policy preference. He was looking for strong leadership that could deliver on promises made to the United States. He was willing to use the media in order to appeal to the public for support against recalcitrant groups. Nonetheless, there was a distinctive gap between his security policy preferences and the popular consensus on Japan's military involvement and use of force. In the end, public voices were heard in electoral politics. Anti-militarist norms set outer limits on Koizumi's initiatives beyond which no leaders would go if they wished to win elections.

His successor, Abe Shinzo, understood that the SDF transformation could not be achieved without clarifying Japan's right to collective self-defence, and he thus created an advisory panel to examine the possibility of Japanese engagement in specific cases of collective self-defence operations. Once the LDP coalition lost its majority in the 2007 upper house election, Abe's idea for constitutional reinterpretation dissipated from the national debate. Prime Minister Fukuda Yasuo, while not initiating the debate on the right to collective self-defence in the National Diet, implicitly admitted the concept of public support for Abe's idea was premature. Some hawkish LDP leaders, Aso Taro and Nukaga Fukushiro, wish to lift the ban on the exercise of collective self-defence, in a bid to promote US–Japan joint military operation on an extended scale. However, as the mechanism of norm compliance is in place, they fear the electoral repercussions of this move. The intrinsic force of anti-militarist norms is not internalised by these LDP leaders, but it is most likely to be accepted by the LDP to avoid political costs.

conclusion

Is Japan really remilitarising?

Why is Japan reluctant to become a military power commensurate with its economic power? This question has been at the heart of the inquiry on Japan's security policy. Constructivists have significantly advanced the answer to this question by highlighting how collective ideas held among the public, or normative rationality, outweighs self-interested, utility-based objectives of policy-making. In their view, the role of human consciousness in social life trumps material factors in Japan's military security policy. At the same time, they neglect to pay close attention to material resources and power, showing how these collective ideas create political resources and opportunities in policy-making. A set of rules and institutions in domestic structures, or the causal mechanism where ideational factors are converted into material forces for the general public, supplies the essential building blocks for explaining the puzzle of militarily reluctant Japan. In this conversion process, decision makers abide by the norms embedded in the collective body of rules and institutions. The collective ideas and understandings are incorporated and embedded within the physical mechanism of norm compliance outside of which most material and political resources do not operate in Japan's military security decision-making.

The findings on norm formation and change derived in this book should also open new connections between constructivism and realism. If norms and ideas are the crucial determinants of Japan's military security policy, then explaining norm formation and change is also crucial to explaining changes in policy. The historical survey of Japan revealed that realists' factors, such as structures, external threats and perception, laid the political foundations for the emergence and maintenance of a new norm, 'reactive pacifism' in the postwar period and the norm change to 'pro-active pacifism' in the post-Cold War environment. It suggests that the analysis of normative impact requires an account of why certain norms emerge and are sustained and why they prevail over others. To this extent, norm evolution conforms to certain structures and power resources.

The Japanese state is weakly autonomous from society in its military security policy. Social norms matter greatly in Japan's military security policy, albeit in a direct and specific way. Research shows that the collective understandings of anti-militarism not only indirectly set parameters for Japan's national security, but also directly affect policy decisions. Political access, constraints and opportunities in domestic structures are the intervening variable for explaining the direct impact of social norms on Japan's military security policy. In postwar Japan, military security has remained the one policy area where national leaders and the general public differ greatly in their beliefs. Persuasion and compliance with norms has not automatically occurred. Given incentives or imperatives that domestic structures create (eg the imperative to be re-elected in a specific electoral system), the conservative politicians acquiesce to the collective expectation of anti-militarism widely shared among the general public. This acquiescence derives from the interactive effects of norms linking agents with domestic structures, such as the set of rules for constitutional revision and national elections.

The formal, domestic structures are the organisational characteristics of political institutions, and their governing principals, decision-making rules and procedures embodied in constitution, law and custom. Social norms become embedded in these formal structures (eg the peace clause of Article 9) as the collective expectation of voters is articulated in political processes (eg electoral politics in SMDs). These embedded norms also shape the instruments available to policy-makers to pursue their self-interests; they constitute the informal rules (eg the 1% of GNP ceiling) by which policy-makers respond to citizens. This is a process of less formal institutionalisation yet does not prevent these informal rules from becoming the effective political limits on Japan's military security policy. Given a clear distance between elite opinions and mass expectation, the intrinsic force of social norms for Japan's military security is less likely to be internalised by national leaders, but to be accepted to avoid political costs.

Within its norm-embedded domestic structures, Japan continues to meet and deflect US requests for military contributions. Yet it is important to note that commitments to the established norms can be weakened by external crises, such as the deterioration of Japan's regional security environment and massive reductions in the presence of US forces in East Asia. The Japanese may react to the changing environment and begin to develop new understandings for problem-solution. Social interaction may lead to new collective understandings. A fundamental change in Japan's military security policy is more likely when these collective understandings are successfully consolidated in the political access, constraints and opportunities that domestic structures provide.

As late as 1990, US pressure for Japan to make more effort on defence almost exclusively focused on Japan's financial contributions to US forces in Japan rather than building up Japan's independent military capabilities. This US preoccupation with Japan's budget, while still ensuring the US security guarantee, provided a supportive environment where the mechanism of norm compliance continued to place constraints on Japan's independent military capabilities and use of force. In other words, domestic constraints and US pressures were easily compatible with each other. In the early 1990s, however, Japan's commitment to the established norms of anti-militarism began to shake with the aftermath of the first Gulf War. The Japanese people were increasingly in favour of a pro-active security policy. This swing in collective beliefs coincided with a shift of US pressure on Japan from budget-sharing to military risk-sharing. Changes in both social norms and US pressures seemed to converge to promote and shape Japan's move towards a 'normal state' and remilitarisation. Is Japan really remilitarising? Let us summarise certain key indexes of Japan's militarisation.

Increasing military spending for remilitarisation

Neo-realists argue that economic growth generates a shift in political power, including military capabilities. Yet, as many authors puzzle, Japan has not turned its economic growth into military power. The 1976 National Defence Program Outline did not emerge from a rational calculation of Japan's strategic need, but rather it was domestically acceptable in political terms. LDP leaders, assisted by civilian bureaucrats, became convinced that it would be extremely important to win the goodwill of voters who feared the development of offensive capabilities and faced greater uncertainty in an economic recession. Japan's anti-defence spending bias supported the idea of limited defence capability in peacetime while the government sought to satisfy the demand for anti-militarism rather than maximise its strategic military capabilities. To maintain Japan's limited defence capabilities, one week after the 1976 NDPO was adopted, the Cabinet officially decided that the defence budget was to be restricted to no more than 1% of GNP. There were no clear strategic needs for setting the 1% ceiling on defence spending, but the 1% ceiling was politically feasible for public acceptance. LDP leaders believed it necessary to hold the defence budget down to less than 1% of Japan's GNP as in the past. The 1% framework became a consensus view among the Japanese public.

Prime Minister Nakasone Yasuhiro (1982–87) appeared to have given an unequivocal commitment to the US–Japan alliance rather than to domestic pressures. On becoming prime minister, he also pledged to build Japan's independent military capabilities. Nonetheless, he was unable to abolish or alter the mechanisms of norm compliance for Japan's military security policy, except for minor changes. Nakasone's act of marginally breaking the 1% ceiling in 1987 did not bring a real change in Japan's defence posture. This symbolic move accounted only for Japan's contributions to US forces based in Japan that were expanding faster than the overall defence budget. Many locally elected LDP politicians reacted to Nakasone's hawkish move, fearing the next electoral implications for the party. After all, the lifting of the ceiling did not lead to Japan's defence budget regularly exceeding 1%. Prime Minister Kaifu Toshiki (1989–91) reintroduced the 1% ceiling in 1990.

It is true that Japan's defence spending in current US dollars rose dramatically after 1985 and surpassed that of France, Germany, Britain and Italy by the 1990s. This increase appeared to support Japan's military rise as neo-realists had predicted. But the abrupt increase was essentially due to the implementation of the 1985 Plaza Agreement in which the G5 rich nations decided to intervene in the foreign exchange markets to drive down the value of the US dollar. Within two years of the agreement, the yen doubled in value against the US dollar. In contrast, Japan's defence spending in yen had increased in an incremental way until 1998 when the annual growth rate began to show almost zero or minus in real terms. Looking closer, Japan's defence spending in yen is crucially important, as the ratio of domestic procurement to total procurement has remained about 90% since 1969. Indeed, the yen-dominated procurement budget began to stagnate in fiscal year 1984.

In theory, defence spending continues to steadily increase as economic growth automatically creates a larger base of 1% of GDP. To this extent, Japan seemed to have improved the strength of the ASDF and the MSDF by acquiring state-of-the-art defence technologies, such as F-15 interceptors, P3C anti-submarine reconnaissance aircraft, the Airborne Warning and Control System aircraft, and AEGIS destroyers, which few states can afford to purchase. However, since 1991 when the bubble economy burst, expenditure on new procurement has continually decreased with a large part of the annual procurement budget honouring previous procurement contracts. The defence debate has still been ritualised along the lines of budgetary constraints. In the last decade (1997–2006), Japan's defence budget has remained under 1% of GDP. As Japan's stagnant economy provided a smaller base of 1% of GDP during this period, its defence budget has suffered from low or minus growth in yen. In fact, the annual growth rate of the defence budget in yen dipped into negative figures for four consecutive years from 2003 to 2006. Acquisition has accounted for less than 20% of the squeezed defence budget in the last decade. This downward trend in acquisition will need to manage the purchase of 'big-ticket' items, such as BMD-related equipment, as well as the acquisition of the hardware committed under the previous mid-term defence program. In essence, the inability of Japan's political leadership to hammer out the future direction of defence strategies (especially those regarding the right of collective self-defence) is likely to waste the limited budget, which could be diverted to unnecessary projects and equipment. The rigid budget limits, based on domestic constraints rather than coping with external threats, are likely to delay the transformation of the SDF.

Developing strategically offensive military capabilities

The distinction between defensive and offensive military capabilities has blurred with the growth of smarter and state-of-the-art weapons. Technological advancement and precision have made it easier to initiate a war and also to allow for the limited or precise use of weapons for a narrowly defined purpose. With these patterns in technology diffusion, from the viewpoint of public scrutiny the nature and scope of defensive capabilities has become extremely important for Japan's military security policy in which it is unconstitutional for Japan to possess what is referred to as offensive weapons.

Despite the technology diffusion, certain military capabilities can be clearly regarded as 'offensive' by nature. To maintain national self-defence, Japan has evidently refrained from acquiring certain capabilities, such as intercontinental ballistic missiles, long-range strategic bombers, and aircraft carriers. Above all, it is unthinkable for Japan to become a nuclear power, which requires ballistic missile development (as tactical nuclear weapons are less useful for the island nation). In May 2002, then Chief Cabinet Secretary Fukuda Yasuo, who succeeded Abe Shinzo as prime minister in 2007, commented that some Japanese might consider Japan becoming armed with a nuclear arsenal if international security got worse. Despite the foreign suspicions that such comments generate, Japan is neither able nor willing to possess nuclear weapons. First of all, although Japan's military security policy is an area where the policy elite and the general public differ greatly in their beliefs, a deep-seated non-nuclear stance transcends differences in their beliefs. Even the strongest nationalists of the LDP, such as Kishi Nobusuke and Nakasone Yasuhiro, clearly state that Japan would choose not to become a nuclear power. Postwar Japan's anti-nuclear sentiment has not faded over time; those who support Japan's possession of nuclear weapons remain only 10% of Japanese voters and the overwhelming majority continue to strongly oppose Japan's nuclearisation. Secondly, Japanese nuclear armament is not strategically in support of Japan's national interests. Defence Ministry officials and SDF officers clearly acknowledge that Japan's nuclearisation could trigger a nuclear arms race and nuclear proliferation in Northeast Asia and thus destabilise regional security. Japan's decision to become a nuclear power would also fundamentally change the nature and scope of Japan's relations with the

United States. The US continues to express its position against nuclear-armed Japan.

Japan has no strategic interest in developing large land armies to defend the island nation. The Ground Self-Defence Force has little capability for ground warfare and even less potential capability for offensive ground warfare. It has neither established airborne forces nor developed air assault capabilities that allow forces to deploy anywhere with little warning. Japan has no amphibious landing forces, either. Both the Maritime Self-Defence Force and the Air Self-Defence Force lack the capability to support land warfare. The Japanese maritime force is not equipped with long-range ground attack missile systems to support land warfare operations, while the Japanese air force does not deploy the most capable tactical, precision-guided munitions to support remote ground warfare.

The ASDF has developed considerable capabilities for air self-defence. Japan's air force has emerged as the second greatest in capability in airborne control and early-warning, next to the United States. With a range of 1,600 miles stretching from air bases in Hokkaido to those in Okinawa, Japanese F-15s have potential capabilities to expand their air power projection to the Taiwan Strait and the Korean Peninsula. However, Japan's air force is not equipped with the capability of offensive aviation. Japan's combat aircraft are not loaded with weapons to perform precision bombing. Japanese F-15s are neither armed to bomb airfields and missile sites nor designed to destroy the enemy's air capability directly.

As far as sea control is concerned, it is often truthfully pointed out that the MSDF has the greatest military capability within the SDF and can be placed among the top two to three naval powers in the world. Japan's naval capabilities have both advanced air defence and anti-submarine warfare operations, which could be deployed outside of Japanese territorial waters to monitor or even attack an enemy fleet. The MSDF's P-3Cs (patrol aircraft), for example, have a radar radius of 1,000 nautical miles for detecting ships and submarines, and project its power across Northeast and even Southeast Asian waters. The MSDF may need to defeat invading enemies at sea, defend Japanese coastlines, clear mines and patrol surrounding waters for any potential threats. However, it is clear that the MSDF is unable to project power ashore through air or missile attacks on foreign soil while projecting defence power over land to protect Japan.

The 2004 introduction of the BMD (Ballistic Missile Defence) is based on the sea-based defence system by Aegis ships and the ground-based Patriot missile system. The BMD requires a new joint structure of the SDF where MSDF's Aegis ships, together with the ASDF's radar, would attempt to intercept missiles, and the GSDF must intervene if they have failed to intercept them. Furthermore, Japan's close co-ordination with US forces would be required to make the BMD system more effective. Yet integrating the two BMD systems may be regarded as exercising the right of collective self-defence. From the viewpoint of the current Japanese government's position, Japan's ballistic missile defence system must remain independent from the US system.

Acceptance of the use of armed force as a means of settling international disputes

The recent swing in collective belief among the Japanese public can be seen to favour Japan's pro-active security policy but within the limits of anti-militarism continuity. The vast majority of Japanese voters believe that Japan's international contribution should not be construed as the use of armed forces. Japanese voters still display a strong aversion to military involvement, as has been shown. By this token, the overwhelming majority of Japanese voters, although being pro-revisionists, do not wish to eliminate Clause 1 of Article 9 of the constitution—the 'renunciation of war'. Opinion polls suggested that most Japanese support SDF participation in UN peacekeeping but oppose expanded participation in UN peacekeeping operations involving the use of force. In other words, the Japanese public clearly does not wish the SDF to become involved in combatant peace enforcement operations, even under UN peacekeeping missions. They solidly accept the use of force only to defend the territorial integrity and political independence of Japan. Therefore, the majority supports the revision of Clause 2 of Article 9—'prohibition on the maintenance of armed forces'—in order to constitutionally recognise the SDF as armed forces defending Japan's soil.

Most lawmakers in Japan fear a strong sense of voters' aversion to military involvement and wish to dilute the military image of the SDF by emphasising the SDF's international contributions to humanitarian relief operations. A handful of hawkish LDP politicians openly argue that Japan should remove its self-imposed prohibition against collective self-defence, which would allow for US–Japan joint military operations on a larger scale. It is highly unlikely that the government will submit the lifting of the prohibition on collective self-defence for ratification by Japanese voters. It is more likely that the Japanese government will covertly try to *reinterpret* the constitutional prohibition in a piecemeal fashion to ease specific US pressures for a strongly alliance-oriented, high-risk strategy. This would neither lead to a fundamental shift in Japan's military security policy nor to large-scale remilitarisation.

Sending the SDF contingents to Iraq showed Japan's high sensitivity to the use of force. Japan dispatched an armed body of the SDF for the first time in 60 years, though in noncombatant operations, to 'noncombatant zones'. It was also the first time that the SDF participated in an area under the administration of an occupying power rather than under UN operations. Japanese political leaders discussed whether there would be any possibility for the SDF to engage in the use of weapons in noncombatant zones. The Japanese government argued officially that weapon use by Japanese personnel must be admitted within the framework of the Japanese constitution. The special measures law for sending the SDF to Iraq provided that SDF soldiers would be permitted to use weapons only to protect their lives, the SDF personnel accompanied by them, and those who were under their management, and must not exceed the proportional use of force in terms of nature, duration and scope of the engagement.

The issue over the use of weapons remains unsolved. The point here is how to minimise any possibility for the SDF personnel's use of weapons, while the ban on SDF participation in combat missions remains firmly in place. The fear of a public backlash has been the dominant factor for Japan's overtly restricted use of weapons. Continued US pressure for military-risk sharing induces a sense of obligation in the Japanese government, yet political sensitivities over the use of force convince the Japanese government to take a minimalist approach. Japan's choice for use of force will continue to be made as a result of political processes in which politicians make decisions exclusively on what the SDF can do without contradicting the Japanese people's strong aversion to military involvement rather than on what it can strategically contribute to US–Japan defence co-operation. Even Japan's responses to the terrorist attacks of 11 September did not fundamentally change its minimalist approach to weapon use. In the case of the SDF dispatch to Iraq, Prime Minister Koizumi was forced to agree that the SDF would be prohibited to transport weapons or ammunition for US troops. The Koizumi cabinet needed to continuously respond to public concerns so that the SDF contingents would neither risk their lives to become involved in combat nor suffer casualties. Prime Minister Koizumi still suffered a disastrous defeat in the 2004 upper house election. Given the public backlash, the Koizumi cabinet suggested that the GSDF contingent would withdraw if security in Samawah degenerated.

Legitimising and legalising the dispatching of armed forces to foreign soil

Japan's pledge to make a visible contribution to international security began earnestly after the 1990–91 Gulf War. The international community strongly condemned Japan for its diplomatic blunder in failing to respond quickly to the Gulf Crisis in a responsible manner. In the aftermath of the war, a clear public majority in Japan emerged in support of making an international contribution (*kokusai kouken*). In the past, Japanese people had been suspicious of any SDF missions overseas that were considered to increase the likelihood of Japan becoming too militaristic. In the mid-1990s, an overwhelming majority supported disaster relief operations overseas; the general public had overcome fears of militarism deriving from SDF missions overseas in humanitarian relief and reconstruction activities. Unlike the collective understanding in the pre-Gulf War period, the Japanese public increasingly acknowledged that it was one thing to worry about overseas deployments involving the use of force; it was quite another to allow overseas deployments for non-military operations. In other words, public support for overseas deployments reflected a collective belief in the admissible field of non-military, humanitarian relief. As mentioned above, it is important to note that despite the aftermath of 11 September and a decade of Japan's participation in UN peacekeeping operations, the Japanese public had neither become more willing to support the SDF's combat operations in UN peacekeeping nor to firmly agree to noncombatant logistical support of US military operations.

The principle of no overseas dispatch, which was integrated into the 1954 SDF Law, had banned the SDF from engaging in any type of overseas operations for four decades. Japan revised the *International Disaster Relief Law* in 1987 to allow the SDF to be deployed overseas for disaster relief activities. In practice, Japan did not send the SDF for disaster relief until after 1991. In 1991 Prime Minister Kaifu also decided to dispatch MSDF minesweepers to the Persian Gulf, although the Japanese government had initially interpreted Article 99 of the SDF Law as that the SDF was authorised to sweep mines in the 'vicinity' of Japan. Since then, the SDF Law has been revised frequently as a result of new special measure laws. As of 2007, the SDF Law specifies the authorised scope of noncombatant SDF operations in the areas outside Japanese territory: peacekeeping operations, emergency evacuation of Japanese residing overseas, rear-area support and ship inspection in the areas surrounding Japan, and provision of goods to US forces in the areas surrounding Japan. The special measures laws have further paved the way for SDF participation in multinational forces that does not fall within the scope of either the *UN Peace Keeping Operations Co-operation Law* or the *International Disaster Relief Law*. The SDF can thus be dispatched to take part in the large scope of noncombatant overseas operations; however, the legal grounds for SDF overseas dispatch are firmly subject to two outer limits that public beliefs have set: the ban on SDF participation in combat operations and the ban on measures construed as use of force.

Japan can legally dispatch the SDF contingents to a wider range of overseas activities. Yet political decisions by the Japanese government to dispatch the SDF overseas have been far more limited than by its mere legal framework. The Japanese government has tested the detailed implementation of those outer limits of what voters were prepared to accept. Even popular Prime Minister Koizumi had to respond to public concerns and avoid the danger of provoking domestic opposition. The crucial part of Koizumi's response to 11 September was to provide rear-area logistical support for US military operations against the Taliban regime in Afghanistan. The Koizumi cabinet tried hard to extend the scope of permissible SDF noncombatant operations, but substantially compromised to prevent the growth of public opposition. Prime Minister Koizumi gave up his original plan to send the GSDF contingents to Pakistan for humanitarian support while prohibiting the transport and supply of arms from rear-area support for the US military. Due to LDP leaders' decisions to avoid further public opposition and mass media criticism, initial plans to dispatch P-3Cs and airborne early warning planes were also cancelled. In the Iraq War the Koizumi cabinet had to withstand the tougher scrutiny of voters. Prime Minister Koizumi initially decided to deploy the GSDF contingents to Samawah to provide rear-area logistical support for US forces but overturned his decision in favour of reconstruction missions. He needed to reassure the public that the Japanese government continued to decrease the risk of the SDF becoming involved in armed attacks and suffering casualties.

The social norm structure of Japan's military security is changing but doing so slowly; this argument challenges the conventional wisdom that Japan is 'remilitarising'. Japan continues to display great restraint in its military security policy. Despite increased military capabilities, Japan has continued to show a strong aversion to military involvement. Since the early 1990s, the Japanese government has managed conflicting pressures awkwardly: domestic norms based on a continuing aversion to military involvement and US pressures on Japan to support US involvement in Asian conflicts. It has stood up through the compliance mechanisms of social norms to the public scrutiny of its military security practices, which US involvement in Asian conflicts has exacerbated. It is the normative content of military security policy that is a primary determinant in shaping Japan's patterns of security policy adjustments. In short, it is highly unlikely that Japan will seek to become a major military power in the foreseeable future. Of course, this is not to argue that dramatic exogenous shocks, such as a new regional threat and a debilitation of the US–Japan alliance, cannot significantly change the nature and scope of existing legal and social norms.

In a longer-term perspective, the slowly changing context of domestic norms threatens to damage Japan's dependence on the US security guarantee. With the possible rise of a new regional security threat, the damaged US–Japan alliance may bring a political crisis to Japan's national leadership and pave the way for large-scale remilitarisation. The answer is yet to be seen.

Appendix 1: Chronology of Japan's security 1946–2008

Terms of Office	Prime Minister	Defence Plans	Policy Shifts	US–Japan Alliance	World Affairs
1946–1947	Yoshida Shigeru		1947 New Constitution enacted		
1948–1954	Yoshida Shigeru			1951 US–Japan Security Treaty signed	1949 People's Republic of China established 1950–53 Korean War
1954–1956	Hatoyama Ichiro		1954 SDF established 1954 Ban on SDF overseas dispatch		1956 USSR Intervention in Hungary
1957–1960	Kishi Nobusuke	1958–60 First Defence Build-up Plan		1960 Revised US–Japan Security Treaty signed	
1960–1964	Ikeda Hayato	1962–66 Second Defence Build-up Plan			1962 Cuban Missile Crisis

145

1964–1972	Sato Eisaku	1967–71 Third Defence Build-up Plan	1967 Ban on arms exports 1967 Three Non–Nuclear Principles	1972 Reversion of Okinawa to Japan	1970 Nixon Doctrine 1972 Nixon's official visit to China
1972–1974	Tanaka Kakuei	1972–76 Fourth Defence Build-up Plan	1972 Ban on collective self-defence		1973 Vietnam Peace Treaty signed
1974–1976	Miki Takeo	1976 National Defence Program Outline	1976 1% of GNP ceiling on defence spending		
1976–1978	Fukuda Takeo				
1878–1980	Ohira Masayoshi			1978 Guidelines for US–Japan defence co-operation adopted	1979 USSR Invasion of Afghanistan
1980–1982	Suzuki Zenko				

APPENDIX 1

Period	PM						
1982–1987	Nakasone Yasuhiro						
1987–1989	Takeshi Noboru					1989 Tiananmen incident	
1989–1991	Kaifu Toshiyuki					1990–91 Gulf Crisis; 1991 Collapse of the USSR	
1991–1993	Miyazawa Kiichi			1992 PKO Law passed			
1993–1994	Hosokawa Morihiro					1993–94 Korean Nuclear Crisis	
1994–1996	Murayama Tomiichi	1995 National Defence Program Outline		1994 Higuchi Report	1995 Nye Report	1995–96 Taiwan Strait Crisis	
1996–1998	Hashimoto Ryutaro				1997 Guidelines for US–Japan defence co-operation		

Period	PM					
1998–2000	Obuchi Keizo					1998 Taepodong Crisis
2000–2001	Mori Yoshiro			2000 Armitage Report		
2001–2006	Koizumi Jun'ichiro	2004 National Defence Program Guideline	2001 Anti-terrorism legislation 2003 Iraq reconstruction assistance legislation 2003 Wartime preparedness legislation 2004 Araki Report	2005 SCC Joint Statement		2001 9/11 Terrorist attacks on the US 2001 War in Afghanistan began 2003 Iraq War
2006–2007	Abe Shinzo		2007 Constitution referendum legislation			
2007–2008	Fukuda Yasuo					

appendix 2

Article 9 of the constitution of Japan and related documents

Chapter II: Renunciation of War

Article 9

Section I: Aspiring sincerely to an international peace based on justice and order, the Japanese people forever renounce war as a sovereign right of the nation and the threat or use of force as means of settling international disputes.

Section II: In order to accomplish the aim of the preceding paragraph, land, sea, and air forces, as well as other war potential, will never be maintained. The right of belligerency of the state will not be recognized.

Basic Policy on National Defense (1957)

Adopted by the National Defense Council and the Cabinet on 20 May 1957.
Source: Japan Ministry of Defense, *Basis of Defense Policy*, available at http://www.mod.go.jp/e/d_policy/dp02.html, last accessed October 2007.

The objective of national defense is to prevent direct and indirect aggression, but once invaded, to repel such aggression, and thereby, to safeguard the independence and peace of Japan based on democracy.

To achieve this objective, the following basic policies are defined:

1. Supporting the activities of the United Nations, promoting international collaboration, and thereby, making a commitment to the realization of world peace

2. Stabilizing the livelihood of the people, fostering patriotism, and thereby, establishing the necessary basis for national security.

3. Building up rational defense capabilities by steps within the limit necessary for self-defense in accordance with national strength and situation.

4. Dealing with external aggression based on the security arrangements with the US until the United Nations will be able to fulfill its function in stopping such aggression effectively in the future.

National Defense Program Outline (1976)

Adopted by the National Defense Council and the Cabinet on 29 October 1976.
Source: Japan Defense Agency, *Defense of Japan 1989*, pp.262–266.

1. Objectives

Japan's possession of a defense capability within the scope permitted by the Constitution is not only a concrete expression of the people's will to safeguard the nation's peace and independence, but also aims - together with the Japan-United States security arrangement - directly at forestalling any aggression against Japan and repelling such aggression should it occur. Concurrently, the very fact that Japan firmly maintains such a defense posture contributes as well to the international political stability of Japan's neighboring region.

A major consideration in this regard is the nature of the defense capability which Japan should possess. Assuming that the international political structure in this region - along with continuing efforts for global stabilization - will not undergo any major changes for some time to come, and that Japan's domestic conditions will also remain fundamentally stable, the most appropriate defense goal would seem to be the maintenance of a full surveillance posture in peacetime and the ability to cope effectively with situations up to the point of limited and small-scale aggression. The emphasis is on the possession of the assorted functions required for national defense, while retaining balanced organization and deployment, including logistical support. At the same time, it is felt that consideration should be given to enabling this defense posture to contribute to the domestic welfare through disaster-relief operations and other such programs.

Japan has steadily improved its defense capability through the drafting and implementation of a series of four defense buildup plans. At this time, the present scale of defense capability seems to closely approach the target goals of the above-mentioned concept.

This outline is meant to serve as a guideline for Japan's future defense posture in the light of that concept. Based on the information given below, efforts will be made to qualitatively maintain and improve defense capability, and fulfill the purpose of that capability, in specific upgrading, maintenance and operation of defense functions.

4. Posture of National Defense

(1) Setup of Warning and Surveillance

Japan's defense structure must possess continuous capability to conduct warning and survelillance missions within Japan's territory and neighboring sea and airspace as well as to collect required intelligence.

(2) Setup for Countering Indirect Aggression and Unlawful Actions by Means of Use of Military Power

(i) Japan's defense structure must possess the capability to act and take the required steps to respond to such cases as intense domestic insurgency with external support, organized personnel infiltration and arms smuggling, or the covert use of force in Japan's nearby sea and airspace.

(ii) Japan's defense structure must be capable of immediate and pertinent action to cope with aircraft invading or threatening to invade Japan's territorial airspace.

(3) Setup for Countering Direct Military Aggression

Japan's defense structure must be capable of taking immediate responsive action against any direct military aggression, in accordance with the type and scale of such aggression. It should be capable of repelling limited and small-scale aggression, in principle without external assistance. In cases where unassisted repelling of aggression is not feasible, it should be capable of continuing effective resistance until such time as cooperation from the United States can be introduced, thus rebuffing such aggression.

(4) Setup of Command Communications, Transportation and Rear Support Services

Japan's defense structure must be able to function in such fields as command communications, transportation, rescue, supply and maintenance, for swift, effective and adequate operations.

(5) Setup of Education and Training of Personnel

Japan's defense structure must be capable of carrying out intensive education and training of personnel at all times for the reinforcement of the personnel foundation of defense capability.

(6) Setup of Disaster-Relief Operations

Japan's defense structure must possess the capability to carry out disaster-relief operations in any areas of the country when required.

The Guidelines for US–Japan Defense Cooperation (1997)

Source: Japan Ministry of Defense, *SCC Joint Statement, 23 September 1997*, available at http://www.mod.go.jp/e/d_policy/index.html, last accessed October 2007.

SECTION V. Cooperation in situations in areas surrounding Japan that will have an important influence on Japan's peace and security (situations in areas surrounding Japan)

Situations in areas surrounding Japan will have an important influence on Japan's peace and security. The concept, situations in areas surrounding Japan, is not geographic but situational. The two Governments will make every effort, including diplomatic efforts, to prevent such situations from occurring. When the two Governments reach a common assessment of the state of each situation, they will effectively coordinate their activities. In responding to such situations, measures taken may differ depending on circumstances.

1. When a Situations in Areas Surrounding Japan is Anticipated

When a situation in areas surrounding Japan is anticipated, the two Governments will intensify information and intelligence sharing and policy consultations, including efforts to reach a common assessment of the situation.

At the same time, they will make every effort, including diplomatic efforts, to prevent further deterioration of the situation, while initiating at an early stage the operation of a bilateral coordination mechanism, including use of a bilateral coordination center. Cooperating as appropriate, they will make preparations necessary for ensuring coordinated responses according to the readiness stage selected by mutual agreement. As circumstances change, they will also increase intelligence gathering and surveillance, and enhance their readiness to respond to the circumstances.

2. Responses to Situations in Areas Surrounding Japan

The two Governments will take appropriate measures, to include preventing further deterioration of situations, in response to situations in areas surrounding Japan. This will be done in accordance with the basic premises and principles listed in Section II above and based on their respective decisions. They will support each other as necessary in accordance with appropriate arrangements.

Functions and fields of cooperation and examples of items of cooperation are outlined below, and listed in the Annex.

(1) Cooperation in Activities Initiated by Either Government

Although either Government may conduct the following activities at its own discretion, bilateral cooperation will enhance their effectiveness.

(a) Relief Activities and Measures to Deal with Refugees

Each Government will conduct relief activities with the consent and cooperation of the authorities in the affected area. The two Governments will cooperate as necessary, taking into account their respective capabilities.

The two Governments will cooperate in dealing with refugees as necessary. When there is a flow of refugees into Japanese territory, Japan will decide how to respond and will have primary responsibility for dealing with the flow; the United States will provide appropriate support.

(b) Search and Rescue

The two Governments will cooperate in search and rescue operations. Japan will conduct search and rescue operations at in Japanese territory; and at sea around Japan, as distinguished from areas where combat operations are being conducted. When U.S. Forces are conducting operations, the United States will conduct search and rescue operations in and near the operational areas.

(c) Noncombatant Evacuation Operations

When the need arises for U.S. and Japanese noncombatants to be evacuated from a third country to a safe haven, each Government is responsible for evacuating its own nationals as well as for dealing with the authorities of the affected area. In stances in which each decides it is appropriate, the two Governments will coordinate in planning and cooperate in carrying out their evacuations, including for the securing of transportation means, transportation and the use of facilities, using their respective capabilities in a mutually supplementary manner. If similar need arises for noncombatants other than of U.S. or Japanese nationality, the respective countries may consider extending, on their respective terms, evacuation assistance to third country nationals.

(d) Activities for Ensuring the Effectiveness of Economic Sanctions for the Maintenance of International Peace and Stability

Each Government will contribute to activities for ensuring the effectiveness of economic sanctions for the maintenance of international peace and stability. Such contributions will be made in accordance with each Government's own criteria.

Additionally, the two Governments will cooperate with each other as appropriate, taking into account their respective capabilities. Such cooperation includes information sharing, and cooperation in inspection of ships based on United Nations Security Council Resolutions.

(2) Japan's Support for US Forces Activities

(a) Use of Facilities

Based on the U.S.-Japan Security Treaty and its related arrangements, Japan will, in case of need, provide additional facilities and areas in a timely and appropriate manner, and ensure the temporary use by U.S. Forces of Self-Defense Forces facilities and civilian airports and ports.

(b) Rear Area Support

Japan will provide rear area support to those U.S. Forces that are conducting operations for the purpose of achieving the objectives of the U.S.-Japan Security Treaty. The primary aim of this rear area support is to enable U.S. Forces to use facilities and conduct operations in an effective manner. By its very nature, Japan's rear area support will be provided primarily in Japanese territory. It may also be provided on the high seas and international airspace around Japan which are distinguished from areas where combat operations are being conducted.

In providing rear area support, Japan will make appropriate use of authorities and assets of the central and local government agencies, as well as private sector assets. The Self-Defense Forces, as appropriate, will provide such support consistent with their mission for the defense of Japan and the maintenance of public order

(3) US–Japan Operational Cooperation

As situations in areas surrounding Japan have an important influence on Japan's peace and security, the Self-Defense Forces will conduct such activities as intelligence gathering, surveillance and minesweeping, to protect lives and property and to ensure navigational safety. U.S. Forces will conduct operations to restore the peace and security affected by situations in areas surrounding Japan.

With the involvement of relevant agencies, cooperation and coordination will significantly enhance the effectiveness of both forces' activities.

National Defense Program Guideline for FY 2005–

Approved by the Security Council and the Cabinet on 10 December 2004.
Source: Prime Minister of Japan and His Cabinet, *National Defense Program Guideline for FY 2005–*, available at http://www.kantei.go.jp/foreign/policy/2004/1210taikou_e.html, last accessed October 2007.

Section IV. Future Defense Forces

1. Role of the Defense Forces

Based on the recognition discribed above, Japan will develop and maintain, in an efficient manner, the necessary Self-Defense Forces posture to effectively carry out missions in the following areas:

(1) Effective Response to the New Threats and Diverse Situations

Japan will deal effectively with the new threats and diverse situations by developing highly responsive and mobile defense force units capable of responding properly to various different situations and by deploying them appropriately in accordance with Japan's geographical characteristics. Should such a situation emerges, the defense forces will respond quickly and appropriately in smooth and close collaboration with the police and other relevant organizations, thereby providing a seamless response to the situation in accordance with circumstances and designated roles. Japan's Self-Defense Forces posture to address the key elements of the new threats and diverse situations will be as follows:

a. Response to Ballistic Missile Attacks

We will respond to ballistic missile attacks by establishing necessary defense force structure, including the introduction of ballistic missile defense systems, to deal effectively with ballistic missile attacks. We will adequately respond to the threat of nuclear weapons by doing so, in addition to relying on US nuclear deterrence.

b. Response to Guerrillas and Special Operations Forces Attacks

We will maintain necessary defense force structure to respond effectively to attacks carried out by guerrillas and special operations forces. We will also enhance readiness and mobility of the defense force units, and deal with such attacks in a flexible manner.

c. Response to the Invasion of Japan's Offshore Islands

We will maintain necessary defense force structure to respond effectively to the invasion of Japan's offshore islands, improve and strengthen capabilities to transport and deploy forces, and deal with the invasion in a flexible manner.

d. Patrol and Surveillance in the Sea and Airspace Surrounding Japan, and Response to the Violation of Japan's Airspace and the Intrusion of Armed Special-Purpose Ships and Other Similar Vessels

We will maintain necessary defense force structure, including ships, aircraft and other assets, to carry out around-the-clock patrol and surveillance in the sea and airspace surrounding Japan. We will also maintain fighter aircraft units to respond instantly to the violation of our territorial airspace, as well as combatant ships and other assets in order to respond to armed special-purpose ships operating in waters surrounding Japan, submerged foreign submarines operating in Japan's territorial waters, and other similar vessels.

e. Response to Large-Scale and/or Special-Type (Nuclear, Biological, Chemical, and Radiological) Disasters

To deal effectively with large-scale and/or special-type (nuclear, biological, chemical, and radiological) disasters, where protection of life and property is desperately needed, we will maintain an adequate force structure with defense force units, as well as specialized capabilities and expertise to conduct disaster relief operations in any part of Japan.

US–Japan Alliance: Transformation and Realignment for the Future (2005)

Source: Japan Ministry of Foreign Affairs, *SCC Document, 29 October 2005*, available at http://www.mofa.go.jp/region/n-america/us/security/scc/doc0510.html, last accessed October 2007.

Section II Roles, Missions, and Capabilities

Both sides reconfirmed that the entire spectrum of bilateral cooperation must be strengthened, consistent with relevant national security policies and laws, and with agreements between the U.S. and Japan. Through their examination of roles, missions, and capabilities, they emphasized the importance of improving several specific areas of cooperation:

- Air defense.
- Ballistic missile defense.
- Counter-proliferation operations, such as the Proliferation Security Initiative (PSI).
- Counter-terrorism.
- Minesweeping, maritime interdiction, and other operations to maintain the security of maritime traffic.
- Search and rescue operations.
- Intelligence, surveillance and reconnaissance (ISR) operations, including increasing capabilities and effectiveness of operations by unmanned aerial vehicles (UAV) and maritime patrol aircraft.
- Humanitarian relief operations.
- Reconstruction assistance operations.
- Peacekeeping operations and capacity building for other nations' peacekeeping efforts.
- Protection of critical infrastructure, including US facilities and areas in Japan.
- Response to attacks by weapons of mass destruction (WMD), including disposal and decontamination of WMD.
- Mutual logistics support activities such as supply, maintenance, and transportation. Supply cooperation includes mutual provision of aerial and maritime refueling. Transportation cooperation includes expanding and sharing airlift and sealift, including the capability provided by high speed vessels (HSV).
- Transportation, use of facilities, medical support, and other related activities for non-combatant evacuation operations (NEO).
- Use of seaport and airport facilities, road, water space and airspace, and frequency bands.

glossary

fukoku kyohei	rich nation, strong military
hibuso	unarmed
hinomaru	(sun circle) flag
jishuboei	autonomous defence
kaishaku kaiken	constitutional reform through reinterpretation
kiban boeiryoku koso	standard defense force concept
Kirishima	one of SDF's Aegis destroyers
koenkai	personal support groups
kokubo zoku	national defence policy group
kokusai koken	international contributions
kokusanka	domestic production of technology
oitsuke oikose	catch up and surpass
omoiyari yosan	host nation budgets
sekihairitsu	the ratio of a candidate's vote to the district winner's vote
Shogun	warlord of Japanese Edo period (1603–1868)
sogo anzen hosho	comprehensive security
zoku	LDP national politicians who are regarded as experts on specific policy areas due to their experience

Acronyms

ARF	ASEAN Regional Forum
ASDF	Air Self-Defence Force
ASEAN	Association of Southeast Asian Nations
BMD	Ballistic Missile Defense
COCOM	Co-ordinating Committee for Multilateral Export Controls
DPJ	Democratic Party of Japan
DRAMs	dynamic random access memory (semiconductors)
DSP	Democratic Socialist Party
EASI	East Asia Strategic Initiative
FSX	Fighter Support Experiment
GSDF	Ground Self-Defence Force
JDA	Defense Agency
JMTC	Joint Military Technology Commission
LDP	Liberal Democratic Party
MITI	Ministry of International Trade and Industry
MOU	memorandum of understanding
MSA	Mutual Security Assistance
MSDF	Maritime Self-Defence Force
NDPO	National Defence Program Outline
NDPO	1976 National Defence Program Outline
NPR	National Police Reserve
NSF	National Safety Force
ODA	Official Development Assistance
PKO	Peacekeeping Operations
PR	Proportional Representation
S&TF	Systems and Technology Forum
SDF	Self-Defence Force

SDPJ	Social Democratic Party of Japan
SII	Structural Impediments Initiative
SMD	single member districts
SSC	US–Japan Security Subcommittee
TfT	Technology-for-Technology
TMD	Theater Missile Defence
UNPCC	United Nations Peace Co-operation Corps
VER	Voluntary Export Restraint

Notes

1 For the legislative process of the *Anti-Terrorism Special Measures Law*, see Midford 2003:329–51; Shinoda 2003:19–31.
2 This legislation involves three bills: a new bill to set out procedural guidelines for a response to armed attacks on Japan; revisions of the Self-Defence Force Law for providing troops easier access to land in an emergency; and revisions to the law on the establishment of Japan's Security Council to strengthen its role.
3 The ruling coalition failed to persuade the Democratic Party that called for the establishment of referendum procedures for not only constitutional revision but also a wider range of other important national issues, and it forced a vote on the bill.
4 'Japan Upgrades its Defence Agency,' *Washington Post* 16.12.2006; *Japan Times* 17.12.2006.
5 In contrast, Japanese leaders' call for Japan to become a 'normal nation' has been closely related to their emphasis on a more independent Japanese stance in world affairs. See Ozawa 1987; Ishihara 1991.
6 See Calder 1988a:411–39. The relationships between election systems and military security in Japan will be discussed later in the text.
7 See 'Nixon's Asia Doctrine,' *New York Times* 3.8.1969.
8 Japanese contributions to US forces in Japan quadrupled in yen from 1975 to 1994, while its expenditure for SDF indicated roughly half that rate of increase during the same period. See MOD 1975–1995. Japan is obligated under the Status of Forces Agreement with the United States to provide facilities and grounds to the US forces in Japan. In 1978 the Japanese government began to expand its contribution to the additional 'host nation support' for the non-obligatory scope of contributions, such as improvement of facilities and housing of US bases in Japan, payment of utility costs for US bases in Japan, and payment for Japanese employees working at US bases in Japan.
9 In 1981 Prime Minister Suzuki pledged to Washington that Japan would strengthen its independent military capabilities in order to defend several hundred miles of surrounding waters and the sea lanes to a distance of 1000 miles. As soon as he had taken office in 1982, Prime Minister Yasuhiro Nakasone called for a strengthening of Japan's independent military capabilities, which he described as an 'unsinkable aircraft carrier' in the Pacific.

10   In the 1986 national election, Nakasone's LDP won 300 out of 511 seats (or 58.7%) in the lower house.
11   *Asahi Shinbun* 2.5.2001; a public opinion survey, conducted by Japan Broadcasting Corporation (NHK), 2–4 March 2002.
12   In September 1985, the central bank governors and finance ministers from the 'Group of Five'—the United States, Japan, Britain, France and West Germany—decided to intervene in the foreign-exchange markets to drive the value of the US dollar down. Within two years, the yen doubled in value against the US dollar.
13   In this book, public opinion data on military security has been taken primarily from public opinion surveys, in particular the 'Public Opinion Survey on the Self-Defence Force and Security,' which has been conducted every three years since 1969 by the Public Relations Office of Japan's Cabinet Office (the former Ministry of Public Management). This allows us to make comparisons over time. To analyse older data (pre-1969) and corroborate and update the information from public opinion surveys, data has also been accessed from opinion polls conducted by media organisations and national research institutes. Among them are polls carried out by national newspapers, that is, the *Asahi Shinbun Mainichi Shinbun, Nihon Keizai Shinbun*, and *Yomiuri Shinbun*. These newspaper's polls are supplemented by those provided from the Public Opinion Research Division of the NHK (Japan Broadcasting Corporation), which has been responsible for public opinion surveys fielded on a regular basis since 1946, and from the Institute of Statistical Mathematics that conducted nationwide surveys on security-related constitutional issues in the 1950s and 1960s.
14   For arguments on Japanese public opinion subject to elite moulding, see Hellmann 1969; Johnson 1995:115–40; Garon 1997; Hook 1996.
15   For an excellent review of this approach, see Page & Shapiro 1983:175–90.
16   See Chai 1997:389–412. US security guarantees have provided Japan's desirable freedom in economic development. This security arrangement is the essence of the Yoshida doctrine, which derives from Yoshida's pragmatism. Yoshida was not a pacifist; as long as national resources could afford, he wished to see Japan's immediate military build-up. Japan's governing principle of military security has developed by imposing normative constraints on self-interested pragmatism of Yoshida's fellow conservatives. As discussed later, the 1% of GNP ceiling on defence spending was not a product of political elites-led institutionalisation of the Yoshida doctrine, but rather their adaptation to widely shared beliefs among the Japanese public.
17   Other scholars also embrace such a 'reactive state' thesis. See Lincoln 1993; Hellmann 1988.
18   For a similar argument whereby no power-centre handles Japan's external affairs, see van Wolferen 1989:25–49.
19   For such general patterns of alliances, see Christensen & Snyder 1990:137–68; Snyder 1984:461–96; Powell 1999.
20   Some scholars emphasise the designated buck-catcher's credibility to defend the buck-passer. See Cha 1999.

21 The benefits of a successfully shared security to a state are positively associated with the greater economic capabilities of the state. See Olson & Zeckhauser 1966:266–79.
22 Those who have applied Waltz's systemic theory have normally combined their arguments with the security dilemma theory and the role of perception to predict and prescribe patterns of alliances.
23 On 25 July 1969, reporters were briefed in Guam about the President's plan to reduce the presence of US forces in Asia. This statement was later formalised as the Nixon Doctrine.
24 This clear policy can be found as early as in 1958. See HCPS 1958.
25 Also see his remarks in HRB 1970.
26 It is noteworthy that the Nixon Administration wished to avoid any pressure on Japan to become a major military power in Asia, while encouraging a moderate increase in defence forces. See National Security Decision Memorandum (NSDM) 13, 28 May 1969, cited in Sugawa 2002:50.
27 For his nationalistic belief, see Nakasone 1954.
28 For the evolution of the Yoshida Doctrine, which was based on the US security guarantee allowing the maintenance of maximum economic investment and minimal defence spending, see Dower 1979; Otake 1988; Pyle 1992.
29 For the course of detailed events, see Schaller 1996.
30 See Miyazawa's speech in Bangkok in January 1993, cited in MOFA 1994:168–73; HRPS 1991.
31 In 1991 the Japan Socialist Party (JSP) dropped 'Socialist' from its English name to become the SDPJ. In 1996 the SDPJ renamed itself the SDP.
32 Japan is obliged by the Status of Forces Agreement to provide facilities and areas to the US forces in Japan. In addition to this obligation, in 1978 the Japanese government, on Defence Agency Director Kanemaru Shin's initiative, began to cover part of the other costs of US forces stationed in Japan. By the mid-1990s, the ratio rose to more than three-quarters of the total costs. This host nation support was known as *omoiyari yosan* (sympathy budgets).
33 For the trend of Host Nation Support budgets, see *Japan Statistical Yearbook* and *Asahi Nenkan*, various years.
34 See the Japanese Defence Agency's publication (JDA 1978), *Boeicho ni okeru Yujihosei Kenkyu ni tsuite* (Regarding Research on Emergency Contingency at the Defence Agency) a document opened to the public on 21 September 1978.
35 At that time, the Japanese government was urged at the US–Japan Security Consultative Committee to act consistently with US policy to contain the Soviet Union at a global level. In November 1978, this resulted in the Guideline for US–Japan Defence Co-operation.
36 For this trend, see 'The United States' sections of *The Military Balance,* 1977/78 edition–1984/85 edition. Also see Preston 1984:547–51.

37 The US Congress passed this amendment which would forbid any further US military involvement in Southeast Asia, effective 15 August 1973.
38 For the logic of trust and mistrust underlying international relations, see Jervis, 1978:167–214; Jervis 1989; Kydd 2005.
39 Figures adopted from OECD, *OECD Economic Outlook*, various issues.
40 Figures calculated from sources provided in IMF, *Government Finance Statistics Yearbook*, various years.
41 HCC 1954b ; HCPS 1954b. Article 8 of the MSA agreement stated, 'The Government of Japan, reaffirming its determination to join in promoting international understanding and good will and maintaining world peace, will take such action as may be mutually agreed upon to eliminate causes of international tension; to fulfil the military obligations which the Government of Japan has assumed under the Security Treaty between the United States of America and Japan; will make, consistent with the political and economic stability of Japan the full contribution permitted by its manpower, resources, facilities and general economic condition to the development and maintenance of its own defensive strength and the defensive strength of the free world: take all reasonable measures which may be needed to develop its defence capacities; and take appropriate steps to ensure the effective utilisation of any assistance provided by the Government of the United States of America'.
42 Figures in this section provided by the Japanese Ministry of Defence.
43 The ARF was the first diplomatic agreement to set up a regional dialogue in East Asia to deal specifically with security matters. It included not only the member states of ASEAN but their regional major powers, such as the United States, China, Russia and Japan.
44 Neo-mercantilism is a policy where a state seeks to gain a balance-of-trade surplus and promote domestic production and employment by reducing imports. Liberal trade policies are less likely to cause political problems with trading partners; they are based on internal adjustments, such as changes in interest rates and taxation. In contrast, neo-mercantilism policies are designed to directly change the terms of exchange for foreign economic transactions, such as import quotas, subsidies, and undervalued currency, so that these external adjustments are more likely to put the burdens on companies and governments abroad.
45 I use the term 'pacifism' rather than anti-militarism to develop my arguments in the following chapters. As illustrated in the next chapter, the word pacifism is well suited for defining Japanese people's collective understanding of peace in a broad sense. In this book, pacifism is defined as a social norm or belief widely shared among the public, and a specific form of pacifism in postwar Japan is seen as a fundamental constraint on military security policy.
46 As mentioned in the Introduction, the Cabinet Public Relations Office has conducted a public opinion survey on national security every three years since 1969. The office has administered a lengthy questionnaire to 3,000 men and women in their 20s and older (except the 2000 survey that was conducted with a sample size of 5,000).

47 Compiled from *Kinema Junpo*, January 1950 to December 1959; Sato Tadao, *Nihon Eigashi* (History of Japanese Films) 1995.
48 The November 1950 opinion poll was conducted by *Asahi Shinbun*. The December 1950 opinion poll and the September 1951 one were taken by *Mainichi Shinbun*. Cited in Morishita 1995:35.
49 For this general trend indicated by public opinion polls of *Asahi Shinbun Mainichi Shinbun* and the Cabinet Office, see NHK 1975:124–9.
50 The results of the opinion polls are from those conducted by *Yomiuri Shinbun* in January 1954 and those by the Cabinet Office in 1956 and 1959.
51 See, for example, *Asahi Shinbun* 15.8.1954:editorial; *Mainichi Shinbun*, 15.8.1955:editorial; *Mainichi Shinbun*, 15.8.1956:editorial. These editorials were written for the memorial day marking the end of the war.
52 The Institute of Statistical Mathematics in Tokyo conducted an opinion survey on constitutional revision 17 times from 1954 to 1962. Until 1959 about 30% favoured 'should revise it soon' and another 30% preferred 'should not revise it at all'. During the same period, only 10% were for 'unadvisable now' to revise it. But this ratio rose sharply to nearly 35% by 1962.
53 In the Sunagawa case of 1959, the Supreme Court ruled that Japan's constitutional ban on rearmament did not prohibit the stationing of US troops on Japanese soil. Following the popular acceptance of the existing SDF, LDP politicians also began to argue that a sovereign nation has the right of self-defence, and thus that any armed forces for self-defence do not violate Article 9. Therefore, Prime Minister Ikeda stated, 'the existing self-defence capability is within the limits of the constitution'. See HRC 1961:(38)25.
54 See editorials in *Asahi Shinbun* 15.8.1963; 15.8.1964; *Yomiuri Shinbun* 15.8.1965; 15.8.1966. For a sense of Japanese victim-hood that many influential Japanese sought to cultivate, see Igarashi 2000; Orr 2001.
55 For a clear argument of this point, see the editorial in *Asahi Shinbun* 15.8.1972.
56 The Cabinet Public Relations Office conducted a public opinion survey on this question in 1963, 1965, 1970, and for every three years since 1978.
57 See Hastings & Hastings (eds), *Index to international public opinion*, various years. There are some exceptions between 1969 and 1990; in 1969 Americans favouring reduction in defence spending rose to over 50% and in 1981 those supporting increases also had a majority.
58 Sources from OECD 1981 and OECD 1980–2001.
59 The Japanese government defines collective self-defence as 'the right to use armed force to stop an armed attack on a foreign country with which the state has close relations, even if the state itself is not under direct attack.' See MOD 2007.
60 For the relationships between Japan's economy and fiscal size, see Statistical Bureau 1973–1980, (ch 3, 5).
61 For military officials' view, see *Asahi Shinbun* 8.9.1975.
62 To accept the 1976 National Defence Program Outline, for example, the then Ministry of International Trade and Industry (MITI) was actively involved in the

advancement of the defence industry. At that time, the Ministry of Foreign Affairs was less optimistic about the assessment of détente than the Defence Agency. See *Asahi Shinbun* Tokyo edition, 10.10.1976; *Nihon Keizai Shinbun* 10.8.1976.

63 In the 1980s when influential LDP politicians led a strong campaign for constitutional reform, two-thirds of LDP Diet members were pro-revision but few wished to include it on their political agenda. Only 14–17% of LDP Diet members wished to actively participate in the campaign. See *Mainichi Shinbun* 20.10.1980; *Asahi Shinbun* 4.11.1980.

64 It should be noted that Pempel has come to acknowledge the increasing influence of politicians over bureaucrats in his later work. See Pempel 1992:19–24.

65 A Special Measures Law for the Promotion of Designated Industries, for example, was proposed in 1963 but it was too discriminatory for any politician to support and died in the Diet. Also see Haley 1991:chp7.

66 In 1951 the Keidanren created a 'Working Group on US–Japan Economic Co-operation' out of which the Defence Production Committee grew to promote Japan's defence industry.

67 LDP national politicians who are regarded as experts on specific policy areas due to their experience are called *zoku* (policy group). See Inoguchi & Iwai 1987.

68 Besides Genda, there were several former uniformed officers who turned into Diet members. Given the fact that the SDF were the largest body of government employees in Japan representing 240,000 personnel, this degree of SDF-related electoral success has been much smaller than expected. In 1977 Horie Masao from the GSDF was elected for the upper house (retired in 1989). In 1986 Nagano Shigeto, GSDF chief of staff, was elected to replace Genda in the upper house. In 1989 Tamura Hideaki from the ASDF became an upper house legislator to replace Horie. In recent years, there have been no Diet members with uniformed officer backgrounds until the 2007 success of Colonel Sato Masahisa, the commander of the Samawah Mission, for the upper house election.

69 The *kokubo zoku* were affiliated with three committees of the LDP's Policy Affairs Research Council, which examined policy initiatives and legislative drafts prepared by the bureaucracy: the National Defence Division, the Security Affairs Research Council, and the Base Countermeasures Special Committee.

70 Sources in this section are from the 'Survey of Cabinet and Party Approval Ratings' conducted by *Asahi Shinbun* Yoron Chosashitsu since July 1946. Those of 'do not know' and 'no response' are excluded from the figures.

71 Miyake Ichiro compiled the JES (Japanese Election Studies) Data to highlight the attributes of floating voters in the 1983 simultaneous elections for the lower and upper houses. Miyake 1995:143–73.

72 Under the NDPO, Japan committed itself to defending Japanese soil against a limited invasion and calling for US help only if unable to stop the invasion on its own. In 1978, Japan made its tentative commitment for the first time to work toward defending its sea lanes out to 1,000 nautical miles.

73 By the late 1970s, Director General of the Defence Agency Kanemaru successfully persuaded LDP leaders to meet US demands for greater cost-sharing for maintenance

of US military forces in Japan. Under the US–Japan Security Treaty, Japan had already been obliged to offer facilities and areas to the US forces in Japan at Japan's expense. In the late 1970s, the Japanese government began to further increase the scope of its contributions, such as improvement of facilities and housing of US bases in Japan.

74 For the budget of the Defence Facilities Administration Agency and Host Nation Support, see Asahi Shinbun Sha, ed, *Asahi Nenkan* (Asahi Annuals), various years.

75 'Joint Communique Following Discussions with Prime Minister Zenko Suzuki of Japan' (May 8, 1981), Ronald Reagan Residential Library, Archives, Public Papers of Ronald Reagan, August 7, 2005, http://reagan.utexas.edu.library.unl.edu/archives/speeches/1981/81may.htm

76 The ratios to total aid flows in this section were adopted from MOFA, *Keizaikyoryoku ni Kansuru Kihon Shiryo* (Basic Document of Economic Assistance), internal reports, February 1983.

77 According to an opinion poll, the *Gaiko ni Kansuru Yoron Chosa* (Opinion Poll on Foreign Policy), conducted in 1981 by the Cabinet Office, 43.1% of respondents believed that Japan 'should actively promote *keizai kyoryoku*' (economic foreign aid), 34.2% that Japan should maintain the status quo of economic foreign aid, and 5.0% that Japan should 'contribute as little as possible'.

78 US Department of State Memorandum of Conversation between Nixon and former Prime Minister Kishi, 6 October 1970.

79 There were US measures to place an import surcharge exclusively on Japanese goods. In August 1971, President Nixon imposed a 10% surcharge on Japanese imports to the US market in order to issue an ultimatum to Japan to restrict textile imports to the United States.

80 The increase in anti-dumping cases in the 1980s was associated with the rise of petitions that cited several countries, including Japan, for dumping the same product, such as steel and semiconductors, in the US market. In the mid-1980s, for example, the US government came under intense pressure to intervene and protect the semiconductor industry. The US Commerce Department, in an unprecedented move, initiated an anti-dumping action and threatened to set a high floor price on DRAMs (Dynamic Random Access Memory—semiconductors). In 1986 Japan conceded and further forced Japanese semiconductor firms to curtail production to the US market.

81 The voluntary export restraint (VER) was extensively applied in the early 1980s when Japanese car makers 'voluntarily' limited their exports of cars to the US market. It was essentially a quantity-fixing cartel in which the MITI, under strong US pressure, arranged the quota. The restraint was said to be not a 'unilateral' but rather a 'mutual' agreement between the United States and Japan.

82 See 'First Annual Report of the US–Japan Working Group on the Structural Impediments Initiative (22.5.1991),' US–Japan Working Group on the Structural Impediments Initiative, 23.9.2005, http://www.mac.doc.gov/japan/source/MENU/Miscellaneous/ta910522.html.

83 In the past, action on trade with Japan had been driven primarily by bureaucratic interests within the executive branch other than congressional and business demands, such as those of the Commerce Department and the Office of the US Trade Representative. However, once Clinton took office in 1993, his top policy advisors began to take trade with Japan as a critical national security concern.

84 MITI's officials at the working level still objected and saw US–Japan defence technology co-operation as a one-way flow of technology in the sense that the United States would continue to sell military hardware to Japan without disclosing the unknown technology, yet Japan would have to give up its home-grown technology to the United States. For Japanese industry, they needed to make sure that their participation in technology transfer agreements would relax technology transfers from the United States to Japan, too.

85 The Joint Military Technology Commission (JMTC), created by the 1983 agreement to oversee technology transfers, initially approved the Toshiba 'Keiko' surface-to-air missile but it was never implemented due to Toshiba's sale of an advanced milling machine that was to be used for Soviet submarines. There were two other cases concerned with shipbuilding technology, which was sold to US military shipyards. All in all, LDP leaders followed the lead of both the JDA and the MITI, which adopted a very restricted approach to dual-use technology transfers.

86 In the early 1990s, despite the differences in bureaucratic interests in Japan, the national bureaucracy as a whole was shifting away from purely home-grown projects. Even Japan's Defence Agency—and especially its Equipment Bureau—clearly understood the increasing necessity of collaboration with the United States to keep up with the growing complexity of large-scale, advanced defence systems, while seeing Japan's dual-use technologies as bargaining chips to be used in negotiations with the United States over national security. See JDA 1994.

87 From Japan's Cabinet Office, 'Kokumin Seikatsu ni Kansuru Yoron Chosa' (Opinion Survey on National Lifestyles). The Cabinet Public Relations Office of Japan's Cabinet Office has conducted an annual public opinion survey on national lifestyle since 1954 (except in 1998 and 2000 when the office did not conduct it). The office has administered a lengthy questionnaire to 10,000 men and women 20 years of age or above.

88 The contents of the pro/anti-revision questions in all the surveys was almost identical, but the sequence of the questions and other related questions differed with each survey. This may explain some differences in the survey results; however, it is evident that the overall trend was pro-revision-oriented.

89 See a public opinion survey conducted by the Japan Broadcasting Corporation 2–5.3.2002; another by *Yomiuri Shinbun* 20–21.3.2004.

90 See a public opinion survey conducted by the Japan Broadcasting Corporation 2–4.3.2002.

91 In February and March 2004, the *Yomiuri Shinbun* administered an opinion survey of 476 lower house members on the constitutional issue. Of the 297 usable responses, LDP members represented 47% and Democratic Party members accounted for 39%. See *Yomiuri Shinbun* 17.3.2004. The Japanese government claimed that Japan has the

'inherent right' of collective self-defence as a sovereign nation, including collective security activities under UN peace enforcement operations and joint military operations with US forces, but it has been interpreting Article 9 as a prohibition of collective self-defence.

92 In April 2004, the *Mainichi Shinbun* conducted an opinion survey of 722 lower and upper houses members on constitutional revision. The party-based breakdown figures are available for the 545 respondents. See *Mainichi Shinbun* 3.5.2004.

93 Thirty-six LDP Diet members defected over electoral reform issues in 1993, and the LDP lost power accordingly. The opposition parties' coalition (except the Japan Communist Party) came to power and rammed through legislation on electoral reform in 1994.

94 The new electoral system for the House of Representatives consisted of 500 seats, 300 elected in single-member districts and 200 (later reduced to 180) in eleven regional proportional representation districts. Each voter has two ballots: one for the name of a candidate in the single-member district and the other for the name of a party in the regional proportional representation district. It was introduced in the expectation that the dynamics of this new system would be driven, not by personal constituency-service, but rather by broad policy-oriented elections.

95 The concept of 'areas surrounding Japan' seemed to implicitly include the Korean peninsula and Taiwan. China questioned the real intention behind this concept.

96 Armitage presented a bipartisan study group report, 'The United States and Japan: Advancing toward a Mature Partnership,' which was known as the Armitage Report. Participants in this group, such as James Kelly and Torkel Patterson, became key players in formulating Bush's policy toward Asia.

97 The law allows the deployment of the MSDF ships to the Indian Ocean in support of coalition forces conducting operations in Afghanistan. In December 2002, the Koizumi government decided to dispatch a SDF's Aegis-equipped destroyer under this law.

98 The *Asahi Shinbun* telephone poll conducted on 28–29 September 2001 showed that 62% supported Japan's co-operation with the United States. See *Asahi Shinbun* 1.10.2001. Another poll conducted by *Nihon Keizai Shinbun* on 21–22 September showed that 70% were in favour of Japan's support for US military action. See *Nihon Keizai Shinbun* 25.9.2001.

99 Cabinet Public Relations Office of Japan's Cabinet Office, a public opinion survey on national security, 1991, 1994, 1997 and 2000.

100 Japan Broadcasting Corporation, a public opinion survey conducted 2–4.3.2002.

101 The permissible activities are listed in the Appendices of the law.

102 These principles specify conditions that a cease-fire be in effect, that the consent of parties in conflict be received, that the SDF observe neutrality, that the only use of force allowed by the SDF be for self-defence, and that the Japanese government withdraw the SDF if hostilities become eminent.

103 The law was amended to enable the SDF to participate in international disaster relief operations overseas and to transport personnel and goods for these operations.

104 To give some substance to the 1987 US–Japan Guidelines for Defence Co-operation, the domestic law is an attempt to clarify what Japan could do to support the Unites States in case of security contingencies in East Asia. It authorises the SDF to use force to protect themselves as well as those who are with them in the same activities, but explicitly prohibits the SDF from taking action that can be construed as use of force.

105 Opponents argued that the extensive air defence capability and joint operationality of the Aegis would violate the prohibition on collective self-defence. The data collected by the Aegis system with air-defence radar were to be linked by computer to US Navy ships. This was viewed as Japan exercising the right to collective self-defence.

106 The Japanese government was known to be overtly preoccupied with their sailors' comfort. It was reported that the Aegis destroyer had an inside temperature of 25°C, providing sailors with more comfort in operations.

107 A *Yomiuri Shinbun* poll also indicated that 43% of respondents opposed dispatch while 30% supported dispatch. See *Yomiuri Shinbun* 15.7.2003.

108 These results seemed to come from public reaction to the Japanese hostage crisis of April 2004 when several Japanese civilians had been taken hostage by an Iraqi group. The Japanese government had decided not to withdraw the SDF from Iraq to meet the demand of the hostage takers. Interestingly enough, the hostage incident appeared to increase support for the presence of SDF in Iraq.

109 Nippon Television Network Corporation, *Nippon Terebi Yoron Chosa* (NTV Public Opinion Polls), available at http://www.ntv.co.jp/yoron/, last accessed July 2007.

110 Prime Minister Abe cited specific cases as pending matters: the questions of whether Japan could (1) launch interceptor missiles to shoot down a ballistic missile fired from North Korea toward the United States, (2) provide cover to US Navy ships under attack in international waters near Japan, (3) provide cover to other militaries co-operating in an international reconstruction assistance project, and (4) provide rear support to the US military when it is engaged in a military confrontation. See *Asahi Shinbun* 28.4.2007.

111 See a report, submitted by an advisory committee to Prime Minister Takeshita Toru on 27 April 1989, 'Seiji Kaikaku ni kansuru Yushikisha Kaigi Teigen' (Proposals for Political Reform by the Panel of Experts), available at http://www.secj.jp/pdf/19890427-1.pdf, last accessed September 2007; another report, submitted by an advisory council on the electoral system to Prime Minister Kaifu on 26 April 1990, 'Senkyo Seido oyobi Seiji Shikin Seido no Kaikaku ni tsuite no Toshin' (Proposals for Reforms of Electoral Systems and Political Financing), available at http://www.secj.jp/pdf/19900426-2.pdf, last accessed September 2007.

112 The new electoral system allows candidates to run from a single-member district and at the same time to be listed as a party's proportional representation candidate. As a result, this double-candidacy system has produced some candidates who lost in a single-seat election but returned by a proportional representation. This system was included in the electoral reform to persuade those who opposed the single-member district system.

113 The figures in this section are calculated according to data provided by MIAC 2007.
114 In 1994 the Political Funds Control Law was passed as part of the political reform legislation, including the new electoral system bill. It was intended to shift responsibility for fund-raising from individual politicians/factions to party headquarters.
115 In 2001 the Cabinet Law was revised to clearly state the Cabinet Secretariat's authority to initiate policy.
116 Some scholars suggest that Koizumi's leadership was a sign of the rising importance of prime ministers in Japan—a phenomenon known as 'presidentialisation'—leading to a personalised government. See Krauss & Nyblade 2005:357–68.
117 The figures are an average based on the *Asahi Shinbun*'s quarterly polls.
118 The figures are an average based on the *Asahi Shinbun*'s quarterly polls.
119 The figures in this section were adopted from Akarui Senkyo Suishin Kyokai, 'Dai Yonju-yonkai Shugiin Giin Sosenkyo no Jittai'.
120 In the 1979 lower house election, 19.7% of voters belonged to the *koenkai*, and in the 2005 lower house election, the ratio had dropped to 10.2%. See Akarui Senkyo Suishin Kyokai 2006:54.
121 The figures in this section were adopted from Akarui Senkyo Suishin Kyokai 2006.
122 In 2002 the United States and Japan started taking the Defence Policy Review Initiative to reposition the US–Japan alliance. This document was a product of the bilateral effort.
123 The Ministry of Finance does not appropriate the cost of US force relocation in the defence budget or treat it separately from the regular defence budget, but it has targeted the Midterm Defence Program 2005–2009 for cutbacks.

Bibliography

Japanese government publications

Cabinet Office, Jieitai Boei Mondai ni kansuru Yoron Chosa (Opinion Poll on the Self-Defense Forces and Security Problems), 1969, 1972, 1975, 1978, 1981, 1984, 1988, 1991, 1994, 1995, 1997, 2000, 2003, 2006 editions.

Cabinet Secretary, Nihon no Anzen Hosho to Boei no Arikata—Nijyu-isseki e Mukete no Tenbo (Ways of Japan's Security and Defense—Visions for the 21st Century) Okurasho Insatsukyoku, Tokyo, 1994.

HCA 1972, Diet House of Councilors, Minutes of the Committee on Audit, 14 September.

HCB 1952, Diet House of Councilors, Minutes of the Committee on the Budget, 6 March.

HCC 1954a, Diet House of Councilors, Minutes of the Committee on the Cabinet, 19 May.

—— 1954b, Diet House of Councilors, Minutes of the Committee on the Cabinet, 27 May.

—— 1972a, Diet House of Councilors, Minutes of the Committee on the Cabinet, 8 April.

—— 1972b, Diet House of Councilors, Minutes of the Committee on the Cabinet, 12 May.

—— 1972c, Diet House of Councilors, Minutes of the Committee on the Cabinet, 18 May.

—— 1974, Diet House of Councilors, Minutes of the Committee on the Cabinet, 30 September.

—— 1982, Diet House of Councilors, Minutes of the Committee on the Cabinet, 19 August.

HCI 1987, Diet House of Councilors, Minutes of the Committee on Investigations of Diplomacy and Comprehensive Security, 21 August.

HCPS 1954a, Diet House of Councilors, Minutes of Plenary Session, 6 February.

—— 1954b, Diet House of Councilors, Minutes of Plenary Session, 2 June.

—— 1958, Diet House of Councilors, Minutes of Plenary Session, 14 February.

HRA 1967, Diet House of Representatives, Minutes of the Committee on Audit, 21 April.

HRB 1952, Diet House of Representatives, Minutes of the Committee on Budgets, 31 January.

—— 1967a, Diet House of Representatives, Minutes of the Committee on Budgets, 26 April.

—— 1967b, Diet House of Representatives, Minutes of the Committee on Budgets, 11–12 December.

—— 1970, Diet House of Representatives, Minutes of the Committee on Budgets, 24 February.

—— 1973, Diet House of Representatives, Minutes of the Committee on Budgets, 1 February.

—— 1986, Diet House of Representatives, Minutes of the Committee on Budgets, 18 February.

HRC 1961, Diet House of Representatives, Minutes of the Committee on the Cabinet, 13 April.

—— 1969a, Diet House of Representatives, Minutes of the Committee on the Cabinet, 24 June.

—— 1969b, Diet House of Representatives, Minutes of the Committee on the Cabinet, 8 October.

HRCI 2003a, Diet, House of Representatives, Minutes of the Special Committee on Iraq, 25 June.

—— 2003b, Diet, House of Representatives, Minutes of the Special Committee on Iraq, 3 July.

HRCRC 2001, Diet House of Representatives, Minutes of the Constitution Research Council, 6 December.

HRCS 1988, Diet, House of Representatives, Minutes of the Special Committee on Security, 9 November.

HRECB 2002 Diet House of Representative, Minutes of the Special Committee on Emergency Contingency Bills, 3 July.

—— 2003 Diet House of Representative, Minutes of the Special Committee on Emergency Contingency Bills, 20 May.

HRFA 1972, Diet, House of Representative, Minutes of the Committee on Foreign Affairs, 24 May.

—— 1982, Diet, House of Representative, Minutes of the Committee on Foreign Affairs, 27 May.

HRPS 1950, Diet House of Representatives, Minutes of Plenary Session, 29 July.

—— 1971, Diet House of Representatives, Minutes of Plenary Session, 24 November.

—— 1972, Diet House of Representatives, Minutes of Plenary Session, 30 October.

—— 1985, Diet House of Representatives, Minutes of Plenary Session, 30 January.

—— 1991, Diet House of Representatives, Minutes of Plenary Session, 25 January.

—— 2003a, Diet House of Representatives, Minutes of Plenary Session, 5 June.

—— 2003b, Diet House of Representatives, Minutes of Plenary Session, 24 June.

—— 2004, Diet House of Representatives, Minutes of Plenary Session, 2 November.

HRUSJ 1960, Diet, House of Representatives, Minutes of the Special Committee on US–Japan Security Treaty, 28 April.

JDA 1976, Defense of Japan 1976, Japanese Defense Agency, Okurasho Insatsukyoku, Tokyo.

—— 1978, Boeicho ni okeru Yujihosei Kenkyu ni tsuite, (Regarding Research on Emergency Contingency at the Defense Agency), Japanese Defense Agency, Tokyo.

—— 1994 'Boei Sangyo Gijutsu Kondankai Hokokusho' (Report of the Advisory Panel on Defense Industry and Technology), Japanese Defense Agency, 18 March 1994.

—— 2001 'Boei Kankeihi no Suii' (Trends in Defense Budgets), Japanese Defense Agency, available at: http://www.jda.go.jp/j/library/wp/2001/siryo/dg13016a.htm, last accessed August 2005.

—— 2005, 'Nihon no Boei Seisangaku nado no Suii' (Trends in Japan's Defense Industrial Production), Japanese Defense Agency, available at http://ida-clearing.jda.go.jp/hakusho_data/2005/2005/html/17s57000.html, last accessed July 2007.

—— 2006, Boei Hakusho (Defence of Japan) 2006 edition, Japanese Defence Agency, Gyosei, Tokyo

METI 2000, Japan Ministry of Economy, Trade and Industry, Boei Sangyo Gijutsu Kiban no Iji Ikusei ni Kansuru Kihonteki Hoko (Basic Directions for the Maintenance and Nurture of Defense Industry Foundations), November 2000, available at http://www.meti.go.jp/report/downloadfiles/g01120bj.pdf, last accessed July 2007.

MIAC 2007, Senyo kanren Shiryo (Data on Elections), Ministry of Internal Affairs and Communications, available at http://www.soumu.go.jp/senkyo/senkyo_s/data/index.html, last accessed September 2007.

MOD 1975–1995, Boei Hakusho (Defence White Paper), Ministry of Defense, available at: http://www.clearing.mod.go.jp/hakusho_web/; site last accessed January 2007

―― 1975–2006, Boei Hakusho (Defense White Paper) Ministry of Defense, available at: http://www.clearing.mod.go.jp/hakusho_web/; site last accessed January 2007.

―― 2004, National Defense Program Guideline for FY 2005, 10 December, Ministry of Defense, available at http://www.mod.go.jp/e/policy/f-work/taikou05/fy20050101.pdf, last accessed September 2007.

―― 2007, 'Fundamental Concepts of National Defense,' Ministry of Defense, available at: http://www.mod.go.jp/e/d_policy/index.html, last accessed July 2007.

MOFA 1979, Gaiko Seisho: Showa 53-nen-ban (Diplomatic Bluebook 1978) Ministry of Foreign Affairs, Okurasho Insatsukyoku, Tokyo.

―― 1983, Keizaikyoryoku ni Kansuru Kihon Shiryo (Basic Document of Economic Assistance), Ministry of Foreign Affairs, internal reports, February 1983.

―― 1993, Gaiko Seisho: Heisei 4-nen-ban (Diplomatic Blue Book 1992) Ministry of Foreign Affairs, Okurasho Insatsukyoku, Tokyo.

――1994, Gaiko Seisho: Heisei 5-nen-ban (Diplomatic Blue Book 1993) Ministry of Foreign Affairs, Okurasho Insatsukyoku, Tokyo.

――1995a, Gaiko Seisho: Heisei 7-nen-ban (Diplomatic Bluebook 1995), Ministry of Foreign Affairs, available at: http://www.mofa.go.jp/mofaj/gaiko/bluebook/1995_1/h07-shiryou-1-2.htm#a3, last accessed May 2007.

――1995b, 'National Defense Program Outline in and after FY 1996' (tentative unofficial translation), Ministry of Foreign Affairs, 28 November 1995, available at http://www.mofa.go.jp/region/n-america/us/q&a/ref/6a.html, last accessed September 2007.

――1996, 'US–Japan Joint Declaration on Security: Alliance for the 21st Century,' Ministry of Foreign Affairs, Tokyo, 17 April 1996, available at: http://www.mofa.go.jp/region/n-america/us/security/security.html, last accessed April 2007.

―― 1997, 'The Guidelines of US–Japan Defense Co-operation,' Ministry of Foreign Affairs, September 1997, available at http://www.mofa.go.jp/region/n-america/us/security/guideline2.html, last accessed July 2007.

―― 2005, Nichi-Bei Shuno Kaidan no Gaiyou (Overview of Japan–US Summit), Ministry of Foreign Affairs, 26 May 2005, available at http://www.mofa.go.jp/mofa/kaidan/s_koi/us-me_03/us_gh.html, site last accessed December 2005.

NDPG 2005, Cabinet Secretariat, National Defense Program Guideline, FY 2005 -, available at http://www.kantei.go.jp/foreign/policy/2004/1210taikou_e.html, site last accessed May 2007.

PMJC 2003, Statement by Prime Minister Koizumi Junichiro 9 December 2003, Prime Minister of Japan and His Cabinet, available at http://www.kantei.go.jp/jp/koizumispeech/2003/12/09danwa.html, site last accessed October 2005.

—— 2007, 'Tero Taisaku Tokubetsu Sochi Ho' (Anti-Terror Special Measures Law), Prime Minister of Japan and His Cabinet, June 2007, available at http://www.cas. go.jp/jp/hourei/houritu/tero_h.html, last accessed September 2007.

US Government publications

SCC 2005, *US–Japan Alliance: Transformation and Realignment for the Future*, US–Japan Security Consultative Committee, 29 October 2005, available at http://www.mod.go.jp/j/news/youjin/2005/10/1029-2plus2/29-e.htm, last accessed September 2007.

SCC 2006, *United States-Japan Roadmap for Realignment Implementation*, US–Japan Security Consultative Committee, 1 May 2006, available at http://www.mod.go.jp/j/news/youjin/2006/05/0501-e02.html, last accessed September 2007.

USC 1977 *Planning US General Purpose Forces: Forces Related to Asia*, Congress, USGPO Washington, DC.

USDD 1983, *Soviet Military Power*, 2nd edition, Department of Defense, USGPO Washington, DC.

—— 1990, *A Strategic Framework for the Asian Pacific Rim: Looking Toward the 21st Century*, Department of Defense, USGPO Washington, DC.

—— 1995, Office of International Security Affairs, *United States Security Strategy for the East Asia-Pacific Region* (February) Department of Defense, Office of International Security Affairs, Department of Defense, Washington DC.

—— 1996, 'US–Japan Defense Equipment and Technology Cooperation,' briefing paper, May, Department of Defense, Office of the Under Secretary for Acquisition and Technology.

USDS 1957, 'Memorandum from the Joint Chiefs of Staff to the Secretary of Defense', Department of State, June.

USHRAS 1988, *Measures of Defense Burdensharing and US Proposals for Increasing Allied Burdensharing*: hearing held 10 May 1988, Congress, House of Representatives, Committee on Armed Services, Burdensharing Panel, USGPO Washington, DC.

USHRIR 1977, *Security Issues in the Far East*, Congress, House of Representatives, Committee on International Relations, USGPO, Washington DC .

USOTA 1990, *Arming Our Allies: Cooperation and Competition in Defense Technology*, Congress, Office of Technology Assessment, USGPO Washington, DC.

USP 1975, *International Economic Report of the President*, transmitted to the Congress (March), USGPO Washington, DC.

USSAS 1979, *United States–Japan Security Relationship: The Key to East-Asian Security and Stability*: report of the Pacific Study Group to the Committee on Armed Services, US Senate, 22 March 1979, Congress, USGPO Washington, DC.

USSFA 1976, *The End of the Postwar Era: Time for a New Partnership of Equality with Japan,* Congress, Senate, Committee on Foreign Affairs, USGPO Washington, DC.

USSWN 1945, 'US Initial Post-Surrender Policy for Japan,' document No. 150/4/A, 21 September, State, War, Navy Coordinating Committee (SWNCC).

WGSII 1991, 'First Annual Report of the US–Japan Working Group on the Structural Impediments Initiative' (May 22, 1991), available at http://www.mac.doc.gov/ japan/source/MENU/Miscellaneous/ta910522.html, last accessed September 2005.

Newspapers

Asagumo Shinbun, 19 March 1970.

Asahi Shinbun, 5 and 6 September 1945, 15 August 1954, 22 December 1954 (Evening edition), 20 May 1960, 22 October 1960 (Evening edition), 15 August 1963, 15 August 1964, 19 and 31 March 1970, 18-25 November 1971, 15 August 1972, 6 June 1975, 8 September 1975, 5 November 1976, 4 November 1980, 8 December 1980, 28 April 1982, 16 December 1989, 27 January 1990, 15 August 1990, 1 October 1990, 1 and 6 November 1990, 18 December 1990, 24 April 1991, 15 August 1991, 28 February 1995, 15 August 1995, 7 January 2001, 2 May 2001, 20 September 2001, 1 October 2001, 27 November 2001, 4 September 2002, 3 and 16 December 2002, 27 January 2003, 25 February 2003, 22, 30 and 31 March 2003, 25 and 26 June 2003, 30 June 2003 (Evening edition), 1 and 22 July 2003, 25 August 2003 (Evening edition), 2 November 2003, 16 March 2004, 17 April 2004, 22 and 29 June 2004, 23 July 2004, 26 October 2004, 21 December 2004, 3 May 2005, 30 November 2005, 28 April 2007, 3 October 2007.

Asahi Shinbun, Tokyo edition, 6 June 1975, 10 October 1976.

Asia Times Online, 19 December 2002.

The Associated Press, 6 December 2002.

Daily Yomiuri, 20 March 1990, 19 August 1990, 22 September 2001, 25 October 2001, 19 November 2001, 24 July 2004.

Japan Times, 15 February 1970, 17 May 2000, 21 September 2001, 23 and 24 December 2001, 6 December 2002, 18 March 2003, 31 August 2003, 13 February 2004, 23 July 2004, 21 June 2006, 17 December 2006, 14 and 26 April 2007, 12 May 2007.

Kyodo News, 28 September 2001, 1 October 2001, 6 November 2001, 13 August 2003, 2 November 2004.

Mainichi Shinbun, 27 May 1946, 15 August 1955, 15 August 1956, 29 March 1970, 16 March 1971, 20 October 1980, 21 October 1990, 14 June 1991, 15 August 1991, 15 August 1992, 15 August 1995, 5 January 1996, 15 August 1997, 3 November 2003, 8 March 2004, 19 April 2004, 3 May 2004, 15 June 2004, 10 October 2005, 2 and 3 May 2007.

New York Times, 3 August 1969, 22 November 1969, 30 August 1990, 19 September 2001.

Osaka Mainichi Shinbun, 5 and 30 September 1945.

Sankei Shinbun, 28 March 1982, 18 April 2002, 5 December 2005.

Singapore Straits Times, 6 December 2002.

This is Yomiuri, 1997 'Nihon-Koku Kenpo no Subete' (All points of the Japanese Constitution), special edition, May.

Tokyo Shinbun, 14 May 2007.

Wall Street Journal, 17 January 1991.

Washington Post, 29 January 1989, 27 March 1990, 20 September 2001, 16 December 2006.

Yomiuri Hochi, 5 and 6 September 1945.

Yomiuri Shinbun, 15 August 1965, 15 August 1966, 28 April 1971, 7 July 1977, 20 May 1980, 20 July 1980, 25 October 1990, 15 August 1992, 6 April 1995, 21 September 2001, 18 November 2001, 4 May 2002, 1 December 2002, 15 July 2003, 24 October 2003, 17 March 2004, 2 April 2004, 28 June 2004, 2 November 2004, 26 April 2006, 23 September 2007.

Books and articles

Advisory Group on Defense Issues 1994, (ed), 'Nihon no anzen hosho to boeiryoku no arikata' (The modality of the security and defense capabilities of Japan—the outlook for the 21st Century), 12 August.

Akarui Senkyo Suishin Kyokai, 2006, 'Dai yonju-yonkai shugiin giin sosenkyo no jittai' (The actual condition of the 44th House of Representative election) Akarui Senkyo Suishin Kyokai, Tokyo.

Asagumo Shinbunsha, 2001 (ed), *Boei handobukku* (Defense handbook), 2001 edition, Asagumo Shinbunsha, Tokyo.

Asahi Shinbun Sha, (various years), *Asahi Nenkan* (Asahi Annuals), Asahi Shinbunsha, Osaka.

Asher, Herbert 1998, *Polling and the public: what every citizen should know*, Congressional Quarterly Press, Washington DC.

Bayard, Thomas O and Kimberly A Elliot, 1994, *Reciprocity and retaliation in US trade policy*, Institute for International Economics, Washington, DC.

Berger, Thomas U 1993, 'From sword to chrysanthemum: Japan's culture of anti-militarism' *International Security*, (17)4 (Spring).

—— 1998, *Cultures of antimilitarism: national security in Germany and Japan*, John Hospkins University Press, Baltimore.

Bobrow, Davis 1989, 'Japan in the world: opinion from defeat to success,' *Journal of Conflict Resolution*, (33) December.

Boei Nenkan Kankokai, 1961, *Boei Nenkan* (Defense Annual Report) 1961 editions Boei Nenkan Kankokai, Tokyo.

——, 1971, *Boei Nenkan* (Defense Annual Report) 1971 editions Boei Nenkan Kankokai, Tokyo.

Boei o Kangaeru Jimukyoku, 1975 (ed), *Waga kuni no boei o kangaeru* (Review of our country's defense) Asagumo Shinbunsha, Tokyo.

Bowen, Roger 1992, 'Japan's foreign policy,' *PS: political science and politics*, (25)1 (March).

Braw, Monica 1991, *The atomic bomb suppressed: American censorship in occupied Japan*, ME Sharpe, Armonk, NY.

Business Week, 7 August 1989.

Calder, Kent 1988a, *Crisis and compensation: public policy and political stability in Japan, 1949–1986*, Princeton University Press, Princeton.

—— 1988b, 'Japanese foreign economic policy formation: explaining the "reactive state"' *World Politics*, (40)4 (July).

Campbell, John C 1977, *Contemporary Japanese budget politics*, University of California Press, Berkeley and Los Angeles.

Carmines, Edward G and James A Stimson 1989, *Issue evolution: race and the transformation of American politics*, Princeton University Press, Princeton.

Cha, Victor D 1999, *Alignment despite antagonism: the US-Korea-Japan security triangle*, Stanford University Press, Stanford.

Chai, Sun-Ki 1997, 'Entrenching the Yoshida Defense Doctrine: three techniques for institutionalization,' *International Organization*, (51)3 (Summer).

Chanda, Nayan 1988, 'Biting the bullet,' *Far Eastern Economic Review*, 29 September.

Checkel, Jeffrey T 1998, 'The constructivist turn in international relations theory,' *World Politics*, (50)2 (January).

Chomsky, Noam and Edward Herman 1988, *Manufacturing consent*, Pantheon, New York.

Christensen, Thomas J 1996, *Useful adversaries: grand strategy, domestic mobilization, and Sino-American conflict, 1947–1958*, Princeton University Press, Princeton.

Christensen, Thomas J and Jack Snyder 1990, 'Chain gangs and passed bucks: predicting alliance patterns in multipolarity,' *International Organization*, (44)2 (Spring).

Comprehensive Security Study Group, 1980, *Sogo anzen hosho kenkyu gurupu Hokokusho* (Study group report on comprehensive security), Comprehensive Security Study Group, Tokyo, July.

Council on Security and Defense Capabilities, 2004, *Japan's vision for future security and defense capability*, Council on Security and Defense Capabilities, Tokyo.

Cronin, Richard P 1994, 'Japanese and US economic involvement in Asia and the Pacific,' *CRS (Congressional Research Service) Report*, (94–764)F (September).

Curtis, Gerald L 1971, *Election campaigning, Japanese style*, Columbia University Press, New York.

—— 1988, *The Japanese way of politics*, Columbia University Press, New York.

Dekle, Robert 1989, 'The relationship between defense spending and economic performance in Japan,' in Makin, John H and Donald C Hellmann (eds), *Sharing world leadership? A new era for America and Japan*, American Enterprise Institute for Public Policy Research, Washington DC.

Destler, IM, Hideo Sato, Priscilla Clapp, and Haruhiro Fukui 1976, *Managing an alliance: the politics of US–Japan Relations*, Brookings Institution, Washington DC.

Destler, IM, Haruhiro Fukui and Hideo Sato 1979, *The textile wrangle: conflict in Japanese American relations, 1969–1971*, Cornell University Press, Ithaca NY.

Dixon, Anne M 1999, 'Can eagles and cranes flock together?,' in Green, Michael J and Patrick M Cronin (eds), *The US–Japan alliance: past, present, and future*, Council on Foreign Relations Press, New York.

Dower, John W 1979, *Empire and aftermath: Yoshida Shigeru and the Japanese experience, 1878–1954*, Harvard University Press, Cambridge MA.

Duverger, Maurice 1954, *Political parties: their organization and activity in the modern state*, John Wiley, New York.

Eckstein, Harry 1988, 'A culturalist theory of political change,' *American Political Science Review*, (82).

Eichenberg, Richard 1981, 'Defense welfare tradeoffs in West German defense budgeting,' PhD dissertation, University of Michigan.

—— 1989, *Public opinion and national security in Western Europe: consensus lost?* Cornell University Press, Ithaca.

Emmerson, John K 1971, *Arms, yen and power: the Japanese dilemma*, Dunellen, New York.

Foreign Broadcasting Information Service, 25 June 1990.

Garon, Sheldon 1997, *Molding Japanese mind: the state in everyday life*, Princeton University Press, Princeton, NJ.

George, Aurelia, 1991 'Japan's America problem: the Japanese response to US pressure,' *The Washington Quarterly*, (14) Summer.

Glaser, Chales L 1996, 'Realists as optimists: cooperation as self-help,' *Security Studies*, (5)3 (Spring).

Gotoda, Masaharu 1990, 'Kaigai hahei o tadasu' (Rectifying the overseas dispatch), *Gekkan Asahi* (December).

Green, Michael J 1995, *Arming Japan: defense production, alliance politics, and the postwar search for autonomy*, Columbia University Press, New York.

Green, Michael J and Richard J Samuels 1994, 'Recalculating autonomy: Japan's choices in the new world order,' *The National Bureau of Asian Research Analysis*, (5)4 (December).

Haley, John O 1991, *Authority without power: law and the Japanese paradox*, Oxford University Press, New York.

Hastings and Hastings, (eds), *Index to international public opinion*, various years.

Havens, Thomas RH 1987, *Fire across the sea: the Vietnam War and Japan, 1965–1975*, Princeton University Press, Princeton.

Hayashi, Shuzo et al 1989, 'Seiji kaikaku no kansuru yushikisha kaigi teigen' (Proposals for political reform by the panel of experts), 27 April, available at http://www.secj.jp/pdf/19890427-1.pdf, last accessed September 2007.

Heginbotham, Eric and Richard J Samuels 1998, 'Mercantile realism and Japanese foreign policy,' *International Security*, (20)4 (Spring).

Hellmann, Donald 1969, *Japanese foreign policy and domestic politics*, University of California Press, Berkeley.

—— 1988, 'Japanese politics and foreign policy: elitist democracy within an American green house,' in Inoguchi, Takashi and Danniel I Okimoto (eds), *The political economy of Japan*, (2), Stanford University Press, Stanford.

—— 1989, 'The imperatives for reciprocity and symmetry in US–Japanese economic and defense relations,' in Makin, John H and Donald C Hellmann (eds), *Sharing world leadership? A new era for America and Japan*, American Enterprise Institute, Washington DC.

Hirano, Sadao 1996, *Ozawa Ichiro to no nijunen* (Twenty years with Ichiro Ozawa), Purejidentosha, Tokyo.

Hirose, Michisada 1981, *Hojokin to seikento* (Subsidies and party in power), Asahi Shinbunsha, Tokyo.

Hiwatari, Nobuhiro 2006, 'Japan in 2005: Koizumi's finest hour,' *Asian Survey*, (46)1 (January/February).

Hook, Glenn D 1986, *Language and politics: the security discourse in Japan and the United States*, Koroshio Shuppansha, Tokyo.

—— 1996, *Militarization and demilitarization in contemporary Japan*, Routledge, London.

Hook, Glenn D and Gavan McCormack 2001, *Japan's contested constitution: documents and analysis*, Routledge, London.

Hook, Glenn D, Julie Gilson, Christopher Hughes and Hugo Dodson 2001, *Japan's international relations: politics, economics and security*, Routledge, London.

Hughes, Christopher 2004, *Japan's reemergence as a 'normal' military power*, Adelphi Paper ISS/Oxford University Press, Oxford.

Hummel, Hartwig 1996, 'Japan's military expenditures after the Cold War: the "realism" of the peace dividend,' *Australian Journal of International Affairs*, (50)2.

Igarashi, Takayoshi 2000, *Bodies of memory: narratives of war in postwar Japanese culture, 1945–1970*, Princeton University Press, Princeton.

Iklé, Fred Charles and Terumasa Nakanishi 1990, 'Japan's grad strategy,' *Foreign Affairs*, (69)3 (Summer).

Imamura, Naraomi 1978, *Hojokin to nogyo noson* (Subsidies, agriculture, and villages), Ie no Hikari Kyokai, Tokyo.

Inoguchi, Takashi 1986, 'Japan's images and options: not a challenger but a supporter,' *Journal of Japanese Studies*, (12)1 (Winter).

Inoguchi, Takashi and Grant B Stillman (eds) 1997, *North-East Asian regional security: the role of international institutions*, United Nations University Press, Tokyo.

Inoguchi, Takashi and Tomoaki Iwai 1987, *Zoku giin no kenkyu* (Studies of Zoku parliamentarians), Nihon Keizai Shinbunsha, Tokyo.

Institute for National Strategies Studies 2000, 'The United States and Japan: advancing toward a mature partnership,' *INSS Special Report* (11 October) 13.

Institute of Oriental Culture 2005, 'The world and Japan' database, available at http://www.ioc.u-tokyo.ac.jp/~worldjpn/, University of Tokyo, last accessed July 2007.

International Monetary Fund (IMF), *Government finance statistics yearbook*, various years.

Iriye, Akira 1991, 'Japan's defense strategy,' *The annals of the American academy of political and social science*, (513)1 (January).

Ishihara, Shintaro 1991, *Japan that can say no*, Simon & Schuster, New York.

Ito, Go 2003, *Alliance in anxiety: détente and the Sino–American–Japanese triangle*, Routledge, New York.

Iwata, Shuichiro 1997, 'Beikoku no gunjisenryaku to nichibei anpotaisei' (US military strategies and the US–Japan security system), *Kokusai Seiji* (International Politics) (115) May.

Japan Statistical Bureau, (ed), *Japan Statistical Yearbook*, various years.

JEI Report 1989, 'Power sharing: future challenge to US–Japan relations?' (Japan Economic Institute) 23 June.

Jervis, Robert 1970, *Perception and misperception in international politics*, Princeton University Press, Princeton.

—— 1978, 'Cooperation under the security dilemma,' *World Politics*, (30).

—— 1989, *The logic of images in international relations*, Columbia University Press, New York.

Johnson, Chalmers 1975, 'Japan: who governs? An essay on official bureaucracy,' *Journal of Japanese Studies*, (2)1.

—— 1995, *Japan: who governs? The rise of the developmental state*, WW Norton, New York.

—— 1996 'The Okinawa rape incident and the end of the Cold War in East Asia,' *IPRI Working Paper*, (16) February.

—— 2005, 'No longer the 'lone' superpower: coming to terms with China,' *JPRI Working Paper*, (105) March.

'Joint communique following discussions with Prime Minister Zenko Suzuki of Japan' (8 May 1981), Ronald Reagan Residential Library, Archives, Public Papers of Ronald Reagan, available at http://www.reagan.utexas.edu.library.unl.edu/archives/speeches/1981/81may.htm, last accessed August 2005.

Kahn, Herman 1970, *The emerging Japanese superstate: challenge and response*, Prentice-Hall, Englewood Cliff, NJ.

Kaihara, Osamu and Takuya Kubo 1979, *Genjitsu no boeirongi* (Realistic defense argument), Sankei Shuppan, Tokyo.

Kamiya, Matake 2002/3, 'Nuclear Japan: oxymoron or coming soon?' *Washington Quarterly*, (26)1.

Katzenstein, Peter J 1996, *Cultural norms and national security: police and military in postwar Japan*, Cornell University Press, Ithaca.

Katzenstein, Peter J and Nobuo Okawara 1993, 'Japan's national security: structures, norms, and policies,' *International Security*, (17)4 (Spring).

—— 2002, 'Japan, Asia–Pacific security, and the case for analytical eclecticism,' *International Security*, (26)3.

Kawato, Sadafumi, Takashi Yoshino, Koji Hirano, and Junko Kato 2001, *Gendai no seito to senkyo* (Contemporary political parties and elections), Yuhikaku, Tokyo.

Keddell, Joseph P Jr 1990, 'Defense as a budgetary problem: the minimization of conflict in Japanese defense policymaking, 1976–1987,' PhD dissertation, University of Wisconsin, Madison, Wisconsin.

—— 1993, *The politics of defense in Japan: managing internal and external pressures*, ME Sharpe, Armonk, NY.

Keohane, Robert O and Joseph S Nye 1977, *Power and interdependence*, Little Brown, Boston.

Keohane, Robert O and Lisa L Martin 1995, 'The promise of institutionalist theory,' *International Security*, (20)1 (Summer).

Kesavan, KV 1984, *Japanese defense policy since 1976: latest trends*, Australian National University Press, Canberra.

Kinema Junpo, January 1950 to December 1959.

Kishi, Nobusuke 1983, *Kishi Nobusuke kaikoroku: hoshugodo to anpokaitei* (Kishi Nobusuke memoir: the merger of conservative forces and security treaty revision), Kosaido Shuppan, Tokyo.

Kosaka, Masataka 1973, *Opinions for Japan's foreign policy*, Adelphi Paper, (97) International Institute for Strategic Studies, London.

Kowert, Paul and Jeffery Lego 1996, 'Norms, identity, and their limits: a theoretical reprise' in Katzenstein, Peter J (ed), *The culture of national security and identity in world politics*, Columbia University Press, New York.

Krauss, Ellis S and Benjamin Nyblade 2005, '"Presidentialization" in Japan? The prime minister, media and elections in Japan', *British Journal of Political Science*, (35).

Kubo, Takuya 1973, 'Heiwaji no boeiryoku' (Defense capability in peacetime), *Kokubo*, (22) April.

Kuroda, Kiyotaka 1989, *Taiheiyo senso no rekishi* (History of the pacific war) (2), Kodansha, Tokyo.

Kuwata, Etsu and Toru Maebara (eds) 1986, *Nihon no senso: zukai to data* (Japan's wars: diagrams and data), Hara Shobo, Tokyo.

Kydd, Andrew H 2005, *Trust and mistrust in international relations*, Princeton University Press, Princeton.

Layne, Christopher 1993, 'The unipolar illusion: why new great powers will rise,' *International Security,* (17)4 (Spring).

LDP Special Study Group on Japan's Role in the International Community, 1992 'Japan's role in the international community—draft report,' *Japan Echo*, (19)2.

Leifer, Michael 1996, *The ASEAN regional forum*, Adelphi Paper (302) Oxford University Press for the International Institute for Strategic Studies, Oxford.

Lijphart, Arend 1994, *Electoral systems and party systems: a study of twenty-seven democracies, 1945–1990*, Oxford University Press, New York.

Lincoln, Edward J 1993, *Japan's new global role,* The Brookings Institution, Washington DC.

Lind, Jennifer M 2004, 'Pacifism or passing the buck? Testing theories of Japanese security policy,' *International Security*, (29)1 (Summer).

Lord, Guy 1973, *The French budgetary process*, University of California Press, Berkeley.

MacArthur, Douglas 1964, *Reminiscences,* Naval Institute Press, Annapolis MD.

Maeda, Yukio 2007, 'Senkyo seido no hi-ikkansei to tohyo handan kijun' (The inconsistency of the electoral system and determinants of voting), *Shakai Kagaku Kenkyu,* (58)5, 6.

Mansfield, Mike 1976, *The end of the postwar era: time for a new partnership of equality with Japan: a report by Mike Mansfield to US Congress, Senate, Committee on Foreign Relations* (USGPO, Washington DC, (August).

Margolis, Michael and Garry Mauser (eds) 1989, *Manipulating public opinion: essays on public opinion as a dependent variable,* Wadsworth, Belmont CA.

Martin, Laurence 1981, 'The domestic content of British defense policy,' in Flynn, Gregory (ed), *The internal fabric of Western security,* Croom Helm, London.

Matsuura, Shigeru 2007, 'Heisei jyu-kyu-nen-do yosan no gaiyo' (Summary of the budget in FY 2007) *Chosa to Joho,* (557) January.

Matthews, Eugene 2003, 'Japan's new nationalism,' *Foreign Affairs,* (82)6 (November/December).

McCormack, Gavan 2004, 'Remilitarizing Japan,' *New Left Review,* (29) September–October, available at http://newleftreview.org/A2525, site last accessed January 2007.

Mearsheimer, John J 2001, *The tragedy of great power politics,* WW Norton, New York.

Mendel, Douglas H Jr 1975, 'Public views of the Japanese defense system,' in Buck, James H (ed), *The modern Japanese military system,* SAGE, Beverly Hills.

Midford, Paul 2000, 'Japan's leadership role in East Asian security multilateralism: the Nakayama proposal and the logic reassurance,' *The Pacific Review,* (13)3.

—— 2002, 'The logic of reassurance and Japan's grand strategy,' *Security Studies,* (11)3 (Spring).

—— 2003, 'Japan's response to terror: dispatching the SDF to the Arabian Sea,' *Asian Survey,* (43)2 (March-April).

—— 2006, *Japanese public opinion and the war on terrorism: implications for Japan's security strategy,* East-West Center, Washington DC.

The military balance 1977–1984, (1977/78 edition–1984/85 edition) Institute for Strategic Studies, London.

Miller, John 2002, 'Japan crosses the Rubicon,' *Asia-Pacific Security Studies,* (1)1.

Miyake, Ichiro 1986, 'Seito shiji to seijiteki imeji' (Party support and political image), in Watanuki, Joji et al, *Nihonjin no senkyo kodo* (Voting behaviour of the Japanese), Tokyo Daigaku Shuppankyokai, Tokyo.

—— 1989, *Tohyo kodo* (Voting behaviour), Tokyo Daigaku Shuppankyokai, Tokyo.

—— 1995, *Nihon no seiji to senkyo* (Japanese electoral politics in disarray), Tokyo Daigaku Shuppankyokai, Tokyo.

—— 2001, *Senkyo seido henkaku to tohyo kodo* (Electoral reform and voting behaviour), Mokutakusha Tokyo.

Miyashita, Akitoshi and Yoichiro Sato (eds) 2001, *Japanese foreign policy in Asia and the Pacific: domestic interests, American pressure, and regional integration*, Palgrave, New York.

Mochizuki, Mike 1983/1984, 'Japan's search for strategy,' *International Security*, (8)3 (Winter).

Morishita, Toru 1995, 'Sengo Nihon kokumin no heiwa ishiki no tenkai' (Developments in the peace consciousness of the Japanese), *Rekishi Hyoron*, (553) May.

Muramatsu, Michio 1981, 'Hojokin seido no seiji gyoseijo no igi (Political and administrative significance of the grants-in-aid system), *Jichi Kenkyu*, (57) September.

Muramatsu, Michio and Ellis S Krauss 1984, 'Bureaucrats and politicians in policymaking: the case of Japan,' *American Political Science Review*, (78).

Murata, Koji 1998, *Daitoryo no zasetsu* (The presidential setback), Yuhikaku, Tokyo.

—— 2007, 'Japan's security policy and US–Japan–China Relations,' in Self, Benjamin and Jeffery Thompson (eds), *An alliance for engagement: building cooperation in security relations with China*, The Henry L Stimson Center, Washington DC.

Muroyama, Yoshimasa 1992, *Nichi-Bei anpo taisei* (US–Japan security regimes), (1) Yuhikaku, Tokyo.

Nakanishi, Terumasa 1990, 'Saying 'yes' to the US–Japan partnership,' *Japan Echo*, (17)1 (Spring).

Nakasone, Yasuhiro 1954, *Nihon no shucho* (Japan's viewpoint) Keizai Orai-sha, Tokyo.

NHK 1995, (Japan Broadcasting Corporation), *NHK supesharu: sengo gojyunen sonotoki nihon wa* (NHK special: Japan in fifty years of postwar), (1) Nihon Hoso Shuppan Kyokai, Tokyo.

—— 1975, Broadcasting Poll Research Institute, (ed), *Zusetsu sengo yoron shi* (Postwar Opinion Polls Illustrated), Nihon Hoso Shuppan Kyokai, Tokyo.

—— 1982, Broadcasting Poll Research Institute, (ed), *Zusetsu sengo yoron-shi* (Postwar

Opinion Polls Illustrated), 2nd ed, Nihon Hoso Shuppan Kyokai, Tokyo.

Nihon Keizai Shinbun, 15 September 1969, 24 March 1970, 7 October 1972, 10 August 1976, 31 August 1980, 15 February 1987, 15 August 1995, 25 September 2001, 25 November 2004, 31 May 2006.

Nippon Television Network Corporation, *Nippon Terebi Yoron Chosa* (NTV Public Opinion Polls), available at http://www.ntv.co.jp/yoron/, last accessed July 2007.

Nye, Joseph S Jr 1995, 'The case for deep engagement,' *Foreign Affairs*, (74)4 (July/August).

Oberdorfer, Don 1997, *The two Koreas*, Addison-Wesley, Reading MA.

O'Hanlon, Michael E and Mike M Mochizuki 1998, 'A liberal vision for the US–Japanese alliance,' *Survival: The IISS Quarterly*, (40)2 (Summer).

Okakura, Koshiro and Kanji Makise 1969, *Shiryo Okinawa mondai* (Documents of the Okinawa issue) Rodo Junposha, Tokyo.

Olson, Mancur 1965, *The logic of collective action: public goods and the theory of groups*, Harvard University Press, Cambridge MA.

Olson, Mancur and Richard Zeckhauser 1966, 'An economic theory of alliances,' *Review of Economics and Statistics*, (48)3 (August).

OECD various issues, *OECD Economic Outlook*, Organisation for Economic Co-operation and Development.

—— 1981, *National accounts of OECD countries, 1962–1979,* Organisation for Economic Co-operation and Development, Paris.

—— 1980–2001 *Social expenditure database* (SOCX), Organisation for Economic Co-operation and Development.

Orr, James 2001, *Victim as hero: ideologies of peace and national identity in postwar Japan*, University Of Hawaii Press, Honolulu.

Orr, Robert M Jr 1990, *The emergence of Japan's foreign aid power*, Columbia University Press, New York.

Otake, Hideo 1982, *The politics of defense spending in conservative Japan*, Cornell University Peace Studies Program, Ithaca.

—— 1983, *Nihon no boei to kokutai: detanto kara gunkaku e* (Japan's defense and domestic politics: from détente to military buildup), San'ichi Shobo, Tokyo.

—— 1986, Nihon no boei to kokunai seiji (Japan's defense and domestic politics), San'ichi Shobo, Tokyo.

—— 1988, *Saigunbi to nashonarizumu* (Rearmament and nationalism), Chuo Koronsha, Tokyo.

—— 1990, 'Defense controversies and one-party dominance: the opposition in Japan and West Germany,' in Pempel, TJ (ed) *Uncommon democracies: the one-party dominant regimes*, Cornell University Press, Ithaca NY.

—— (ed) 1991, *Sengo nihon boei mondai shiryoshu* (Documents of security problems in postwar Japan), (1) San'ichi Shobo, Tokyo.

Otsuki, Shinji and Masaru Honda 1991, *Nichibei FSX senso* (The US–Japan FSX war), Ronsosha, Tokyo.

Ozawa, Ichiro 1987, *Blueprint for a new Japan: the rethinking of a nation*, Kodansha America, New York.

Page, Benjamin I and Robert Y Shapiro 1983, 'Effects of public opinion on policy,' *American Political Science Review*, (77)1.

Park, Yung Chul 1986, *Bureaucrats and ministers: contemporary Japanese government*, University of California Institute of East Asian Studies, Berkeley.

Pekkanen, Robert and Ellis S Krauss 2005, 'Japan's "coalition of the willing" on security policies,' *Orbis*, (Summer).

Pempel, TJ 1974, 'The bureaucratization of policymaking in postwar Japan,' *American Journal of Political Science*, (18) November.

—— 1992, 'Bureaucracy in Japan,' *PS: Political Science & Politics*, (25).

—— 1998, *Regime shift: comparative dynamics of the Japanese political economy*, Cornell University Press, New York.

Pharr, Susan J 1993, 'Japan's defensive foreign policy and the politics of burden sharing,' in Curtis, Gerald L (ed), *Japan's foreign policy after the cold war: coping with change*, ME Sharpe New York.

Powell, Robert 1999, *In the shadow of power: states and strategies in international politics*, Princeton University Press, Princeton.

Preston, Anthony 1984, 'The changing balance in the Pacific,' *Jane's Defense Weekly*, 29 September.

Purrington, Courtney and AK 1991, 'Tokyo's policy responses during the Gulf Crisis,' *Asian Survey*, (31)4 (April).

Pyle, Kenneth B 1992, *The Japanese question: power and purpose in a new era*, AEI Press, Washington DC.

Rae, Douglas W 1971, *The political consequences of electoral laws*, Yale University Press, New Haven.

Reed, Steven R 1991, 'Structure and behaviour: extending Duverger's Law to Japanese case,' *British Journal of Political Science*, (20).

—— 2007, 'Duverger's Law is working in Japan,' *Japanese Journal of Electoral Studies*, (22).

Reuters, 30 November 2002.

Richardson, Bradley M and Scott C Flanagan 1984, *Politics in Japan*, Little, Brown, Boston.

Rifomu Kurabu, 1980 'Nichibei sogo anzen hosho e no teigen' (A proposal for US–Japan comprehensive national security), *Kikan Chuo Koron Keizai Mondai*, (19) Fall.

Risse-Kappen, Thomas 1991, 'Structure and foreign policy in liberal democracies,' *World Politics* (43)4 (July).

Rosecrance, Richard 1986, *The rise of the trading state: commerce and conquest in the modern world*, Basic Books, New York.

Rosenau, James N 1961, *Public opinion and foreign policy*, Random House, New York.

Rubinstein, Greg A 1999, 'US–Japan armaments cooperation,' in Green, Michael J and Patrick M Cronin (eds), *The US–Japan Alliance: past, present, and future*, Council on Foreign Relations Press, New York..

Sakata, Michita 1975, 'Sakata's scenario,' *Far Eastern Economic Review*, 14 November.

Samuels, Richard J 1994, *'Rich nation, strong army': national security and the technological transformation of Japan*, Cornell University Press, Ithaca, NY.

—— 2007, 'Securing Japan: the current discourse,' *Journal of Japanese Studies*, (33)1.

Samuels, Richard J and Christopher P Twomey 1999 'The eagle eyes the Pacific: American foreign policy options in East Asia after the Cold War,' in Green, Michael J and Patrick M Cronin (eds), *The US–Japan Alliance: past, present, and future*, Council on Foreign Relations Press, New York.

Sato, Eisaku 1997, *Sato Eisaku Nikki* (Diary of Eisaku Sato), (4) Asahi Shinbun, Tokyo.

Sato, Seizaburo, 'From national defense to security', Gaiko Forum (Summer 2000), available at http://www.gaikoforum.com/essay/seizaburosato.htm, last accessed April 2007.

Sato, Tadao 1995, *Nihon eigashi* (History of Japanese films), Iwanami Shoten, Tokyo.

Satoh, Yukio 1991, 'Asian–Pacific process for stability and security,' in *Japan's Post Gulf International Initiatives*, Ministry of Foreign Affairs, Tokyo.

Scalapino, Robert A and Junnosuke Masumi 1962, *Parties and politics in contemporary Japan*, University of California Press, Berkeley.

Schaller, Michael 1996, 'The Nixon "shocks" and US–Japan strategic relations, 1969–74,' US–Japan Project Working Paper Series, Working Paper 2.

Senkyo Seido Shingikai (Council for Electoral Systems), 'Senkyo seido oyobi seiji shikin seido on kaikaku ni tsuite no toshin' (Proposals for reforms of electoral systems and political financing), 26 April 1990, available at http://www.secj.jp/pdf/19900426-2.pdf, last accessed September 2007.

Shinoda, Tomohito 2003, 'Koizumi's top-down leadership in the anti-terrorism legislation: the impact of political institutional changes,' *SAIS Review*, (23)1 (Winter-Spring).

Smith, Sheila A 1999, 'The evolution of military cooperation in the US–Japan Alliance,' in Green, Michael J and Patrick M Cronin (eds), *The US–Japan Alliance: past, present, and future*, Council on Foreign Relations Press, New York.

Snyder, Glenn H 1984, 'The security dilemma in alliance politics,' *World Politics*, (36)4 (July).

—— 1997, *Alliance politics*, Cornell University Press, Ithaca NY.

—— 2002, 'Mearsheimer's world—offensive relaism and the struggle for security,' *International Security*, (27)1 (Summer).

Snyder, Jack L 1991, *Myth of empire: domestic politics and international ambition*, Cornell University Press, Ithaca, NY.

Soeya, Yoshihide 1998, 'Japan: normative constraints versus structural imperatives,' in Alagappa Muthiah (ed), *Asian security practice: material and ideational influences*, Stanford University Press, Stanford.

Sorrels, Charles A 1977, *Planning US general purpose forces: forces related to Asia/ US*, Congressional Budget Office USGPO, Washington DC.

Stockwin, JAA 1987, 'Japanese public opinion and policies on security and defense,' in Dore, Ronald and Radha Sinha (eds), *Japan and world depression*, St Martin's Press, New York.

Sudo, Sueo 1992, *The Fukuda Doctrine and ASEAN: new dimensions in Japanese foreign policy*, Institute of Southeast Asian Studies, Singapore.

Sugawa, Kiyoshi 2002, 'Nakasone's jishuboei: limits of autonomy, 1970-1971,' in Clemons, Steven Hiromi Murakami and Clyde Prestowitz Jr (eds), *Japan and the United States reconsidered: evolution of security and economic choices since 1960*, Economic Strategy Institute, Washington DC.

Suzuki, Motoshi 1999, 'Shugiin shinsenkyo seido ni okeru senryakuteki tohyo to seito shisutemu' (Strategic voting and party systems in the new electoral system for the lower house), *Leviathan*, (25) Fall.

Takao, Yasuo 1999, 'Welfare state retrenchment—the case of Japan,' *Journal of Public Policy*, (19)3 (September–December).

Tatsumi, Yuki 2004, 'Japan's first step toward a national security strategy: assessing the Araki Commission Report,' *PacNet*, (47A), 22 October.

Toshitani, Nobuyoshi 1962, 'Kenpo dai-kyujo to kokumin no hoishiki' (Article 9 and the legal consciousness of the public), *Shiso* (Thought) June.

Tow, William T 1983, 'US–Japan technology transfers: collaboration or conflicts?' *Journal of Northeast Asian Studies*, (2)4.

Tsuji, Kiyoaki 1964, 'The bureaucracy preserved and strengthened,' *Journal of Social and Political Ideas in Japan*, (2) December.

Tsutsumi, Hidenori 2007, 'Shosenkyokuka ni okeru kohosha hyoka to tohyo kodo' (The evaluation of candidates and voting behaviour in the single-member districts), paper presented at the 11th National Meeting of the Japan Public Choice Society, 7–8 July, Hiratsuka, Japan.

Twomey, Christopher 2000, 'Japan, a circumscribed balancer: building on defensive realism to make predictions about East Asian security,' *Security Studies*, (9)4.

Umemoto, Tetsuya 1985, 'Arms and alliance in Japanese public opinion,' PhD dissertation, Princeton University.

Ushio, Shiota 1986, 'Kane to boei' (Money and defense), *Chuo Koron*, (101)5 (May).

Van Evera. Stephen 1998, 'Offense, defense, and the causes of war,' *International Security*, (22)4 (Spring).

Van Wolferen, Karel 1989, *The enigma of Japanese power: people and politics in a stateless nation* Macmillan London.

Wada, Haruki 2002, 'Sengo nihon heiwashugi no genten' (Origins of Japan's postwar pacifism), *Shiso*, (944) December.

Walt, Stephen M 1987, *The origins of alliances*, Cornell University Press, Ithaca NY.

Waltz, Kenneth N 1979, *Theory of international politics*, Random House, New York.

—— 1993, 'The emerging structure of international politics,' *International Security*, (18)2 (Fall).

—— 2000, 'Structural realism after the Cold War,' *International Security*, (25)1 (Summer).

Watanabe, Akio 2001, 'Nichibei domei no goju-nen no kiseki to nijuiseiki e no tenbo' (The fifty years' course of US–Japan Alliance and the prospect for the 21st century) *Kokusai Mondai* (International Affairs) (490) January.

Watson, Bruce 1982, *Red navy at sea: Soviet naval operations on the high seas 1956–1980*, Westview Press, Boulder.

Welfield, John 1988, *Empire in eclipse: Japan in the postwar American alliance system*, Athlone Press, London.

Wildavsky, Aaron 1975, *Budgeting: a comparative theory of the budgetary process*, Little Brown, Boston.

Wlezien, Christopher 1995, 'The public as themostat: dynamics of preferences for spending,' *American Journal of Political Science*, 39.

Wohlforth, William 1993, *The elusive balance: power and perceptions during the Cold War*, Cornell University Press, Ithaca NY.

Wong, Kar-yiu 1989, 'National defense and foreign trade: the sweet and sour relationship between the United States and Japan,' in Makin, John H and Donald C Hellmann (eds), *Sharing world leadership? A new era for America and Japan*, American Enterprise Institute for Public Policy Research, Washington DC.

Yamamoto, Masaru 1990 'The Japan that can say yes: groping for a world role,' *World Policy Journal*, (7)3.

Yasumoto, Dennis T 1986, *The manner of giving: strategic aid and Japanese foreign policy* Lexington Books, Lexington MA.

Yomiuri Shinbunsha 2001, *Yoron Chosabu*, 'Beikoku terojiken ni kansuru denwa kinkyu zenkoku yoronchosa' (National opinion poll on the terrorist attacks against the United States), 24–25 September.

Yoshida, Shigeru 1957, *Kaiso junen* (Memoirs of ten years) (2) Shinchosha, Tokyo.

—— 1962, *Yoshida memoirs: the story of Japan in crisis,* Houghton Mifflin, Boston.

Yuasa, Hiroshi 1986, *Kokkai giinzoku* (Diet member policy tribes) Kyoikusha, Tokyo.

Zakaria, Fareed 1998, *From wealth to power: the unusual origins of America's world role*, Princeton University Press, Princeton.

Index

Abe, Shintaro, 92
Abe, Shinzo, 5, 26, 105, 119, 120, 131, 137, 172n110
Aegis destroyers, 2, 109, 110, 136, 138, 171n97, 172n105, 172n106
Afghanistan, 2, 32, 90, 110, 111, 142, 171n97
  Soviet invasion, 32, 35, 90,
Aichi, Kiichi, 23, 42, 71
Air Self-Defence Force (ASDF), 2–3, 67, 82, 115, 128, 136, 138, 168n68
Akagi, Munenori, 68
Allied Occupation, 43, 50, 55, 58, 77, 87
  demilitarisation, 50, 58, 87
al-Qaeda, 2, 111
anti-militarism, xiii, 5, 10, 12, 18, 33, 47, 48, 49, 51, 53, 54, 68, 80, 87, 90, 115, 131–135, 139, 166n45
  victimisation, xi, 54
  see also constructivism
anti-terrorism, 2, 119
  Anti-Terrorism Special Measures, 2, 5, 8, 105, 106, 108–109, 111, 120, 163n1, 171n97
  non-combat zone, 109
  rear-area support, 2, 5, 105, 107–109, 110, 111, 141, 142
anti-war movies, 56–57
Araki Commission Report, 128–129
  integrative defence strategy, 128,
Arita, Kiichi, 41, 42
Armacost, Michael, 92
Armitage, Richard, 1–2, 3–4, 110, 171n96
  Armitage Report, 104, 106
Aso, Taro, 105, 131
Association for Family Members of Japan's War Dead (*Nihon Izokukai*), 84

Association of Southeast Asian Nations (ASEAN), 44, 91, 166n43
ASEAN Regional Forum (ARF), 44–45, 166n43
Aum Shinrikyo, 99
Australia, 24, 118
avoidance politics, 82, 84–85, 127

ban on arms exports, 8, 10, 38, 46, 70, 79, 95–96
ban on overseas dispatch, 8, 16, 65–67, 72–73, 105, 141–142
  see also SDF
Basic Policy for National Defence, 22, 79
Berger, Thomas U, 17, 21, 47, 48, 87
Biruma no tategoto (The Burmese harp), 57
Bretton Woods, 21, 89
Britain, 4, 55, 62, 104, 118, 136, 164n12
Brown, Harold, 31
'bubble' economy, 39, 99, 136
bureaucracy-dominant model, 77–78
Bush administration, 25, 106
Bush, George, 25, 38, 92, 94
Bush, George W, 2, 4, 104–105, 111, 112

Cabinet Office (Japan), 59, 74, 135, 173n115
Calder, Kent, 9, 11, 18, 163n6
  reactive state, 18
Carlucci, Frank, 92
Carter, Jimmy, 31–33, 91
Case-Church Amendment, 32, 166n37
Chai, Sun-Ki, 17, 48–49
Cheney, Dick, 25
China, 18, 23, 24, 25, 34, 43, 67, 75, 87, 89, 90, 128, 166n43, 171n95
  anti-Japanese demonstrations, 128
  US rapprochement, 24, 89

civilian control, 7, 31, 48, 54, 76, 78
  civilian officials, 7, 34, 54, 76
  uniform officers, 7, 54, 76–77, 78, 82, 168n68
Clinton administration, 25, 97
Clinton, Bill, 30, 44, 94–95, 170n83
coalition-building process, 14, 15, 69, 105
Cold War, 24, 26, 29, 30, 38, 87, 89, 102, 104, 131
collective self-defence, 4, 8, 12, 16, 71–73, 105, 110, 119, 120, 129, 131, 137, 138, 139, 167n59, 171n91, 172n105, 172n110
  ban on collective self-defence, 4, 8, 12, 16, 72, 101, 104, 110, 113, 119, 132, 139
  see also security policy
constitution, 4–5, 21, 29, 30, 38, 48, 50, 51, 53, 55, 58–59, 66, 67, 72, 78, 109, 118, 134, 137, 140
  amendment, 4–5, 6, 53, 58, 66
  Article 9, 3, 4, 6, 7, 8, 16, 48, 50, 51, 53–54, 55–56, 58, 66, 67, 72, 79,100, 101, 134, 139, 167n53, 171n91
  Article 66, 76
  Article 96, 7, 16, 79
  Constitution Research Council, 69
  constitutional reform by reinterpretation (*kaishaku kaiken*), 79, 168n63
  national referendum, 4–5, 7, 77, 105, 118, 119
  referendum law, 5, 105, 118, 119, 163n3
  reinterpretation, 28, 119, 120, 131, 139
  revision, 7, 10, 12, 55, 57, 58–59, 66, 67, 69, 77, 79, 100, 101, 105, 118–120, 129, 134, 139, 163n3, 167n52, 170n88, 171n92
constrains on security policy
  budgetary, 35, 129, 130, 131, 136
  constitutional, 63, 66, 87, 100, 107, 129

domestic, 6, 9, 10, 11, 12, 35, 130, 135, 137
external, 6, 8, 11, 12, 35, 52, 87–98, 137
legal-formal, 77, 79, 100, 111, 142
normative, 17, 48, 164n16, 166n45
political, 79, 130, 131
constructivism, xiii, 13, 17, 47–52, 133
  anti-militarism, xiii, 48–49
  ideational factors, xiii, 17, 49
  independent impact of norms, xiii, 12, 47–48, 99
  internalised, 50, 54, 132, 134
  intersubjective, 47, 50
constructivists, xiii, 12, 49, 50, 133
Cronin, Patrick, 102
Curtis, Gerald, 123

Defence Agency, 4, 8, 24, 31, 34, 35, 38–39, 41, 54, 75, 76–77, 79, 81, 82, 97–98, 131, 168n62, 170n85, 170n86
  Development Planning Division, 41
  Procurement Demand Division, 41
defence budget/expenditure, 6, 8, 10–13, 20, 23, 24, 33, 39, 40, 42, 46–47, 51, 61–62, 73–76, 79, 81, 83, 84, 88, 89–90, 91, 92, 97, 119, 127, 130–131, 135–136, 163n8
  acquisition, 14, 30, 34, 35, 36, 129, 130, 136
  anti-defence spending bias, 15, 74, 80, 84, 85, 125, 129, 135
  blame avoidance, 11, 15
  defence burden, 13–14, 19, 21, 24, 32, 33, 41, 42, 48
  deficit financing, 13
  domestic constraints, 13, 75–76
  GDP/GNP, 8, 10, 11, 13–14, 24, 30, 32, 33, 36, 40, 41, 73, 136
  'host nation support', 30, 39, 91, 163n8, 165n32, 165n33
  incrementalism, 14, 35, 74, 136
  macro-economic constraints, 13, 73, 74, 81
  missile defence, 131

net support, 62, 167n57
personnel, 14, 30, 131
security environment, 13, 62, 73–76
social spending, 63, 73–74, 84,
US dollars, 14, 136
yen, 14, 35, 36, 39, 136, 163n8
see also GNP/GDP ceiling on defence spending
Defence Build-up Plan, 23
  First, 1958–60, 41, 67
  Second, 1962–66, 41
  Third, 1967–71, 41, 69, 75
  Fourth, 1972–76, 23, 24, 41
defence technology, *see* military technology
Democratic Party of Japan (DPJ), 5, 114, 118, 121, 124, 127, 163n3, 170n91
Democratic Socialist Party, 71
détente, 34, 35, 76, 89
developmentalism, 10, 54,
Diet (national legislature), 4, 26, 27, 33, 34, 41, 54, 58, 66, 67, 68, 71, 73, 79, 112, 113, 114, 115, 117, 118, 120, 129, 131
  resolution, 22, 65, 71, 78
Dulles, John Foster, 40, 67

East Asia, 17, 18, 20–21, 24, 25, 30, 32, 37, 39, 42, 43, 44, 46, 90, 102, 134, 137, 172n104
East Asia Strategic Initiative, 25
Eisenhower, Dwight, 68, 88
elections, 12, 23, 42, 70, 77, 134
  candidate-centred, 120–124, 125
  collective goods, 84–85
  continuous disputes, 127
  discrete disputes, 127–128
  'hard votes', 80, 83, 84, 123, 127
  'floating voters', 80, 82–84, 120, 125, 168n71
  lower house, 29, 34–35, 66, 83, 114, 117–118, 120, 121, 123, 125, 126, 127, 173n120
  national policy issues, 120–124, 125, 127

party-centred, 120–124, 127
personal support networks (*koenkai*), 80, 120, 127, 173n120
ratio of a candidate's vote to the district winner's vote (*sekihairitsu*), 122
subsidies, 125, 127
upper house, 23, 58, 83, 84, 114, 115, 116, 120, 131, 140, 168n68
voting behaviour, 83, 122–127
electoral systems, x, xiii, 6, 7, 16, 73, 77–78, 79–80, 134, 171n94, 172n112
  multi-member district (SMD), 7, 79, 80, 118, 120, 122
  proportional representation (PR), 84, 121, 122, 126, 127, 171n94, 172n112
  reform in 1994, 101, 106, 120–123, 123–128, 171n93, 172n112, 173n114
  single-member district, 79, 118, 120–123, 124, 126, 127, 134, 171n94, 172n112
  single non-transferable vote, 80, 120
  'winner-takes-all', 118
Emperor Hirohito, 54–55
European Union (EU), 45

Flanagan, Scott, 78
FSX (Fighter Support Experimental), 37–39, 81, 97
Fukuda Doctrine, 44
Fukuda, Takeo, 27, 31, 32–33, 34, 42, 72, 91
Fukuda, Yasuo, 120, 131, 137

Genda, Minoru, 82, 168n68
Giarra, Paul, 103
GNP/GDP ceiling on defence spending, 8, 10, 11, 34, 35, 46, 51, 73–76, 79, 85, 89, 134, 135, 136, 164n16
Great Hanshin Earthquake, 99
Green, Michael L, 102
Ground Self-Defence Force (GSDF), 3, 30, 41, 67, 115, 116, 118, 128, 138, 140, 142, 168n68

Guidelines for US–Japan Defence
  Cooperation
  1978 guidelines, 103, 165n35
  1997 guidelines, 103, 104, 172n104
  'areas surrounding Japan', 103, 104,
    141, 171n95
Gulf War (1990–1991), 2, 5, 11, 26–27,
  28, 44, 52, 99, 135, 140–141

Haig, Alexander, 91
Hashimoto, Ryutaro, 30, 44, 103
  Clinton–Hashimoto summit, 103
Hatoyama, Ichiro, 57, 58, 66, 67, 79
  rearmament, 57
Higuchi, Hirotaro, 29, 102
  Higuchi Commission Report, 29, 102
Himeyuri no to (Himeyuri Lily Tower),
  57
Hiroshima, x, 21, 54, 59
Hokkaido, 30, 31, 138
Hook, Glenn D, 17, 47–48
Horiuchi, Mitsuo, 109, 110
Hosokawa, Morihiro, 29, 101–102
House of Councillors (Japan), 4, 118
House of Representatives (Japan), 4, 5, 7,
  8, 101, 118, 171n94

Indian Ocean, 2, 106, 108, 109, 110,
  171n97
Ikeda, Hayato, 21, 58–59, 66, 68, 69, 79,
  167n53
  income-doubling plan, 68, 69
International Disaster Relief Law, 108,
  141, 171n103
International Peacekeeping Operations
  (PKO) Law, 8, 28, 111, 141
  see also United Nations
Iraq, 2–3, 26, 28, 104, 105, 110, 111,
  113–118, 127, 140, 172n108
Iraq Humanitarian Reconstruction
  Assistance Special Measures 3, 5, 8,
  112, 113–114
  noncombat zone, 3, 113, 140
  Samawah, 3, 115, 116, 118, 140, 142,
  168n68

see also anti-terrorism
Ishiba, Shigeru, xii, 105
Ishihara, Shintaro, xii, 25
Ishikawa Heavy Industries, 39
Ishikawa, Yozo, 38
Ito, Masayoshi, 91

Jackson, Karl, 37
Jamaica, 91, 92
Japan Coast Guard, 1
Japanese voters, 15, 35, 71, 78, 90, 91,
  93, 98, 111, 114, 116, 124–127, 134,
  135, 137, 139, 142
Jervis, Robert, 20, 166n38
Johnson, Chalmers, 78
Johnson, Lyndon, 88
Juni no hitomi (Twenty-four eyes), 57

Kades, Charles, 55
Kahn, Harman, 17–18
Kaifu, Toshiki, 25, 26, 136, 141, 172n111
Kanemaru, Shin, 27, 31, 35, 165n32,
  168n73
Kato, Koichi, 109
Katzenstein, Peter J, 17, 48, 49, 76–77,
  78, 87
Kawasaki Heavy Industries, 39
Keddell, Joseph, Jr, 9, 21
Keidanren (Federation of Economic
  Organisation), 23, 80–81
  Defence Production Committee, 80–81
Kelly, James, 4, 171n96
Kennedy, John F, 88
Keohane, Robert O, 45
Kike wadatsumi no koe (Listen to the
  voices from the sea), 56
Kishi, Nobusuke, 21, 58, 67–69, 93, 137,
  169n78
Koga, Makoto, 113
Koizumi, Jun'ichiro, xii, 2, 3, 4, 101,
  104–105, 106, 107, 109, 110, 111, 113,
  114, 115, 116, 117, 118, 121, 125, 128,
  131, 140, 142
populism, 107, 126
public support, 107, 117, 126

top-down leadership, 2, 106, 117, 124, 125, 131, 173n116
Koizumi cabinet, 104–105, 107, 109, 110, 111, 112, 114–116, 126, 128, 140, 142, 171n97
Komeito, 27, 71
Kono, Yohei, 44–45, 102
Korea, 67
  North, 59, 60, 128
  South, 31, 32, 33, 71–72
Korean peninsula, 30, 33, 34, 104, 138, 171n95
  nuclear crisis, 52, 99
  'Taepodong shock', 59–60, 99, 128
Korean War, 57, 58, 65, 66, 67
  procurement boom, 65, 66, 81
Kubo, Takuya, 34, 76
Kurihara, Yuko, 82
Kurisu, Hiromi, 31
Kuwait, 26, 28, 115

Latin America, 92
Law to ensure Japan's peace and security in the situations in the areas surrounding Japan (Regional Crisis Law), 108, 111, 172n104
Layne, Christopher, 18
Liberal Democratic Party (LDP), 3, 4, 5, 7, 8, 9, 10, 14, 15–16, 22, 23, 24, 26, 27, 29, 34–35, 38, 39, 41, 42, 44, 50, 51, 59, 69, 70, 71, 72, 74–80, 81–82, 84–85, 96, 101, 102, 106, 109, 110, 113, 114, 115, 118, 120, 121, 126, 127, 131, 132, 170n91, 171n93
  candidates, 80, 83–85, 120, 122, 123–125, 127
  candidate selection, 121, 122, 124
  election defeat in 1993, 101, 125, 171n93
  factions, 70, 106, 124, 125
  leaders, 10–11, 74, 79, 103, 110, 124, 127–128, 131, 132, 135, 142, 168n73
  national defence policy group (*kokubo zoku*), 81–82, 124, 168n67, 168n69
  neo-conservatives, 105

Policy Affairs Research Council, 85, 168n69
political funds, 124, 173n114
politicians, 14, 23, 27, 28, 39, 42, 44, 50, 59, 72, 74, 77, 84–85, 96, 101, 109, 120, 136, 167n53, 168n63
  pork-barrel, 74, 85, 122, 125, 127, 137, 139
liberalism, 42–47, 49
  institutionalism, 43, 44
  interdependence, 45
  multilateralism, 29, 43
  multilateral security, 28–29, 37, 42–45, 102
  neo-liberalism, 12
Lind, Jennifer, 17, 19

MacArthur, Douglas, 54, 55, 66, 67
Mansfield, Mike, 89
Maritime Self-Defence Force (MSDF), 14, 26, 41, 67, 110, 128, 136, 138, 141
Mearsheimer, John J, 18
Midterm Defence Program Estimates, 32, 79, 130, 131, 173n123
Mihara, Asao, 31, 82
Miki, Takeo, 8, 34–35, 70, 75, 76, 89
militarism, 1, 12, 15, 49
military technology, 26, 95–98
  aerospace industry, 37–38, 47
  autonomous development, 39, 46, 170n84
  co-development, 37–39, 97
  defence industry, 69, 80–81, 97
  dual-use technologies, 81, 95, 97, 170n85, 170n86
  indigenisation (*kokusanka*), 69, 96, 98
  Joint Military Technology Commission (JMTC), 170n85
  missile defence-related technology, 8
  partnership, 38, 97–98
  R&D, 47
  Systems and Technology Forum (S&TF), 95
  Technology-for-Technology (TfT), 97

transfer, 10, 38, 39, 95, 96, 97, 170n84, 170n85
Ministry of Defence (formerly Defence Agency), 137, 166n42
Ministry of Finance, 35, 74, 81, 173n123
Ministry of Foreign Affairs, 4, 43, 81, 92, 97, 168n62
Ministry of Economy, Trade and Industry (formerly Ministry of International Trade and Industry), 81, 95, 97–98, 167n62, 169n81, 170n84, 170n85
Aircraft and Ordinance Office, 81
missile shield, *see* Theatre Missile Defence
Mitsubishi Heavy Industries, 23, 39, 80, 81
Miyake, Ichiro, 122, 168n71
Miyazawa, Kiichi, 27, 28, 29, 165n30
Mochizuki, Mike, 43
Mori, Yoshiro, 1, 123
multilateralism, 28, 29, 102
  see also liberalism
Murayama, Tomiichi, xii, 29, 30, 102, 103

Nagasaki, x, 21, 54, 56, 59
Nagasaki no kane (The bells of Nagasaki), 56
Nakanishi, Terumasa, xii, 25–26
Nakasone, Yasuhiro, 10–11, 22–23, 24, 39, 74, 85, 92, 95–96, 101, 105, 135–136, 137, 163n9, 164n10
Nakayama, Taro, 28–29
National Defence Program Outline (NDPO), 11, 79
  1976 NDPO, 11, 30, 32, 33–35, 75, 85, 89,102,103, 130, 135, 167n62, 168n72
  1995 NDPO, 44, 103, 130
National Defence Program Guideline (NDPG), 18, 128–132
  new threats, 128–130
  terrorism, 129
nationalism, 1, 25
New Frontier Party (Shinshinto), 121
New Komeito Party, 4, 118

New Party Sakigake, 29
Nikkeiren (Japan Federation of Employers' Association), 23
Nixon, Richard, 8–9, 21, 24, 41, 59, 71, 93–94, 165n26, 169n78, 169n79
  Guam, 8–9, 21, 165n23
Nixon Doctrine, 21, 22, 93, 165n23
Nixon's shock, 23
  US presidential election in 1968, 93
Nixon–Sato Joint Communique, 71–72
  Korea clause, 71–72
  Taiwan clause, 71–72
Nonaka, Hiromu, , 109, 110, 113
normal nation, xii, 6, 11, 29, 99, 100, 105, 106, 135, 163n5
norms, ix, x, xi, xiii, 7, 11, 12, 14, 15, 16, 17, 47–52, 65, 75, 98, 99, 105–106, 108, 115, 118, 119, 128, 131, 132, 133–135, 142, 143, 166n45
  agents, 17, 99, 134
  change, xi, 12, 50, 51, 99–132, 133
  collective expectation, 6, 7, 8, 10, 14, 16, 47, 51–52, 59, 63, 65, 99, 101, 105, 108, 112, 119, 133–134, 137, 139, 164n16
  collective understanding, x, 12, 50, 52, 56, 57, 99, 119, 133–135, 141, 166n45
  compliance, ix, xiii, 7–8, 10, 12, 14, 15, 16, 17, 50–51, 65–85, 105, 123–128, 132, 133–135, 136, 142
  consensus, 52, 87, 99, 131
  construction, 15, 51, 99
  formation, 12, 50, 53–63, 133
  institutionalisation, 7–8, 15, 48–49, 65, 87, 99, 125, 133–134, 164n16
  intrinsic force, 16, 17, 51, 65, 132, 134
  material/political leverage, 7, 65
  structures, 12, 17, 47, 48, 52, 65, 87–98, 99, 119, 133–134
North Korea, xi, 1, 11, 59, 60, 172n110
  see also Korea
nuclear accident, 99
nuclear deterrence, 18, 22
nuclear weapons, 21–22, 54, 56, 60, 71, 137

three non-nuclear principles, 8, 21–22, 54, 71, 79, 137
  see also security policy
Nukaga, Fukushiro, 110, 132
Nye, Joseph, 29, 45, 102–103
Nye Report, 29–30, 103

Official Development Assistance (ODA), 91, 92, 93, 169n77
Ohira, Masayoshi, 91
Oil Crisis, 10
Okinawa, x, 21, 22, 25, 70–71, 93–94, 138
  group suicide (*shudan jiketsu*), x
  Kadena Air Base, 70
  reversion, 21, 22, 70, 93–94
  US Marine Corps, 25
Olson, Mancur, 19, 40, 84, 165n21
Ono, Yoshinori, 116
Ozawa, Ichiro, xii, 26, 27, 28, 29, 39,

pacifism, 6, 17, 49, 50, 51, 54, 58, 59, 63, 65, 66, 73, 77, 87, 106, 166n45
  inward-looking, xi, 99, 100
  Japan-specific, 49, 53, 54, 99
  'one country pacifism', 100
  pragmatism, 49, 59, 63, 99
  passivism, 49, 59, 63, 99
  pro-active, 133
  reactive, 133
  unarmed (*hibuso*) Japan, 50, 54, 55, 58, 63
party politics, 101, 102, 107
Patterson, Torkel, 4, 171n96
Pempel, TJ, 78, 168n64
Persian Gulf, 26, 28, 108, 141
  minesweepers, 26, 28, 108, 141
Pharr, Susan, 9, 17, 18–19, 91
  defensive-state strategy, 9, 19
  substitution policy, 91
  see also realism
Philippines, x, xi, 25, 32
Plaza Agreement, 14, 136, 164n12
political access and opportunities, x, xiii, 16, 17, 51, 65, 99, 133, 134

post-Cold War, xii, 17, 18, 25, 28, 30, 38, 42, 43, 52, 59, 94, 103, 104, 105, 106, 107, 133
public opinion, x, xiii, 6, 12, 13, 14–15, 22, 26, 28, 39, 41, 51, 53, 57, 62, 69, 82, 85, 101, 105, 106–120, 164n14
  elitism, 15
  opinion survey, 12, 22, 27, 28, 42, 53, 55, 57, 58, 59–63, 66, 83, 99, 100–101, 107–108, 109–112, 115–119, 139, 164n13, 167n52, 169n77, 170n88, 170n91, 171n92, 171n98, 172n107, 172n108
  pluralism, 15
  Cabinet Public Relations Office, x, 42, 59–62, 107, 164n13, 166n46, 167n56, 169n77, 170n87
  shared beliefs, 6, 53, 59, 73, 99

Reagan, Ronald, 32, 35, 38, 92, 169n75
realism, xiii, 17–42, 47, 49, 133
  alliance politics, 13, 19, 20–42
  back-passing, xii, 19, 20, 42, 164n20
  bilateralism, 19, 42–43, 44
  collective goods, 13, 19, 91, 104
  cost-benefit analysis, 13, 19
  cost minimising, 19, 34, 40, 42
  defensive realism, xii–xiii, 13, 17, 19, 20–42
  defensive state, 19, 20, 30, 37, 40
  defensive-state strategy, 19–20, 30, 35, 42
  'free ride', 13, 19, 20, 37
  neo-mercantilism, 46–47, 166n44
  neo-realism, 12, 13, 14, 18, 20, 135
  offensive realism, xii–xiii, 18
  perception, 20, 133
  structuralism, 18, 75
realists, xi, xiii, 12, 13, 14, 75, 105
rearmament, 6, 41, 46, 48, 57, 58, 66, 67, 77, 79–80, 90, 91, 92, 133
  see also Hatoyama, Ichiro
remilitarisation, 5–16, 17, 18, 40, 51, 79, 80, 90, 120, 133–143
Renewal Party, 29, 101

Richardson, Bradley, 78
Rosecrance, Richard, 45–46
   trading state, 45

Sakamoto, Yoshikazu, 102
Sakata, Michita, 34– 35, 75, 82
Samuels, Richard J, 46–47, 96, 105
   mercantilist realism, 46–47
Sanada, Hideo, 72
Sato, Eisaku, 8, 21, 22, 23–24, 69,
   70–71, 72–73, 93
Sato, Seizaburo, 26
Saudi Arabia, , 26
security policy, xi–xiii, 1–16, 17–52, 48,
   79, 80, 82, 84, 105, 111, 120, 123, 125,
   129, 131, 133–134, 137, 139, 142
   autonomous defence (*jishuboei*), xii,
   22–23, 24, 25, 39, 41, 42
   'Britain of Asia', 4, 106, 111
   collective self-defence, 4, 8, 16, 71–73
   comprehensive security (*sogo anzen
   hosho*), 91, 93
   exclusively defence-oriented
   (*senshuboei*), 23
   independent military capabilities, 5, 9,
   10, 19, 23, 30, 34, 41, 46, 57, 63, 82,
   90–91, 128, 135, 163n9
   international contribution (*kokusai
   koken*), 112, 139, 140
   non-nuclear principles, 8, 21–22, 71
   nuclearisation, 137–138
   offensive military capabilities, 6, 92,
   135, 137–139
   proactive, 4, 6, 10, 12, 28, 49, 51, 98,
   101, 105, 107, 135, 139
   reactive state, 9, 164n17
   resource diplomacy, 44
   sea lanes, 30, 32, 34, 38, 39, 163n9,
   168n72
   self-defence, 7, 31, 53, 66, 69, 72, 73,
   87, 98, 119, 137,138, 167n53
   standard defence force concept (*kiban
   boeiryoku koso*), 33–34, 75, 76
   unarmed neutrality, xii, 50, 60, 63

   see also constraints on security policy
   and strategic foreign aid
Self-Defence Force (SDF), xi, xii, 2–3, 8,
   10, 22, 23, 26–28, 29–33, 35, 40–41,
   42, 43–54, 58, 59, 60–62, 66, 68, 71,
   76, 79, 84, 92, 100–102, 105–109, 111,
   113–117, 119, 120, 127, 128, 130, 131,
   137–139, 140, 142, 167n53, 168n68,
   172n104, 172n108
   ban on overseas dispatch, 3, 6, 8, 16,
   28, 46, 51, 54, 65–67, 72–73, 109
   Five Principles on SDF participation in
   UN-related peacekeeping operations,
   108, 139, 171n102
   National Police Reserve, 67
   National Safety Force, 67
   overseas dispatch, 2, 12, 26–27, 41,
   71–72, 106, 107, 108, 110–115, 118,
   119, 125, 127, 128, 140–142
Self-Defence Force (SDF) Law, 40–41,
   54, 141, 163n2
   Article 3, 66
   Article 99, 108, 141
September 11, 2, 105, 106, 107, 108,
   128, 140, 141, 142
Shidehara, Kijuro, 55
Shultz, George, 92
Sino–Japanese Friendship Treaty, 30
Sino–Soviet relations, 34
Social Democratic Party of Japan
   (SDPJ), 29, 102, 165n31
Socialist Party, 57, 69, 82, 165n31
Soeya, Yoshihide, 17
Soviet Union, xii, 9, 24, 25, 30–31, 32,
   34, 38, 39, 55, 59, 70, 88, 89, 90, 92,
   94, 103–104, 165n35, 170n85
   collapse, xii, 24, 25
   Far East, 30–31, 32, 35, 59
   military buildup, 9, 30, 31, 34, 35, 59
   Navy, 31, 32
   Northern Territories, 31
   Russian advance, 92
   see also Afghanistan
special interests, 11, 13, 80, 82, 120
   agriculture, 11

defence industry, 13, 80
veterans' groups, 84
strategic foreign aid, 9, 11, 91–93, 104
Sudan, 92
Sunagawa case, 68, 167n53
Suzuki, Zenko, 8, 35, 38, 92, 95, 163n9, 169n75

Taiwan, 32, 71–72, 171n95
Taiwan Strait, 104, 138
Takashima, Masuo, 72
Takayanagi, Kenzo, 69,
Takeshita, Noboru, 39, 92, 172n111
Taliban, 2, 111, 142
Tanaka, Kakuei, 23, 24, 75
textbooks, xi
Theatre Missile Defence (TMD), 26, 97
  Ballistic Missile Defence (BMD), 30, 128, 129, 130, 136, 138–139
Tokyo, x, 23, 68, 80, 81, 102, 103
Toshiba Corpopration, 23, 39, 170n85
Tsuji, Kiyoaki, 77
Tsuru, Shigeto, 102
Turkey, 9, 92
two-party system, 120, 121
two-track approach, 28

United Nations, 3, 5, 26, 28, 43, 70, 106, 111
  1992 peacekeeping operation legislation, 8, 28, 111, 141
  combatant peace enforcement, 12, 28, 101, 107, 139, 171n91
  noncombatant peacekeeping operations, 28, 101, 107, 141
  Security Council, 3, 27, 70
  Security Council Resolution 1368, 108
  United Nations Peacekeeping Operations (PKO), 3, 26, 44, 102, 119, 128, 139, 140
United Nations Peace Cooperation Corps (UNPCC) bill, 27
United States, xii, xiii, 2–10, 13, 19, 20–30, 32, 34, 35, 37, 38, 41, 42, 43–46, 61–63, 66–68, 69–71, 93, 95–98, 102–107, 109–112, 114, 115, 120, 131, 138, 139, 142, 163n8, 164n12, 166n43, 168n72, 169n81, 170n84, 170n86, 172n104, 173n122
  Congress, 9, 25, 32, 37, 38, 39, 40, 89, 90, 93–95, 166n37
  Department of Commerce, 169n80, 170n83
  Department of Defence, 10, 25, 29, 32, 90, 97, 103
  Department of State, 4, 32
  global military strategies, 104, 105, 106, 118
  hegemonic power, 18, 21, 93
  Japan's military dependence, ix, xii, 8, 22–23, 29, 51, 76, 87, 88–89, 92, 93, 94, 143
  Navy, 31, 172n105, 172n110
  Office of the US Trade Representative, 170n83
  Pentagon, 1, 4, 102
  security guarantee, xii, 6, 8, 9, 10, 12, 17, 18, 22, 29, 43, 46, 51, 52, 87, 90, 94, 96, 104, 135, 143, 164n16
  unilateralism, xii, 26
  US bases in Japan, 9, 10, 11, 22, 24, 38, 40, 61, 66, 68, 70, 91, 104, 136, 163n8, 169n73
  war on terrorism, 2, 105, 106, 107, 110
US–Japan Security Treaty, xii, 3, 4, 9, 10, 18, 20, 23–26, 34, 58, 60–61, 67–69, 71, 87–98, 169n73
  Article 5, 103–104
  burden-sharing, 4, 8, 9, 24–25, 35, 88–89, 89–93, 95, 98, 104
  cost-sharing, 32, 104, 135
  free-ridership, 24, 46, 87–88, 90, 104
  joint military operations, 68, 101, 103, 110, 132, 139, 171n91
  Mutual Security Assistance (MSA), 40, 41, 65–66, 69, 166n41
  power-sharing, 4, 104, 105, 120
  renewal in 1960, 67–69, 88
  risk-sharing, 4, 11, 26, 98, 104, 135, 140

Security Consultative Committee
(SSC), 4, 129, 165n35
US military reduction, 20–30, 32, 38,
44, 134
US pressure, 6, 8, 9, 10, 11–12, 27,
35, 46, 65, 81, 82, 87–98, 104, 105,
109, 110, 125, 134–135, 139, 140, 142,
169n81
US–Japan Joint Declaration on Security,
30, 44
US–Japan trade relations, 88–89, 91,
93–95, 169n79, 170n83
anti-dumping sanctions, 94, 169n80
Japan's trade surplus, 90, 93
Seven Point Program, 93
Structural Impediments Initiatives
(SII), 94, 169n82
textile wrangle with Japan, 93–94
US trade deficits, 37, 88
Voluntary Export Restraints (VER),
94, 169n81

victimisation, 21, 54, 55, 57, 59, 100,
167n54
see also anti-militarism
Vietnam, 70
Vietnam War, 21, 59, 61, 70, 88, 89
Vogel, Ezra, 102–103,

Waltz, Kenneth, 13, 18, 20, 165n22
wartime preparedness, 4, 5, 6, 13, 31, 60,
99, 104, 105, 128, 163n2
Weinberger, Casper, 32, 38, 39, 95
West Germany, 41
Wilson, Charles, 88
Wolfowitz, Paul, 104, 109–110

Yamazaki, Taku, 109
Yanai, Shunji, 1–2
Yoshida Doctrine, xii, 15, 22, 51, 91,
164n16, 165n28
pragmatism, 51, 66, 68, 164n16
Yoshida, Shigeru, 23, 43, 44, 51, 53, 57,
66, 67, 69, 164n16